# ENSEMBLE THEATRE MAKING

*Ensemble Theatre Making: A Practical Guide* is the first comprehensive diagnostic handbook for building, caring for, and maintaining ensemble. Successful ensembles don't happen by chance; they must be created, nurtured, and maintained through specific actions. Achieving common goals in rehearsal and performance requires group trust, commitment, and sacrifice. *Ensemble Theatre Making* is a step-by-step guide to these processes.

Candid and direct, it considers:

- how to plan and prepare for ensemble work
- the essential building blocks of ensemble
- how to identify ensemble behaviors
- techniques for responding to and positively redirecting those behaviors.

Tools, techniques, and recipes for rethinking ensemble redefine it as a grounded practice, rather than a question of luck. Above all, this significant new work brings decades of experience to the sometimes mystifying questions of what creates ensemble bonds, how to protect them, and how to fix them when they break.

**Rose Burnett Bonczek** is a professor of theatre arts and program head of the BFA in Acting at Brooklyn College, City University of New York, USA, where she specializes in improvisation, directing, and theatre pedagogy. She received the Claire Tow Distinguished Teacher award in 2009–10. She has directed professionally and in educational theatre for over 35 years, and is the festival director and co-producer of Gi60: The International One Minute Play Festival, Live US edition.

**David Storck** is a professor in the School of Performing Arts at the Savannah College of Art and Design, USA, where he specializes in improvisation and character development. He directs improvised and scripted shows, both professionally and in educational theatre. Since 2000 he has taught ensemble-building workshops to everyone from school children to corporate executives and fellow educators.

# ENSEMBLE THEATRE MAKING

## MAKING

A Practical Guide

*Rose Burnett Bonczek and
David Storck*

Routledge
Taylor & Francis Group

LONDON AND NEW YORK

First published 2013
by Routledge
2 Park Square, Milton Park, Abingdon, Oxon OX14 4RN

Simultaneously published in the USA and Canada
by Routledge
711 Third Avenue, New York, NY 10017

Routledge is an imprint of the Taylor & Francis Group,
an informa business

*British Library Cataloguing in Publication Data*
A catalogue record for this book is available
from the British Library

*Library of Congress Cataloging in Publication Data*
Bonczek, Rose Burnett, 1958-
Ensemble theatre making : a practical guide / by Rose Burnett Bonczek
and David Storck
p. cm.
Includes bibliographical references and index.
1. Ensemble theater. I. Storck, David, 1962- II. Title.
PN2297.A2B66 2012
792.02'2--dc23
2012013458

ISBN: 978-0-415-53008-8 (hbk)
ISBN: 978-0-415-53009-5 (pbk)
ISBN: 978-0-203-11708-8 (ebk)

Typeset in Times New Roman
by Saxon Graphics Ltd, Derby

MIX
Paper from
responsible sources
FSC
www.fsc.org    FSC® C004839

Printed and bound in Great Britain by the MPG Books Group

FROM ROSE:
To Mike, for proving Tom Robbins right every single day.
I love you for free ...

FROM DAVID:
To Averie and Maddie Bear,
my girls. I love you.

# CONTENTS

# ACKNOWLEDGMENTS

The authors would like to gratefully acknowledge the following:

Our ensemble of early readers who made invaluable contributions to the content and to our spirits: Lisa Anderson, Dr. Valerie Clayman Pye, Rosa Fernandez, Mike Flanagan, Ramona Floyd, Sarah Good, Jenny Grosdas, Sarah Hirshan, Melanie Hopkins, Vera Khodasevich, Arthur Kriklivy, Rosanne Manfredi, Roger Manix, Wayne Maugans, Anthony Ponzio, Ian Wen, Welker White.

Special thanks to Adam Smith for his invaluable technical support and problem solving.

We would also like to thank the following for their support, be it resources, morale, guidance, or stories: Steve Ansell, Jan Ansell, Charles Bales, Dr. Beverly Brumm, Ruben Carbajal, Sabrina Cataudella, Ed Clarkson-Farrell, Michael Colby Jones, Chris Donovan, Elaine Fadden, Tim Fannon, Dr. Helen Huff, Julie Jensen, Jacquie Kahn, Kevin Kennison, Jennifer Light, Rob Light, Michael LoPorto, Terril Miller, Colleen Mond, Michael Posnick, Paul Rooney, Pat Ruff, Mickey Ryan, Bill Sellman, Judy Sellman, Francisco Solorzano, Jeffrey Sweet, Christopher Thomasson.

Thanks to the colleges, universities, and organizations that supported and inspired us: Brooklyn College, Department of Theater, especially Thomas A. Bullard, Amy Hughes, Kip Marsh, Jackie Smerling, Tobie Stein, Laura Tesman, Judylee Vivier and Bill Tramontano, and Jerry Mirotznik; Fordham University at Lincoln Center, Department of Communication; James Newman and Summer Repertory Theatre; Marc Adam Smith, Brad Barton, and everyone at Gotham City Improv; members of Burn Manhattan; members of the Heartless Floozies; members of Ms. Dee's Comedy Iced Tea; Manhattanville College Department of Dance and Theatre; Performing Arts Department at Savannah College of Art and Design.

Thank you to the students who volunteered to be in our cover photograph: Anna Bowman, Maddy Buxton, Elizabeth Byland, John Dorsey, K. C. Van Elslander, Courtland Jones, Patrick Myers, Miranda Stevens, Cody Vaughn, Meghan B. Zern, Robert Zerweck, and to our fantastic photographer, Adelle Drahos.

Our deep thanks to Ben Piggott for his faith in this book, and for his keen editorial eye in making it a better book; and to Sam Kinchin-Smith for guiding us through the maze with wonderful support and good cheer always.

And to the pubs of New York City that never kicked us out: Bayard Street Pub, Limerick on 23rd, Baker Street Pub, Ginger Man, Old Town Bar.

And of course, to all our teachers, directors, collaborators, students, and our supportive families.

# INTRODUCTION

## Is this where the party is?

It has been said that directing a successful production is not unlike being the host of a successful party. It begins with inviting the right people (casting). Once the party has begun, your job is to fuel the guests; provide good food, keep their drinks fresh, and let them do what they do best: be themselves. Don't micromanage or steer conversations or force your agenda. Stay attentive to needs and be open to pleasant surprises. If someone gets drunk and obnoxious, put them in a cab. If there's a spill, clean it up. What we're talking about here, without using the actual term, is creating a strong ensemble.

Welcome to the party.

The snacks are on the table, the bar is out on the deck, and you can find the bathroom on your own. We'll keep everything stocked and we expect you to do what you do best: be yourselves. You may be happy to sample a bit of food for thought, or to totally devour some of the conversation here, or you may be attending just to get our recipe for how to throw a party like this yourself. Whatever the case, take some time to relax and enjoy the party and the other guests before you call it a night.

## Who are the hosts?

### Rose

My first real introduction to ensemble work was at State University of New York at New Paltz in the 1970s. As a freshman, I had this "new" teacher, Dr. Beverly Brumm, who introduced us to Grotowski, improvisation, trust exercises, and sound and movement. I was ridiculously fearful in those days. I was terrified, mortified, and thought I would just die if I had to do these exercises. One day in class (during sound and movement circle), Bev looked me in the eye and said, "Rosie man, you gotta get in there." And

1

I did. And in that moment, I found the thing that I'd been missing until that point in my life that would forever guide me as an artist and a teacher. Along with my heart-stopping fear, I found the support of an ensemble. I looked around me, and not only saw the support in the ensemble's eyes, I *felt* their encouragement beaming at me. Their support and belief in me was *so* loud it was as if I could actually *hear* them say, "You can do this!" And I did. And I wanted more. For the next 35 years I directed, taught, and devised theatre that was rooted in ensemble – but that day in Bev's class was the beginning that brought me to these pages.

### David

In 1992 I was dragged (probably kicking and screaming) to Tom Soter's drop-in improv class by a co-worker, Janice Capuana. My previous acting experience hadn't prepared me for the level of interdependence and collaboration that I was to find among improvisers. I took to it right away, and threw myself in – headlong. By 1998 I was a regular performer at the Upright Citizens Brigade Theatre. It was during that time that I began to sense something about the nature of ensembles. All of them endured ups and downs in work and relationships, yet whenever one was in a slump, it seemed that we would focus on "fixing the work." Rarely did we find ourselves focused on "fixing the group," unless there was talk of how to kick someone out.

The prevailing notion at the time was that if the work was going well, the group got along, and that if the work wasn't going well, members started to grumble and point fingers. It was a relationship of direct cause and effect. I had begun to suspect that there was another possibility: that keeping the ensemble in good shape was what would lead us to consistently strong work. We always did our best work when our confidence was high and we were functioning together effectively.

In 1999 Gotham City Improv came calling with an offer to direct their second-stage company. By then I was pursuing this ensemble-first approach in all my work. Six months later, I suddenly found myself in the position of artistic director, with oversight of the training program, while also directing both performance companies. After the Board meeting where this was decided, I remember sitting down at my desk. I wrote on a post-it note and stuck it to my computer where I couldn't miss seeing it every day. It said, "It's the ensemble, stupid." That saying took me back to an old but vivid memory of what I consider my first ensemble experience. I was in sixth grade at Washingtonville Middle School, where each week I would make my way to Mr. Sileo's music room for a trumpet lesson. I would play alone or sometimes Mr. Sileo would play along on his cornet. After a few months, he invited me to join the sixth grade band. Little did I know that the music I had been learning all this time were the handful of songs that the band was working on. My first day of band rehearsal arrived and I took my spot at the end of the 3rd trumpet section. Mr. Sileo lifted his baton and we launched into *The Blue Rock*. Suddenly I was filled with a feeling like none I had felt before. My small part of simple notes was part of a much greater piece. I actually stopped, I was so startled; and looked around. Here were probably 60 or so students, each playing their own simple parts, like me. But together we were making something more complex, more interesting, more fulfilling. We were a band! We were rockin'! We were *connected*. It was an incredible sensation and a turning point from which I couldn't go back. After that, whenever I played alone, I felt ordinary. But when I played with the band, I felt extraordinary. It is that feeling that this book is all about.

## Co-hosts

We first met in 2004 at Brooklyn College when David arrived as a graduate student and Rose was the resident improvisation teacher. We discovered that we came from wildly different experiences with improv, teaching, and ensemble theatre making, and we had many terrific talks about the human dynamics in ensemble, and the role of ensemble in our work. Through these exciting discussions, we embarked on a journey that took us from teacher-student to friends to collaborators *and* friends. Most of these early discussions ended with one of us saying, "You should write a book."

In 2006, a collective of directing alums began to meet on a semi-regular basis at the Old Town Bar in Manhattan to talk shop. We all acknowledged that directing was a fairly lonely profession and we looked forward to those gatherings: to talk about productions and group dynamics, tell hilarious stories about things going wrong *and* wonderful stories about things going right, AND for the pints of Guinness. For an all too brief period, Mike Flanagan, Jimena Duca, Jonathan Hadley, Rhett Martinez, Christopher Thomasson, and Rose had a "directors salon" in which one of the most popular topics was ensemble: when does it work, when doesn't it, and what the hell could we do next time? What does it take to be a "good" ensemble leader? What makes the difference? Unfortunately, life began to present different opportunities to the group just as David joined us. Rhett and Jimena moved away, Jonathan joined the military, er, *Jersey Boys* National Tour, and Mike, David, Christopher, and Rose met now and again. We'd poke sadly at our french fries and say, "We miss those talks." Finally, Rose turned to David and said, "You need to write that book. That book is what all these great conversations were about." David smiled and said, "I'll write it if you write it with me."

We decided to meet once every other week in the pub of our choice. And we thank the many pubs of New York City (especially Old Town Bar) for never throwing us out as we camped for hours on Wednesday afternoons with notebooks, laptops, and empty pint glasses. And thus it went until we were confident enough to share some of the material with others.

When we first told them we were working on a book about ensemble, the most common question was: "How soon can you finish? I need it *now*." The second most common was, "Can I read some of it?" We had an incredibly generous group of friends and colleagues who we put the bite on to be early readers. Their feedback was invaluable: their notes shone light on so many dark corners, and their tremendous support and encouragement lifted our spirits. We've got to single out two crazy, that is, *special* people. One day, our dear friend and fellow director Mike Flanagan, after spending three hours cheerfully reviewing a chapter with us, making fantastic editorial and content observations, made the fatal mistake of saying, "You know, I'm also a writer, and I teach writing as well as theatre. I'd be happy to look at anything else you might have and give editorial suggestions and critique." We said, "What do you charge?" Without missing a beat he said, "Burgers and beer." We hired him on the spot. Mike's amazing editorial skills, suggestions, friendship, and fellowship have made an immeasurable contribution to this book. Like a great director, you don't notice the contribution when the work is that stellar. Mike, you're a great director.

Later in the process, super-woman Valerie Clayman Pye returned a rough draft of a monster chapter *overnight* with countless handwritten notations. She had only recently finished her own dissertation, yet she handed us the monster chapter with a smile saying, "This was great! I'm so excited to be a part of your process. Is there anything else I can look at for you?" When we sputtered, "Oh, we couldn't impose … ," she waved us off and said, "Oh come on. I *love* this. Give me more." So we did. Val's perspective as a theatre practitioner *and* scholar opened up doors we might not have walked through without her insights. Thank you, Val.

Mike and Val gave their time joyfully and selflessly, and their presence is felt throughout these pages. They're the party guests who arrived early to help us decorate, prepare the food (Val's homemade pizzas are to *die* for), and set the table for all of you. We are the luckiest hosts in the world.

## What kind of party is this anyway?

Most of us are familiar with the phenomenon wherein something special can happen when you get people to function effectively as a group. They become more than just the sum of the individuals: a new entity is born; greater accomplishments are possible. It's a super-force that heightens our capabilities as individuals and serves to illuminate the furthest potential of human endeavor. We recognize this phenomenon perhaps most readily in the military, in athletics, and in the arts. It's this last area that we'll be addressing: artistic, collaborative ensemble theatre making. Hereafter, we'll refer to this simply as ensemble.

In our experience, ensemble has often been regarded as "lightning in a bottle," "chemistry," "kismet," or just plain luck, all of which implies that there is little we can do to create it or nurture it. Don't you believe it; our combined 60+ years of experience tells us that ensemble is something we can exert a tremendous influence on. As teachers, directors, and program leaders, we are the "chemists" that help the chemical reactions reach more satisfying and consistent results. As an ensemble leader, you can take specific actions to achieve a more consistently collaborative dynamic in your group, whether you're working in a theatre production, an improv troupe, a cohort-based class of actors, or a community performance group. By identifying ensemble behaviors and developing techniques to respond to those behaviors, you'll have a stronger tool kit that can be applied across artistic and educational disciplines. That special quality found through ensemble will not be *lost* through planning and preparation; it will be *enhanced*.

A word to our ensemble of readers: what we're offering here is not a dissection followed by prescription; it's an exploration into our experiences that will offer some knowledge and tools to help you bring ensemble from the realm of luck into more grounded practice. We're sharing our approaches and stories to *encourage* you to find more consistent results, not *ensure* consistent results; otherwise, we might as well be a military unit. You may also recognize the *absence* of your experience in our stories. Where do you see yourself in these pages? What do you recognize here that you want to say "yes and ... " to? How do some of these observations and stories help you with your *own* self-discovery?

## What else do I need to know before coming in?

A word of explanation on our use of the words "you, I, we, our, and us." When we say "we," "our," and "us," we mean not only Rose and David, but also you the readers, unless specifically indicated otherwise. In some instances, we (David and Rose) will be referencing personal experiences, in which case we'll write "we (David and Rose)" to distinguish the instance.

We will only use "I" in instances where the identity of the narrator has been clarified, such as a personal anecdote that could only be told by either David or Rose. And when we say "you," we mean you, the collective readers.

You, the partygoers.

Now take off your coat, grab a drink, and enjoy yourself.

# 1

# WHAT IS ENSEMBLE?

They may ask me to change what I *do*, but not who I *am*.

–Michael Colby Jones

In our work, an ensemble may be a cast, a class, members of a program, students, amateurs, or professionals. Sometimes we choose the members (casting); sometimes they are thrust upon us (whoever signed up for our class). The members may be similar or as varied as the Earth's population (male, female, young, old, tall, short, Ukrainian, Bolivian, you name it), but what's the common denominator? They're all groups of one size or another and all of the members are in pursuit of a common artistic goal (to tell a story, put on a show, learn a technique, practice skills, etc.). Of course, each member is sure to have individual goals as well, but as long as all members share the group's primary goal, there is a basis for collaboration.

It's interesting to note that the *Collins English Dictionary* traces the word ensemble to the Latin origin meaning "at the same time." The intent of the word was not to merely say collection, group, or team with something in common, but to include a sense of deep connection between the members that enables them to think and act "at the same time." So whether you call it "being in sync," "the group mind," or "being on the same page," you're talking about ensemble. Sadly, it seems the general understanding of the word has come to be diluted from "at the same time" to something less potent or altogether different. Mention ensemble today and some associate it with large casts (an ensemble show), or less featured members of a cast (singers and dancers who round out a musical), or even clothing ("that's a lovely ensemble she's wearing").

Our experiences tell us the same. Haven't our good ensemble experiences been filled with that feeling of "at the same time"? And isn't that what's been missing from some of our less successful experiences? Yet we still call them ensembles. So let's be clear that there is a generic sense of ensemble frequently used and a more specific sense that we're talking about in this book. This specific sense of ensemble, with the strong bond among members, is the one that makes us feel a part of something special and it is what we're after.

Think about how often you're in an ensemble, in the generic sense. Everywhere you look there are ensembles. Your work at a faculty meeting is ensemble work (even if it doesn't always feel that way). A carpool is an ensemble (when one member is late and keeps the others waiting, they feel it). Spontaneous ensembles erupt all the time (for example, a random assemblage of airline passengers, stuck on a tarmac for hours, formed an ensemble to force the pilots to return to the airport). They happen all the time, yet our approach to them still tends to be: "I *hope* the special bond will appear with this group!" Why do we only hope? Why don't we take action? Or if we do, why do we wait for dire circumstances to occur (like being stuck on a tarmac for hours)? Maybe we're focused on what we see as a more primary goal: putting up a good show or teaching our students. Or maybe we just don't know how – it wasn't part of our training. Or maybe we see it as something ephemeral, like love, not knowing when or where it will strike. And it's not that we haven't ever tried. Who hasn't tried to deal with a loner or rebel who disrupts an otherwise tight group? But the solution isn't always easy or apparent. This doesn't mean you have to settle for "I hope" – there are steps you can take to create positive group dynamics, and to maintain a strongly bonded ensemble.

## Seeking a bond

As leaders forming an ensemble, we try to say the right things on the first day: something inspiring, something to build confidence, something to instill a strong work ethic, and then we hope for the best as the work begins. We hope for lightning to strike. Yet think about it: lightning *doesn't* strike by happenstance. Literally, certain meteorological conditions need to exist for lightning to strike. What if you could create those conditions? What if you turned your rehearsal studio or classroom into a "lightning rod" for great ensemble?

Perhaps some of you have already found ways to take that hope and transform it into something tangible in your process. Perhaps you already know how to build a great ensemble, but want to know why it seems to fall apart after a while. *Uh oh, the honeymoon is over. I smell conflict. What was I thinking? They're not looking at each other today. Someone sucked the air out of the room.* How do you maintain the great ensemble you've already got? We (David and Rose) have seen directors and actors throw in the towel and say "Well, we just lost it, and don't click anymore" as if they have no power to effect change. But change *is* possible. You wouldn't throw up your hands (even with fingers crossed) and say "I *hope* this is what happens" in any other category of your work. You would research it, create a plan, take specific actions, and assess those actions as you go. The irony is that we sometimes hold back from taking action because we fear killing whatever good chemistry remains. But as the old song says, wishin' and hopin' alone won't make it happen. If the ensemble is in trouble, go in there and do something about it. Ensemble can be created, nurtured, maintained, and even repaired.

So move from hoping to taking action. You will not only have greater success, but also greater joy in your ensemble. Which isn't to say that you won't still have unsatisfying experiences, but those will grow fewer and farther between. And if you examine those temporary failures, they will help you refine the actions you're taking, and lead you even further from hoping to doing.

## The personal nature of ensemble

We're filled with joy when we belong to an ensemble that works well together. We thrive on the reliability of it. We feel respected, liked, and loved – by the ensemble, and the leader. We relax knowing who will be at that rehearsal or in that class, because we've created relationships, a working dynamic, and a play dynamic. We look forward to spending time with these playmates, no matter what the common goal is. The work doesn't feel like "work" because we're shouldering it together and because our passions are reflected and multiplied. It gives us a sense of security, a sense of belonging to a community. And without this, we tend to hold parts of ourselves back from the world:

- *I don't want to share my idea with the others because I might look stupid.*
- *If I tell her that, she might reject me.*
- *Look how they're looking at me – they all hate me.*
- *How can I be sure that person won't use what I say against me?*

We live in a world filled with judgment and so we look for sanctuaries that protect us from it. We find that protection in the form of a safe ensemble. It is a place where, for better and worse, we can be ourselves and be accepted.

From your earliest days, you were a member of your first ensemble: your family. You loved, you struggled, you learned, and you grew together. As you grew, you looked to form your own families, in the form of ensembles; from the band of friends you chose, to the clubs you joined, to the profession you entered. We all strive to connect with other human beings who make us better versions of ourselves. As ensemble leaders, we also strive to connect with other human beings so that we can make them better versions of themselves. And isn't that similar to the role of a parent?

While chatting one day, we (Rose and David) discovered that we had both been asked the question "Why did you choose to be a director?" To our astonishment, we found that our answers were almost identical: We direct so that we can create positive family experiences. With each show, we create a new family and live another family experience. We want to do it again and again; nurture that family, guide them to be healthy and supportive of one another. We want to be the best "parent" possible. As directors, we get the opportunity to make that happen.

So many others that we've met in our profession have shared similar feelings. They're not only seeking to tell their stories – they're seeking a family to help them in the telling. That chosen community provides a safe and supportive foundation from which the individual can grow stronger, more confident, be accepted, and do their best work. They also know that, like a family, no matter what they do, that chosen family is going to show up at rehearsal the next night. They will never abandon that play or the people involved. Think of the scene in the most recent remake of *King Kong*, when impresario Carl Denham (Jack Black) has brought Jack the playwright (Adrien Brody) on board ship, and orders the ship to pull out from the dock to keep the writer an artistic prisoner who will write the screenplay for his movie. The playwright races topside, sees that they're slowly pulling away from the dock, turns to Denham and screams "You can't do this to me! I won't write your screenplay! I love the theatre!" Denham retorts, "No ya don't. If you loved theatre, you woulda jumped."

We in the theatre are a committed bunch, aren't we? Why is that? Good ensemble forges a stronger than usual bond between its members; a bond that remains in place long after members go their separate ways. Some of us are familiar with this bond because we've been fortunate enough to experience it. The rest of us have heard legendary stories about great theatre collectives or productions, championship teams, or soldiers in combat. Members of these ensembles are often heard to describe the bond as "I would lay down my life for him," or "We could read each other's minds," or "I always know that she will be there for me." Members credit this bond for the extraordinary achievements that they accomplished together or the horrific hardships they were able to endure. The times spent within the ensemble are often recounted as "the greatest time in my life." In each case, the individuals survived or thrived because the bond allowed them all to be at their best, better than they were capable of alone. We all have the potential to make each other better versions of ourselves, and good ensemble realizes that potential.

## Home

If an ensemble is a family, then its environment is a home. Your classroom or rehearsal studio is a home. As an ensemble leader you prepare your environment as you would your home and instill in your ensemble members that they should treat it as they would *their* home. Is everyone taking turns vacuuming? Not treating the furniture as if it's going to be used in a demolition derby? A good ensemble environment is conducive to the work. What environmental needs does your ensemble have? A place where they can be loud? An intimate space? A bare space or one with specific pieces? Suit the environment to your purposes, not just from a practical point of view (let's have chairs so people can sit), but also according to the needs of the ensemble that day. Perhaps the ensemble is stuck, so you change the environment to support inspiration and discovery (maybe adding an unusual object or changing a configuration of flats or set pieces). Perhaps the ensemble needs to get more focused, so you change the environment to support that (remove the object which was previously inspiring, but is now distracting). In short, provide your "family" with a "home" that supports them and can adapt to their changing needs.

Let's remember too that home is not just a physical environment, but a state of mind as well (I feel "at home" here). Let's call it a "psychic home," as distinguished from a physical home. A good ensemble and its leader provide a safe psychic home for its members as much as they do a physical one. The creative benefit of a safe psychic home is that it enables risk-taking. If everyone feels accepted and secure, they'll take risks knowing that failures will be met with support and encouragement. Don't we get more creative results when artists are willing to take risks? And don't students learn more valuable lessons when they're willing to raise their hands and try an idea instead of holding back? A safe home empowers everyone in it. We know, intuitively, that greater potential exists in such environments and we seek them out.

Keep in mind that we're talking about the kind of failure that comes from creative risk-taking, as opposed to the kind that comes from lack of preparation, poor judgment, irresponsible behavior, or selfishness. In fact, a great way to begin a rehearsal or new class is to ask the members how *they* define failure. You can challenge them to *re*-define it by the end of your time together.

Establishing and maintaining a safe psychic home requires you to be a mixture of supportive and constructively critical. However, the ensemble members need to be free of criticisms from each other. (Only in solid, long-established ensembles have they earned enough trust and respect from each other to attempt this.) Remember, as leader, you're in charge: enforce the rules, maintain the boundaries, use discipline when necessary, and always provide support (love). Ensemble members gain a sense of security from knowing that someone is looking after their well-being.

### David

One of my improv teachers was Amy Poehler. Our class took place in a small loft in New York that had been converted into a theatre space. It was tiny, dirty, the floor had buckled to the point we were half afraid it would collapse, there was no air conditioning, it was noisy, and the elevator rides elicited nervous jokes about plummeting to our deaths. And yet, it was a special place that we all loved and look back on fondly. (It has since closed, but don't worry, New York is full of such spaces.) To those of us who studied and performed there, it was home, one of the most wildly creative homes I have ever known. It wasn't home because of the physical surroundings, that's for sure. And it wasn't home because of the great improv that it produced. It was home because of how we thought of it and how we treated it. And that came from Amy. Our class was on Sunday mornings and as the course wound down, some people would show up late, or eat while watching others work, or leave their garbage around. Attitudes were becoming lax and in a very short time, it started to affect our work. Amy would have none of it. She said (and I'm paraphrasing here from memory),

"You know, I'm not a particularly religious person, in the traditional sense. I don't go to church. But I do have a religion – improv is my religion. And this place is my temple. It is sacred to me and what we do here is sacred to me. And it doesn't matter what the space is, it's how you treat it. Don't come in here and piss all over my temple by treating it or the work we do with anything less than reverence. It means that much to me, and if it doesn't mean that much to you, then you shouldn't be here." Now young improvisers can be a pretty laid back, slack bunch of people – especially on a Sunday morning. But on that morning, something changed. Old classmates still talk about that morning and tell that story. Amy Poehler wasn't famous then, we just knew her as our teacher. And I didn't realize it at the time, but she was also an ensemble builder.

## What does it mean to be in an ensemble?

Remember the earlier story from *King Kong* about the strong commitment found in theatre artists? Yes, we are a committed bunch. But let's ask ourselves, "What are we committing to?" Commitment to the ensemble is different than commitment to the project. By committing to an ensemble, you're already committing to the project – and more. This notion goes back to the earliest form of theatre: rituals and storytelling around a fire. No one dancing around the fire or telling about that day's hunt was hoping for a good review or looking to get an agent. They were sharing, playing, bonding, and reinforcing the security they got from each other's company. They were fellow tribe members committed to ensuring their collective survival through sharing stories of events (more on this in Chapter 2). In families, we don't commit to a project, we commit to each other. And through that, the family thrives. Soldiers in battle commit more to each other than to some political purpose behind a war. They commit to helping each other survive.

These examples have very high stakes, usually life and death. And being a committed bunch of theatre folk, we play "life and death" stakes too. So then why do we have fewer instances of tightly bonded ensembles than soldiers in war? Is it because their stakes are real and ours are imagined? Perhaps that's a factor. But perhaps it's because we tend to commit to the project or individual goals more than to each other. Our commitment isn't weak, it's just misplaced: our focus tends to be toward the end result of why we've come together (usually a performance). To be a strong ensemble, and to have a good performance, it's crucial that the greater focus be on *each other*. Have you ever seen a play where the actors were doing wonderful individual work, but it seemed as though they were in different plays and the story wasn't coming across? That's what can happen when there isn't enough commitment to *each other*, when there is too little value seen in a partner's contributions. Just like those soldiers from our

12

example, not everyone fares well and the battle is often lost. In the case of the play, the equivalent might be bad reviews and poor box office. For that ensemble, the aftermath may include finger pointing, recriminations, and a further splintering of the group, if not an outright break-up. Of course, even a tightly bonded ensemble with members who commit to each other can suffer from bad reviews and poor box office on a production, but that ensemble is more likely to stick together, learn from the experience and try again with renewed determination. That is, they are more likely to *survive*. They might even be a tighter ensemble for *having* survived.

## What do you need to create the bond?

A strong ensemble is rooted in the behavior and choices of you and your ensemble members. Chief among these are commitment, sacrifice, and support. Of course we recognize that a "team attitude" is generally required, and often spoken of, but how many people really take it seriously and reflect it in their actions? There's a difference between talking about it and doing it. Just as we tell improvisers, "stop telling the other character how mad you are, *show* them how mad you are." Why does this simple idea prove so elusive? Because we are individuals with egos, agendas, artistic preferences, and competitive urges, and these forces tend to work against a healthy ensemble.

Of course, there are a host of behaviors that contribute to good ensemble, but let's be practical and focus on commitment, sacrifice, and support. You'll find that other behaviors are linked to one or more of "the big three."

### *Commitment*

We all know about the value of commitment in any endeavor. The key point is to recognize that commitment is easy to come by when things are going well. The true measure of commitment is: can you commit when it's *hard* to commit? A show that's going badly is a good testing ground for commitment. Remember our soldiers? When bodies are falling all around them, do they run away? No. They commit harder and fight to the death for each other. That's the level of commitment we're looking for. "But," you say, "this isn't life or death, it's just an abridged production of *The Wizard of Oz* to be performed for pre-schoolers." Now, we certainly don't equate Dorothy's adventure in Oz to a battle in a war. We know it's not life or death; but like Carl Denham, we approach it *as if* it were life or death, with the same level of commitment. Often we hear about survivors of horrific events who refer to fellow survivors as friends for life, committed to each other, because of the terrible experience that they shared. In time, another realization comes to light: that they are not just committed to each other because they survived – they survived because they committed to each other. The stronger the commitment, the stronger the ensemble. Members should agree not to let one another down, ever; and if one person falls, the others will pick them up.

## David

One of the most memorable improv shows I've ever seen was absolutely terrible. Try as they might, nothing the group did that night seemed to work. The scenes went from bad to worse. The audience grew more uncomfortable as the minutes passed. This is a situation where I frequently see group members turn on each other. In those cases, the shows get downright ugly. In this case, however, the group stuck together. The final scene of the show turned out to be on a ship. As you might expect, before long someone shouted, "we're sinking!" It was an effort to inject some energy, stakes, and excitement into the scene. But alas, things continued to deteriorate. The scene had become a metaphor for the entire show. As the players began to lower themselves to the floor to indicate the sinking of the ship, they were all desperately trying to get in a funny one-liner that might offer some small measure of redemption. The lights slowly began to fade. At that moment, three members of the group who were not in the scene, but standing nearby, jumped on to the sinking ship. They all went down with the ship. It may have been an awful show, but it was one of the most exhilarating demonstrations of ensemble that I've ever seen. They were committed to each other, no matter the circumstances, even through this great adversity. Those three performers could have remained to the side, away from the mess on stage, but they chose to jump in with their mates, knowing they could do nothing to help other than to show "we're with you." Those are the groups that survive.

### *Sacrifice*

This is what we really mean when we say team attitude, but team attitude sounds better. Let's face it, very few people *like* to sacrifice. It's doubtful that any of us wake up in the morning and say, "Let's see what sacrifices I can make today!" We are *willing* to make sacrifices, though, when something is important enough to us. Ensemble ain't easy, folks, and if you're drawn to this work, it's because you have a value system in your work that makes ensemble important to you and you're willing to fight for it. You are a true believer. True believers are willing to compromise and even relinquish some of their individual desires if they are not compatible with the needs of the ensemble. In the end, those sacrifices pay unimaginable dividends, so reward lies ahead for those willing to make the sacrifices. If an individual isn't willing to make the necessary sacrifices, then they're either not right for, or not ready for, ensemble.

Sacrifice extends to the ensemble leader as well. Are you willing to make the same sacrifice: putting the needs of ensemble above any individual desires you may have? Of course there are some qualifiers to this, as you'll read in Chapter 3, but if you're not a true believer, you won't be an effective leader.

If you're working on a play, sacrifice means that everyone's first priority is to tell the story. Actors shouldn't put their performance above the story. The prop mistress shouldn't put her handiwork above the story. And the director's ideas for flashy symbolic moments that stop the action shouldn't be put above the story. Everyone's contributions, ideally, should disappear into the story.

### David

An improviser friend of mine was in a very successful group that was renowned for its spectacular performances. They were funny, smart, dramatic, playful, truthful, artistic, satiric, thought-provoking – everything you'd hope for. All members of the troupe were extremely talented in their own right and had impressive backgrounds. Audiences, even those accustomed to the heights of improv, were wowed by their performances. This particular fellow was talking about sacrifice one day. "We're all good," he said, "we all have big egos and want to be the star, the funniest, the most clever, the audience favorite. But we agree to sacrifice that individual need in order to make the show the star. In the end, it comes back to me, to all of us. The show is so admired that my ego is stroked when I'm able to say, 'I am a part of *that*. I helped create *that*.' Collectively, we exceed the sum of our parts and create something better than each of us, alone, could create. So make the sacrifice. It will come back to you tenfold."

### *Support*

The need for support may seem straightforward and obvious on the surface, but beware of underestimating the difficulty of support. What we're talking about is far more than a pat on the back or a few words of encouragement. It takes a developed awareness of others. By taking the focus off of ourselves and putting it on our partners, we begin to identify ways to give them support. A pat on the back or a word of encouragement is simply generic support. Focusing on our partners allows us to provide specific support. This is why listening skills are so valuable, in acting and in almost any endeavor requiring interaction. They tie our responses to our partner *in the moment*.

All of this is easier said than done. Why? Well, as we've all discovered by now, selfishness and other "me" centered behaviors are plentiful. We see them every day in our life and in our work; they're natural. That's why we shouldn't underestimate the difficulty of support – because of the natural tendency to look out for number one. We can all slide into the pit of "me" pretty quickly if we're not careful. When you spot this type of behavior, you need only to gently redirect that person's focus. And they need to beware of it in themselves too. If all members are giving support, then all members will feel supported.

Good support in an ensemble also strengthens the other two parts of the big three. The more supported we feel, the easier it is to commit and make sacrifices. We begin to feel that we're all in this together, which is the start of the bonding that we're after.

### David

Many of my ensemble experiences have come in improvisational theatre. One of the oft quoted tenets of improv is, "I make you look good, you make me look good," meaning we support each other. I saw an example of this many years ago watching an improv show that included a terrific performer named Neil Flynn. Another fellow in this show was not listening very well and repeatedly added things to scenes that didn't make sense, or worse, contradicted information that had already been established. On each occasion, Neil would find a way to justify the new information and keep the scene on track. However, he did it without getting any laughs at the other fellow's expense, which would have been the easy and selfish way of handling it. In fact, he actually made the other fellow's ideas look brilliant, incorporating them in a way that added to the richness of the scene. Neil's focus was not on himself or being funny, but on making each scene as good as it could possibly be and supporting a partner who was having a tough night. Who wouldn't want to work with someone like that? His willingness to support makes him an appealing creative partner.

Commitment, sacrifice and support are the qualities upon which trust is built. Honor those qualities and you build trust; violate them, and you lose that trust. In ensemble, trust is the coin of the realm; with it, members can truly risk, fail, play, discover, and create. Trust is the recognizable form that the bond takes; it's how we know the ensemble *is* bonded. To return to our soldiers, their bond is based on the mutual goal of survival. But trust is what makes it happen. *I trust these guys with my life.* They commit to each other, they support one another, and they sacrifice for one another. They *trust* one another. That's the bond.

### David

A few years ago, I was a guest performer in an improv show. I was joining an established ensemble, which is an interesting challenge, even if only

16

for one night. The members of this ensemble had been together for many years and had as tight a bond as I've come across. During an early scene, I found myself standing inside a small, upside-down stage box that came up almost to my knees. Also standing inside that crowded little box was one of the other performers, a terrific improviser named Jay Rhoderick. We had nothing to hang on to but each other. As the scene progressed, Jay began swaying back and forth, and of course, I had no choice but to sway with him – we were interlocked. He increased the swaying to the point where the box was now rocking back and forth. As I tried to counter his swaying to slow it down, he pushed harder, as if he were actually trying to swing us so far that we'd fall. We were in a precarious position – if we were to fall, we wouldn't be able to cushion our landing by sticking out our arms. We would crash hard on to the stage, and I thought, certainly crack our heads open. In that instant I thought Jay must have gone mad. I'm all for taking risks and committing, but this felt reckless and dangerous. The other members of the ensemble were across the stage singing a song together. They were focused on their song and didn't seem to notice that we were about to come crashing down. Finally, with one great last push, we began falling to the stage. I closed my eyes and braced for impact. The next thing I knew, we had landed safely in the arms of the singers, who simultaneously finished the song with a great crescendo. It was an electrifying moment for the audience and a heart-stopping moment for me. At the same time, it opened my eyes to how much more trust, commitment, and support I was capable of and how deeply it affected the level of work that is possible. Imagine the freedom to be able to risk that much, knowing that you're safe because you have absolute faith in your partners to both be aware of your situation and ready to leap in and save you. I admit, it's scary at first, but in the next moment, it becomes both liberating and addictive. I've been trying to stretch the boundaries of how far an ensemble can go ever since.

If an ensemble member is not willing to sacrifice, commit, and support, then you must ask that person, "Why are you here?" As Amy Poehler said, "If it doesn't mean that much to you, then you shouldn't be here."

## What ensembles do

This gets us to the very nature of what ensembles do. They collaborate. As ensemble leader, you must collaborate with your ensemble, not dictate to it. You're not relinquishing your authority or allowing a non-unified vision; there is plenty of room to collaborate without yielding your leadership (more on this shortly). Encourage your members to collaborate in the process. Let them have a voice. Provide them with opportunities to get personally invested. Be flexible. Listen. Try things. Admit your own mistakes. Be open to the end result being different from what you originally intended. Allow the goal to benefit from the growth that collaboration brings. Will it get messy along the way? Almost always. Will you feel adrift at times? Probably. Will failures occur? Certainly. We wish we could tell you otherwise, but ensemble work, like family life, gets messy. Things go wrong. Your job isn't to prevent these from happening, it's to shepherd the members through these things safely. Messy experiences are actually quite valuable – just look how memorable they are. When you tell a great family story, isn't it always about the time the chestnuts blew up in the oven on Thanksgiving? Or when you tried to help your older sister sneak out of the house late at night and she got stuck in the window frame and mom grounded you both? Embrace the mess.

## Your role in the ensemble

You are the leader; you guide the ensemble. But how much guidance should you give? How much is too much? Too little? It's easy to spot when things aren't working, but it's not always easy to spot *why* they aren't working. Here are three big reasons why ensembles don't succeed:

- One or more members lack commitment, sacrifice, and/or support, resulting in no trust, no bond.
- The leader doesn't allow members adequate collaboration.
- The leader allows the collaborative spirit to overrun proceedings and doesn't keep things on track.

So what do those last two items mean? It's the difference between holding the reins too tightly or too loosely, and the inability to adjust the tension as needed. This is where we return to the concept of collaborating without yielding leadership, authority, or vision. Like so many things in life, there is a balance to be struck. That balance is nearly always in flux, so keep a constant eye on it and adjust as necessary. Is the ensemble flailing or lost? Give guidance. Are they chafing at your guidance? Give them freedom to explore, to try their own ideas, and to fail. Are they suffering from low confidence? Show them you believe in them. As always, communicate with them and make them communicate with you (they're usually eager to). Keep working to maintain the balance.

It would be a lot easier to just be fully democratic (good cop) or fully autocratic (bad cop), wouldn't it? But you can probably imagine how inconsistent your results would be. Nurturing a creative collaboration requires a more deft form of leadership, where balancing authority with sharing is the ideal. Not necessarily balancing them in equal measure, but in proportions that suit the moment. By keeping your finger on the pulse of the ensemble, you can develop a sense of what's needed. This nuanced approach is demanding, but the reward is devotion from the ensemble members.

## David

At one point in his career, my father worked in the same college athletic department as Bobby Knight, the famous basketball coach, who is perhaps just as famous for his temper as he is for his coaching success. A bit lesser known, though, is the undying loyalty and dedication Bobby inspired from so many of his players. How, with his fiery temper, could Bobby Knight inspire such responses? My dad was fond of explaining it by telling this story ... A close relative of one of Bobby's players passed away and the young man needed to fly home for the funeral. Unfortunately, a terrible snowstorm had closed the airports and many of the roads. As the story goes, Bobby got in his car, picked up the young man and drove him hundreds of miles, through the night, through the blizzard, so that he could be home in time for the funeral. He was there for his players, committed to them (on *and* off the court), giving them the support they needed and making sacrifices for them. He treated them like family. He set the example. He was a leader.

You can read more about your role as a leader in Chapter 3.

## Conclusion

For those of you who like a summary, here it is ...

- Good ensembles have a strong bond between members. This bond is trust.
- Trust is earned through the behaviors of commitment, sacrifice, and support.
- Once the bond is solid, great collaboration that leads to extraordinary results can happen.

## David and Rose

In writing this book, we have encountered many challenges, one of which is choosing specific language. Just as the word ensemble is fraught with dilution and wide interpretation, so too are other words that we'd love to use. For instance, "magic." We both use this word in our conversations on ensemble to describe that euphoric state of collaboration and the extraordinary results that come from great ensemble work. But if you'll notice, we've been quite careful to say that great ensemble isn't necessarily the result of magic (or lightning striking), but of an approach to the work based on specific behavior and choices. Hence our dilemma: it's not magic, but it's "magic." All of this bears mentioning because we both feel so strongly that there is something special in great ensemble. Wonderfully, deliciously, inspiringly, upliftingly magical! (Ahhh – we finally said it!) It's why we do this. But just to be clear, the "magic" is the end result of a lot of commitment, sacrifice, support, and hard work. So now let's go back and revise our last sentence before this aside: Once the bond is solid, *magic* can happen!

The leader's job is to ensure commitment, sacrifice, and support, and to maintain the balance necessary for positive collaboration.

# 2

# ANTHROPOLOGY OF
# ENSEMBLE

*Why* do we need a book about ensemble? We used to be able to *do* this for our *survival*, not just enjoyment. The individual *and* the community would *die* if they didn't do this …

–Roger Manix

We used to be able to do this. What happened? We still know ensemble when we see it, we feel it when it's happening, and we go on alert when it's not. We resort to that word "magic" at times because we can't touch it, eat it, or quantify it; and yet it's *real*. We feel it in our bones in the most primal way. And those primal instincts and responses haven't changed all that much in the past 100,000 years give or take. Working in an ensemble (or anywhere, really), you see and feel them manifested *every day*.

These ancient instincts, responses, and signals pop up in our classrooms, rehearsal studios, and company meetings. Yet we've come to associate primal responses as being inferior to intellect. Or worse, when someone shares an instinctual response that can't be quantified, they're told, "Oh, that's all in your imagination!" Fear, protection, and bonding are as ancient as the hills, and yet they're judged and evaluated through a *modern* lens. Evolution itself has become almost synonymous with individual achievement (thank you Industrial Revolution), while communal support and ensemble are relegated to something touchy-feely, or something you only need during times of crisis. So when we've felt that pull toward an ensemble experience, we may have been told (or found ourselves thinking), "Well, that's nice; but it's not *practical*." Or worse, "Well, that's not the *serious* approach."

Here's a news flash: the archaeological and anthropological evidence in our brief human history tells us that it doesn't *get* much more serious than ensemble (and yes, ensemble predates modern society by a long chalk). By examining how our ancestors thrived as communities, and survived *because* they were communities, we can learn more about today's ensembles, and get over this idea of ensemble and instincts as impractical magic. The actions of our ancestors teach us the value of fear, its relationship to survival, and how fear may have contributed to creating the first ensembles.

21

In our modern world, we've been taught to be ashamed of being afraid. Fear is considered a personal failure, and if you're afraid, you're weak, you're a coward. These negative contemporary connotations are in direct contrast to our past relationship with Fear as our Protector and Survival Guide. Through a deeper understanding of the connection between the ancient and the contemporary, we can recognize responses that arise from our primal survival instincts, and we can address fears in a healthier way so that the community – the ensemble – will thrive.

We're not sociologists, nor are we aiming for a scientific debate; but we've distilled some information here that is essential to our conversation about ensemble. We've experienced these things over and over in our rehearsals and classrooms; someone is blocking impulses, or they're making a tentative choice instead of a committed one. We try to guide them through it, and they say, "I don't know why; I just freeze up," or "I'm just trying to get it right." In their body language, we observe them alternating between trying to connect to the ensemble for support, and then pulling away and isolating. This is an old tango between the partners Fear and Trust that have been dangerously dancing for many thousands of years. Being aware of and understanding this ancient dance can bring us closer to positively redirecting behaviors we observe in the ensemble *every day*. So when did this dance begin?

## It all started around a campfire

We began as more solitary souls who hunted and gathered, competed for resources, for food, and for mates. The individuals who won those competitions survived. Anthropologists tell us that at some point, small groups began banding together to share resources and combine their skills, thus increasing their chances of survival. A tribe fared better than individuals, and therein the earliest concept of community may have been born. Together, we stood a better chance of finding food and shelter, we were safer and stronger, we lived longer, and our goal was simply "to survive." The very experience of *being* with others around the proverbial campfire may well have changed lives, and made life a little less daunting. Perhaps we needed one another to survive on a psychic and emotional level as well as a physical one (as we do now). Creating a group bond taught us that our chances of survival were ensured through communal living.

There continues to be an eternal yearning for community that draws us from solitude to a group, whether life is on the line or not. That yearning, however ephemeral it might feel at times, stirs within each of us. We crave family, companionship, connection, and love. We thrill when we stumble upon a group that has the "right" chemistry; they embrace us, and consider us an invaluable member. We identify it as magical, a place to feel safe and warm; to be ourselves to the fullest extent. The fire that we gather around now *is* one another. And in that gathering, aren't we responding to an ancient instinct to seek "survival?"

We recognize when we're a part of an ensemble, a team, or a community. At the heart of that bond, we retain a dual identity both as an individual, and as a vital

22

member of the ensemble. In every sense it's the best of both worlds. That instinctual sense, which protected us from danger by encouraging the group bond so many thousands of years ago, is now stirred, fed, and satisfied. The ensemble itself feels stronger because of our contribution and commitment.

## Rose

While volunteering on an archaeological dig, I personally witnessed some of the world's oldest evidence for ensemble and communal rites being discovered in Neolithic court tombs in Ireland. Among the world's oldest communal ritual sites (some tombs date to 4200 BC), these stone structures earned their name from their distinctive feature of an exterior, public forecourt which one must pass through before accessing smaller interior chambers. A majority of these sites have yielded evidence of specific arrangements and patterning of individual bones that creates an impression of societal beliefs and rituals.

For four summers I volunteered with Dr. Carleton Jones of the National University of Ireland on a court tomb dig at Roughan Hill, County Clare, believing I would gain deeper insights into the history of storytelling and theatre. Later analysis revealed that our court tomb had been in continual use from 3600 BC to 2800 BC. Bone analysis showed that everyone from the community was represented: male and female, from infants to 45-year-olds. During season three, I was working in the oldest chamber and discovered a patterning of bones that seemed to form a "complete leg." There was a patella (knee cap), then a tibia (shin bone) placed below it, a calcaneous (heel) below that, and so on to the toe bones, all laid out in perfect order of a single leg. My supervisor, Jessica Beckett, quickly determined that every bone representing this single leg was in fact, from different individuals. When I picked my own jaw up off the ground, I peppered Jessica with questions. What were the Neolithic people trying to communicate about the nature of community in the design of a single "body?" Were they expressing the life force of the community itself as a single entity? Jessica smiled and said, "I think that would be something cool to explore with actors in a ritual workshop."

Carleton and I had been discussing ways in which art and theatre could inform science, and after many pub-fueled discussions, we decided to conduct a series of workshops. I gathered a group of actors back in New York and Carleton provided cultural and historic information on the time period for them. In one workshop, I created a ground plan of our court tomb, and placed objects that represented some of our more significant finds in the precise locations where they were discovered. I designed a series of exercises focusing on ritual improvisation, one of which instructed the actors to create a ritual that would *result* in the evidence ending up in its specific location. One actor focused on the "community leg." The ritual he created involved the entire group: he had each person place a "bone" that had belonged to one of their own family members/ancestors onto this communal "body," building an entire individual out of the bones of community members that had died. After a whole representation of the human figure had been created by the "community" (including the "leg" we found), each member took a turn to lie on top of the whole human figure, face up to the sky. Some of this had been planned by the actor, some of it improvised, as the ritual took on a life of its own.

In the post-exercise discussion, I asked the actors about their discoveries. There was a lot of emotion while they endeavored to express what they had tapped into. Responses included: "I felt that even when someone had died, it was important to find a way to keep them alive in the community." "Handling the bone connected me with my ancestor, and helped me connect with my living tribe." "Placing my contribution made me feel a part of something larger." "It strengthened how important my own contribution to the tribe was." Finally, one actor who had been quiet for some time, said: "I think I just realized something profound ... when I laid down on the 'bones' of all the people, in that individual human shape, I felt the power and support of the people who came before me, and of the people I was surrounded by *now*. It made me feel safe, loved, a part of a larger family. I felt powerful, like I could do anything if I had that." She paused, and then said, "It's what *we* do. It's ensemble. It's a story. It's a story of *us*. I think I just found out why I have to do theatre. I need my tribe."

I had been looking for answers about the history of theatre. What I found was an even more exciting possibility for the history of ensemble.

## From ancient to modern

We're still trying to find ways to keep our tribe and ancestors alive through the ritual of storytelling, coming together as a tribe to express something in a theatre instead of a court tomb. Family, tribe, community, we don't need to be taught the value of this; it's hardwired in our DNA. We build communities for our protection and survival, and there is no greater force that creates community than Fear. (In this chapter, when referring to Fear as an entity, character, persona, or personal noun, we'll capitalize it. When referencing fears in general terms, or as the verb "to fear," it will be lower case.) In fact, our response to fear *is* community; tragedies, natural disasters, and wars bond people together in a nearly instantaneous way. Community and Ensemble *defeat* Fear. However, as ancient fears (animals, weather) are supplanted by contemporary ones (fear of failure and fear of rejection), our belief patterns evolve. Our personal fears protect us from harm when we believe that community, or our family, has failed us. In the modern world, the cave is *within* us, and our response to what we fear drives us into that cave to feel safe from what lies outside. We may be momentarily protected, but we're also isolated from the tribe and all the support that it offers.

The desire to overcome personal fear is often a prime motivating force for someone to join an ensemble, though it can be difficult to trust that the tribe will support their efforts to emerge from the cave (or Comfort Zone). Staying in the cave has kept us alive and safe; that's why it can feel so counterintuitive to risk danger by going outside. What's outside the cave? Maybe there's food (that can make you stronger), maybe there's fire (that can make you safer), and maybe there are other people who can help you defeat the myth or the reality of your Fear. As we work to create and maintain ensembles, we need to understand the dynamics of fear, how to confront it and take action. Those of you who have furrowed your brows, try not to worry; you already know the antidote. The antidote to fear is building trust, safety, risk-taking, and oh yes, ensemble. See? Now you don't need to read the rest of the book. Kidding.

### Rose

Fear is an old enemy, and an old friend, of humankind and has a long history as our Great Protector. Hardwired into our DNA are those ancient fears that kept us safe from being eaten by saber tooth tigers (when you see that thing with the big teeth, *run*), or safe from being hit by lightning (don't go outside during an electrical storm). Deep within our psyches we have fears of dark places (what beast lurks there?), of storms (being cold and wet feels pretty bad) or heights (falling *hurts*). These ancient fears were fueled by our survival instincts, which made the difference between life and death for our ancestors. Developing the Fear, and listening to it, *benefited* our ancestors, and protected them from dangers unique to their environments. Most fears are specific to a people and their time period: smilodons in 12,000 BC, plague in AD 1400, war in 1939. Through instincts and intelligence, each generation is challenged to develop specific sets of fears that will protect them and increase their chances of survival.

So what happens when those fears that ensured our survival are no longer needed? Does the absence of life-or-death fears make *personal* fears loom larger? Are our instincts still working to develop fears that uniquely evolve in response to personal dangers? And is that Fear trying to keep us *alive*, even though the threat has become extinct? The role of Fear as our Protector explains why some fears still feel as if they're a matter of life or death.

When fear is inhibiting an individual, it's inhibiting the ensemble, so you need to support them in working through it. We start that process by acknowledging their Fear as a very real entity, examining the personal history of that "relationship," and coming to a deeper understanding of it as a way of diminishing its power. That's the intellectual battle; once we understand its nature, the psychic and emotional battle can be won with the support and trust of the ensemble.

## David

When working in a collaborative, creative venture, a person's confidence level is always at risk. Artists and students will often play it safe rather than take a risk. This is most commonly due to an overly conditioned fear of failure and/or rejection. So keen is their Fear that they go to great lengths of denial and rationalization. Somewhere along the line, our society evolved into one that puts a premium on not only success, but on perfection. We hold our icons up as pillars of perfection in some area of expertise, only to search for the flaws that render them "mortal." Michael Jordan is considered the greatest basketball player of his generation, if not of all time, but when he dared to take a risk and play baseball, the criticism he received was a virtual tidal wave.

Who would want to take risks in this environment? It's a hypercritical, competitive society that feeds our fear of failure. Instant access of information through tweeting, blogs, and social media spreads the word faster, even if "the word" isn't true. Mistakes are pounced upon immediately, followed by rampant denial, cover-up and finger-pointing in an attempt to deflect blame or responsibility. The term "managing risk" is now a popular one in corporate America. How can you be free to let your imagination soar if you're continually editing and censoring it?

This is a toxic environment for learning and collaborating. How can we, as directors and educators, work to overcome this now commonly bred quality among our students and artists? Let's start with the good news: just by pursuing an artistic field, we're taking a risk. And as artists, we can't afford to run from fear, because our job is to explore uncharted lands. This demands that we run *toward* fear and the unknown, not *away* from it. As legendary improv leader Del Close said, "Follow the fear." Those who we work with are among the bravest souls out there. Even if they're not taking risks, somewhere deep down, they *want* to!

Follow the fear. If you play it safe, you will rarely make new discoveries. But if you have the courage to follow the fear, you will continually find yourself in new uncharted lands. Even if you're not practicing improvisation, you can put this idea to good use. Following the fear doesn't necessarily make you foolhardy or capricious, it makes you an explorer.

Following the fear can be liberating and empowering, especially creatively. It leads to discoveries and breakthroughs. Once you learn to follow the fear, to take risks consistently, you are equipped with a faster, more powerful creative process. Let's not forget that fear is a great motivator and a great focuser; why not help students learn to harness that power and use it more constructively?

### David

I used to look upon fear the same way most people do. I now have a deep appreciation for fear. It has an upside, a very *big* upside. I embrace the unknown; I take risks far more than ever before. I follow the fear because I'm addicted to making discoveries. Sure, I have to navigate failures, but I'd have to do that anyway (while wasting a lot of time and energy trying to avoid or deny them).

## Ensemble defeats Fear: first steps

We've known teachers and directors who, when they encounter fear in actors or students, simply say, "They need to get over it. It's paralyzing them, and they can't work." This may be true, but telling someone to "get over it" isn't actually going to *help* them get over it. If their Fear is so big that it's paralyzing them, trust us, they're well aware that they need to "get over it." What they may not know is why their Fear feels so overwhelming, why *telling* themselves to "stop being afraid" isn't working. How many times have you heard a fearful student or an actor say, "I feel like I'm going to die." This makes complete sense given the role of the Fear Protector. They're not crazy; they're *listening* to those messages that kept the tribe alive. Unfortunately, those old messages got linked to other events in their lives, and this now prevents them from trusting themselves, and the ensemble. This is why their Fear can feel so huge; their instincts believe they're literally saving them from death.

Given this understanding, you can guide ensemble members to become aware that:

- they're not crazy; they're actually listening to their biology
- their Fear Protector was actually their friend at some point, which dispels some of the shame that comes with fear
- they won't die if they confront their Fear.

The payment that Fear demands in return for protection is Power, just like the big kid on the playground who had your back in exchange for lunch money. Empower your Fear, and Fear keeps you safe. Until, of course, you become strong enough to protect yourself, and you want your power back. Telling someone to "get over it" isn't going to help. Support and gradual, consistent examination of the thing their Fear protected them from *will* help. Specific recommendations are listed later in this chapter.

Of course, don't even think about muddying the waters between essential therapeutic treatment and art. Someone who is suffering as a result of profound trauma should be counseled to seek professional help. Remember, our work may be therapeutic, but it should never *be* therapy. For those haunted by more commonplace but nonetheless paralyzing fears, you can guide them to a deeper understanding of their relationship to it. Beginning the conversation with your ensemble members about their Fear Protector can put them on the path to healthier creative freedom. Introduce the ideas and information; the rest will be up to them.

### David

Everyone has a comfort zone. Think of it as a circle that extends beyond your body. Let's say, for example, that your comfort zone extends three feet beyond your body. Just extending an arm then involves taking a small risk. I encourage my students to welcome their comfort zones and use them when necessary. It remains okay to play it safe *when necessary*. Cocooning inside their comfort zone gives them an opportunity to recover from a difficult failure or to regain confidence. However, once confidence is re-established, I tell them to start stepping outside of their comfort zone again. A step or two to begin with, and a little farther each time. I encourage them to try staying beyond the Comfort Zone until they sense the danger again. Ultimately it's not how far they go each time, but how frequently they can do that. Through repeated attempts, they're developing the thick skin to keep going. Then they achieve a real breakthrough and attain the persistence to stand repeated failure.

By continually challenging the boundary of their comfort zone, they increase its size. After taking several risks on something, they'll become more accomplished at that endeavor, or feel more comfortable trying. They've extended their comfort zone, and now have a new area with which they feel comfortable. This is a life-long pursuit, and it not only applies to ensemble members, but to us as leaders.

Part of our job as directors and educators is to watch for signs of fears. Is a student gliding along, resting on their strengths rather than working on their weaknesses?

Ban them from using their strengths for a time. Force them to struggle with areas they need to develop. Is a student suffering from low confidence? Encourage them to play within their comfort zone, praise them for their strengths, and build that confidence level. In essence, prepare them once again to address their weaknesses. After repetitions of exercises or rehearsals, they'll take greater risks. They've seen what the consequences are, and more important, what they *aren't*.

### Rose

There's an Augusto Boal exercise that is a powerful (and vulnerable) exercise in confronting fears head on: Mask of the Hero, Mask of the Fear. Actors are asked to write down the thing they were most afraid of in childhood: the boogey man, fire, scary clown doll, etc. If it's fear of the dark, ask them to write down what it was lurking in the dark that they were afraid of. Then, ask them to list the personality traits that their Fear possessed (physically strong, relentless, fearless, crafty, patient). Splitting the group in half, the first group goes into the space and is asked to focus on the top three traits associated with their Fear. You then guide them through a physical exploration of becoming their Fear as a *character*, embodying those identified traits. It's very important that they explore their Fear as a character, not *themselves* being terrorized *by* their Fear. This is non-verbal, though at some point in the exploration, sound is permitted with the physical exploration. The goal is not for the explorers to "indicate" who or what they are to the observers, but to explore their Fear and allow it to inhabit them as they would a character or mask.

Have the actors begin from neutral, walking in the space, connecting with their personal center of energy first. Gently coach them to focus on the traits and where those traits inhabit them physically. This should all be solo exploration, no interaction with others – yet. After they've established the physical life, traits, and demeanor of the character, permit interaction (still no words, sound and movement only), but coach them to move on to a new exchange, and then another. What do they discover in the interactions with the other Fears? Does a primary desire emerge? Eventually, coach them to return to private exploration, and then to neutral. Then, ask the observers to name *observed traits only*, and to resist the temptation to "guess" who or what the Fear was. Instructions are the same for Mask of the Hero. Privately, participants write down the identity of their childhood hero, a list of their traits, and then one group at a time goes into the playing area to focus on physically embodying the top traits of their Hero, and so forth. After the discussion, the observers then become the explorers, and vice versa.

Several things usually happen. First, the explorers report that the observed traits were indeed true for the character, but they hadn't actually included them on their list. Focusing on the specific listed traits released *other* characteristics. Second, they find that exploring their Fear as a *character* helped them to understand their Fear and to recognize *positive* traits their Fear possessed. Physical strength, intelligence, confidence, and (ironically) fearlessness are all pretty desirable traits. They realize that their Fear has strong traits that they would *like* to have, or that they *already* have. Third, they discover how closely linked their childhood Fear is to the things they fear now (e.g., if their parents divorced when they were young and their Fear was loneliness, they connect that to their adult Fear of Rejection). And if you've done Mask of the Hero first, participants note that their Fear and their Hero have more intersections than they would have guessed. They grew up not only wanting to become their Hero, but subconsciously to become their Fear as well; both held great power. Invariably the participants discover how much their childhood Hero and Fear influenced who they are, as well as what kinds of roles they're drawn to.

This exercise deepens their understanding of their Fear, and of their relationship to that Fear. Reactions can be powerful; sometimes it's not pretty to discover that you've been giving your power away to something that really isn't all that scary. It can also be liberating when someone embodies their Fear, and discovers how much they've grown. This is probably one of the most vulnerable exercises I know, and it's quite stunning when the ensemble realizes that:

- everyone has Fears
- they've just taken a huge risk and shared their Fear with the ensemble.

Again, discuss the characteristics, not the Fears themselves. If the actor wants to share the identity of their Fear, encourage them to hold on to that information until after class.

## Most common fears and recommendations

One of the biggest fears that actors and students have is the very fear that their Fear is so huge, it will never go away. In a sense they're right; their Fear may always strangle their creative work – so long as they continue to fight it *alone*. This adversarial relationship is very, very real. We've known people who describe their Fear as a tangible force that paralyzes them, and refer to its power in terms so frightening that when asked to be specific, they quickly say, "I don't know."

This isn't "I don't know" as in lack of information, it's "I don't know" as in "*I can't go there.*" Something very tangible, and very *real* exists in that "*there.*" Their Fear has been given so much power that they not only personify it, but also *externalize* it. And let's face it; who hasn't spoken out loud to their Fear as if it were a living creature? If we enter a dark house at night, haven't we said "Okay Monster, just stay in that corner over there and let me pass until I get to the light switch." And on a day when you have an important audition or interview, haven't you spent time at the mirror looking at your image saying, "You can do this. You can *do* this." Aren't we talking directly to our Fear of Failure?

Most fears boil down to the Big Four: Fear of Failure, Fear of Rejection, Fear of Judgment (subset of Rejection), and Fear of Looking Stupid (subset of Failure). The following descriptions and recommendations will help you understand and redirect these fears when they emerge.

### *Fear of Failure*

Probably one of the greatest of them all. The owner of this fear usually grew up with impossibly high standards, or lived in circumstances where the consequences of failing were unreasonably, or dangerously, high. Suffering from this fear nearly always manifests in the person holding back from significant risk-taking, and being harshly judgmental about choices they do make. Commitment suffers, and they are often stuck in playing the middle ground.

### *Fear of Failure: recommendations in any environment*

Once you've established a supportive environment, promote risk-taking. How? Champion failure; applaud it! Point out the relationship of subsequent successes to earlier failures. Demonstrate that failure is a necessary part of any creative process. If you work hard to avoid failure and minimize risk, you can't fully create; you're limiting yourself.

### David

I developed an exercise (initially inspired by my friend Alex Brewer's "MacGyver" exercise) to help improv students embrace the inevitability of failure through learning how to deal with it instead of avoiding it. It's called "I Know What To Do!" The students stand in a line facing me. One student, Susan, steps forward and announces that she has a very simple problem. ("Uh oh, my shoe is untied.") Immediately and without thinking, another student must leap forward and proclaim (as if a superhero character), "I know what to do!" (In reality, of course, they probably have absolutely no idea what to do.) Immediately after this, and again, without thinking (or worse, pre-planning), he points to three others in the line and assigns them each a random task of what to retrieve ("Doug: get me a roll of duct tape!" "Steven: get me a big rock." "Anna: Bring me the King of Greenland!"). Doug, Steven, and Anna run off to some part of the room and run back, now "carrying" the fulfillment of their assignments ("Here's the duct tape – it's yellow!" "Here's the big rock, it's made of volcanic limestone." "Meet the King of Greenland, King Mortimer Hortensio III."). Notice that I've asked them to add some small piece of information if possible (the duct tape is yellow). Doug, Steven, and Anna must fulfill their assignments as quickly and easily as possible. There may be a tendency to say things like, "I couldn't get duct tape, but here's some masking tape." Try to discourage this; their job is not to complicate things, but to support the superhero character. All of the above should happen quickly, with no opportunity to think of "appropriate" responses. At this point, the superhero must use the three items to improvise a solution to Susan's initial problem. Doug, Steven, and Anna are allowed to help. The superhero might say, "Susan, meet King Mortimer Hortensio III of Greenland. He will distract you from your troubles while I fix your shoe. Now put your foot up on this big rock so I can get a closer look at its 'untiedness.' Doug and Steven: use that duct tape to bind Susan's shoe to her foot." At this point, Doug and Steven furiously mime wrapping Susan's foot in duct tape, while Susan pretends to be talking with the King. Seconds later, Doug and Steven finish with a flourish and all five smile in pride and amazement (Tada!) at the "ingeniously" solved problem. In this example, the students actually came up with a fairly reasonable solution. More often they're far more ridiculous.

Most of the students will look amazed at how much fun the exercise was and how the solution actually seemed to work (even if in an odd way). A few skeptics will look frustrated, as if to say, "Well, that's dumb." I now tell them that the exercise is *designed* so that they will fail. "If anything at all went right, it's a miracle. How can you possibly fashion a reasonable solution that combines at least four ideas, with no time to think? It's a ridiculous premise that some of you took quite seriously, and now you feel dissatisfied with the outcome. Now that you know it's ridiculous, do it again and don't take it so seriously – have fun!" At this point, they eagerly leap into subsequent rounds free from worrying about "being right"; free from Fear of Failure. They play; they open up their imaginations and come up with wildly creative "solutions" to simple problems. Some students will take longer to feel completely comfortable than others, but eventually, they discover that their Fear is unfounded and they're better than they thought they'd be. Over time, you'll notice that the solutions become more clever. Free from having to "be right," they actually get much closer to "being right," all the while making split-second decisions. The players also become better at working together as a team. In the end, the players move from feeling scared about failing to actually having fun and being creative. They're still largely failing (because the exercise is so hard), but every so often, a brilliant and unexpected solution comes out and they see that they're getting better by tolerating some creative failures.

This kind of approach can then be brought into other areas of the work you are doing. Be careful about what you say that might inhibit the ensemble members. Remember, *you* have to allow failure as much as they do. Watch your students be bad at something without intervening or correcting too much. Be patient; let them fail, acknowledge that they haven't quite "gotten" it yet, and let them keep trying. Don't be too quick to hand them your solution. Tell them to stick with it, and through practice and repetition their failures will pay off with more desirable results. Of course, there are times when you need to intervene, but don't forget to balance this with the freedom to learn through trial and error.

An atmosphere where failure is embraced and supported leads to greater risk-taking; but is all risk-taking good? Just ask those folks who send around the Darwin Awards every year. Responsible risk doesn't necessarily mean hedging your bets or pulling back; it means that no one has permission to take advantage of this atmosphere to misbehave. A supportive environment that embraces risk is an extraordinary gift, a privilege that is earned through hard work and trust. Therefore, it comes with responsibilities that must be honored if it is to continue. There's a difference between taking a creative risk and behaving like a jackass or indulging in foolishness. Beware those who would take advantage of this environment and use it selfishly.

### *Fear of Rejection*

Those who experience this believe that they may not be accepted by the ensemble/ family, and will be abandoned. "Can I ever do enough to get to stay?" Being cast out, not picked, and ultimately not "loved," covers just about every human condition that forms our emotional core, so of course it affects us in the pursuit of our art (and in life). This can also directly impact the role that the person takes on in the ensemble itself (see Chapter 5).

## *Fear of Rejection: recommendations for the classroom*

Whether a scene study or improv class, take the time to focus on exercises that examine the building blocks of what you're specifically exploring. It will help students discover what uniquely inhibits their process, and thus they will be more open to learn the skills. Using a specific series of exercises, and repeating them, helps students chart their growth and confidence. They will redefine what "risk" means by returning to familiar territory again and again.

- Blind Offers (see Appendix A): This exercise reinforces that every offer will be accepted, that a partner will always be able to "do" something with that offer, and that the offer, and the individual, is "enough." This begins lessening the fear of "not being enough."
- Come Join Me (see Appendix B): There is no right or wrong choice; the group builds from the initial offer, no matter what. This reinforces that every offer will be accepted, and the student will experience how much the ensemble was able to create from their simple but specific action. This, and the very act of having the ensemble join them in the playing area, works wonders to reduce fears.
- What Are You Doing? (see Appendix C): Also reinforces that every offer will be accepted, and be "enough" for their partners to work with.
- Sound and Movement (see Appendix D): Everyone experiences their offer being received and built upon by both a partner and the entire group.

## *Fear of Rejection: recommendations for rehearsal/production*

You may have the kind of rehearsal process for which some of the above exercises can be included. If not, consider the following:

- At the first read-through, include the following in your opening remarks:
  - Though you might feel it's a given, *please* say out loud: "I need everyone to share all they've got; please listen to your first impulses and responses; we need to see *all* of your choices so that together we can create the strongest story possible. Never assume where a wonderful idea is going to come from." By nurturing openness and acceptance, you're discouraging any rejection that could be a trigger for someone's Fear. You've stated for the record that you will not reject anything, though you will *assess* it. This way you're all starting together with a creative contract that all of you will try not to reject anything, or push a choice aside for fear of it being rejected.
  - Define terms that are essential to the process: e.g., you might say that the only wrong thing is to do *nothing*.
  - State your commitment to creating a safe and supportive environment within which everyone will be able to do their strongest possible work. You are agreeing to take on the role of Protector, which pre-empts Fear Protector behaviors.

- If later in rehearsals you observe someone withholding choices, Fear of Rejection is often the culprit. See Chapter 6 for further specifics.
- Depending on the nature of the scene where you observe the behavior, doing status work can be invaluable. Keith Johnstone's chapter on status in *Impro* should be required reading for us all. His concept of status focuses on hierarchy in relationships, one's value within the social pack, and the active raising and lowering of our status within that pecking order. Status relies on the see-saw principle: if someone's status is going up, someone else's is going down; it's active. Johnstone describes someone playing high status as, "Don't come near me; I bite," and someone playing low status as, "Don't bite me. I'm not worth the trouble." Using status terms can help take an actor's focus off of their Fear's trigger (Confrontation? Intimacy?). Focusing on high or low status within the scene instead of focusing solely on the objective can give enough expansion to their comfort zone to allow them to explore what they're avoiding.

### *Fear of Judgment*

This often arises in those who were (or perceived they were) denied something in life. Those who experience this fear believe that "Someone" out there has set a series of impossibly high standards, and they try to meet those *imagined* standards instead of trusting their own. They second-guess what the imagined expectations are, and tie themselves in knots trying to predict the unknowable. This is particularly self-destructive, as it sets them up for failure. Johnstone references "The Watcher at the Gates of the Mind," and Fear of Judgment puts that Watcher on 24-hour guard duty. No one gets in or out without knowing the password.

#### *Fear of Judgment: recommendations for either classroom or rehearsal*

- West Side Story (see Appendix E): There is no way for the ensemble to predict what the offer will be, and it moves so fast that there's no time to judge impulses. And because the "team" joins each initiation, there is a sense of immediate acceptance; from their own partners and from the opposing team. Everyone leads and follows equally. With no elimination, the only possible way to fail is to do "nothing." And since everyone takes equal turns, that can never happen.
- Physical exercises such as Kitty Wants a Corner (the non-elimination form, *always!*), Sound and Movement, or the Blindfold Series (see Appendix G). Words tend to be closely associated with harsh self-judgment. Exercises that require physical communication allow actors to experience how much they communicate with less than what they *think* they need.

#### *Fear of Judgment: recommendations specific to rehearsal/production*

- See previous note in Fear of Rejection on opening remarks for first read-through. Depending on the age and experience of your cast, you could add: "Though I appreciate everyone's commitment and desire to want to make a contribution to the show, please leave any directorial guidance to me – even if your best friend is begging you for *your* notes. Let me do my job, so I can support you doing *your* job." The temptation for actors to give each other notes can be exacerbated by low budget (which can limit rehearsal time), by familiarity, or by a rivalry. Your statement makes the structure clear in a supportive way. Though it won't erase *imagined* judgment, it will help someone know that they'll only be experiencing verbal assessment from you.

- See Chapter 6 for behaviors regarding withholding, and actors who block partners. Fear of Rejection is often the culprit. The actor's very desire to *be* a good scene partner is often what makes them close off, because of worry that their offer won't be "enough" for their scene partner.

### Fear of Looking Stupid

This often evolves when someone has been singled out for high expectations, was pressed to be an over-achiever, or was made to bear greater responsibility than they could reasonably handle at a young age. The consequences for failing were likely rejection, derision, or disappointment from a family member or a teacher. The Fear was created to protect them from these consequences. In their acting, it evolved into "If I never take a risk, I will never look stupid."

#### Fear of Looking Stupid: recommendations for the classroom

- West Side Story: the physical silliness that can arise, and its speed, helps everyone see that the expectations are the same, and most important, that no one thinks anyone is "looking stupid."
- Kitty Wants a Corner: again, the non-elimination form. This is low-stakes risk-taking, which feels incredibly high at the outset. At first they fear that being "Kitty" is punishment and they learn quite the opposite.
- Family Portraits (see Appendix H): This physically challenging (and hysterically funny) exercise doesn't give anyone time to worry about what they look like. And because there are only group turns, they always have a "Family" in tow.
- Silly Walk Relay Race (see Appendix I): Rose has used this as a mid-term exam in her graduate improv class. Seriously, it relieves stress and pressure from outside work, and there is honor in being the silliest walker. Everyone does it, everyone cheers on their team, and what defines "silly" becomes completely redefined.

#### Fear of Looking Stupid: recommendations for rehearsal/performance

- See previous note in Fear of Rejection on suggestions for first read-throughs. The welcome mat has been placed out, you've stated that there is no such thing as a stupid idea by inviting *all* offers, and you've prohibited judgmental remarks. "You look stupid" *is* a judgment; a very specific and common one though, which is why we give it its own space here.

- Positive reinforcement and an honest, well-timed compliment can do wonders. Identify the parts of the play that seem to stimulate their Fear. (Is their character asked to take extreme action? Are they in a physically romantic scene?) Positive notes can guide them to what *is* working. And don't push them too hard, too early. If you press for a result early in the process, you leave the actor nowhere to go, and they fear looking stupid as they try to push beyond that initial "result."
- If you narrowly define how a specific moment should go before the actors have had a chance to explore it (and no line readings, ever), they fear looking stupid because they don't yet understand what that moment is *about*. They feel they're looking stupid because they're *feeling* stupid. If you notice you've done this, stop them immediately. Tell them you were wrong (even if you weren't) and start from scratch. Encourage discovery and investigation, and if you *were* right about the initial direction, guess what? They'll find it themselves, and it will be much richer because of their ownership of the discovery. And if you were *wrong*, they'll show you that by arriving at a dynamic that will be better than what you originally proposed. Dare to be proved wrong. About everything.

### *Individual fears becoming the ensemble's Fear*

It's a good thing when fear drives someone to seek support in finding their tribe; not so good if they want to "hide" within the safety of the group. There's a subset of fears that can arise, and even if the Fear is triggered by how much the individual wants the ensemble to succeed, these fears will ultimately affect the entire group. These include:

- *I'm going to let the ensemble down.* A person becomes tentative with choices and starts to isolate, which means they're not listening to partners, and may start to seek an inordinate amount of reassurance from you and the ensemble. Everyone goes through insecure times, and ensembles are generous because we all know "our day is coming." But. If it continues unabated, having to constantly tell a member of the group that they're worthy is going to get old very fast.
- *I'm going to make all of us look bad.* Can also lead to tentative choices, avoiding risk, or making the same kinds of choices repeatedly. This invariably leads to constant apologies. We've all experienced someone who repeatedly says "I'm sorry" for every little thing. This may have begun as an isolated insecurity, but it evolved into a habit for which they reject taking responsibility for any choices at all.
- *I'm going to be responsible for all of us failing.* Actually a fairly egotistical position. Though their Fear is real, they need to be reminded of their role in

the ensemble. The ensemble succeeds, and fails, as a team. Its success doesn't rise and fall on the actions of one individual.

- *I'm going to be banished from the group.* The ultimate Fear of Rejection from the tribe. They join this group because they want to be a part of something, but the entire time they live in fear of the day they'll be rejected by the group. A vicious cycle.

These dynamics can challenge even the most supportive ensemble. We don't always have time to address the individual's Fear in the midst of group work (nor is it always appropriate). In nearly every situation though, whether someone is holding back, or imposing their Fear on the ensemble, there are two sentences we use that have made a positive impact every single time. They provide an immediate shorthand that applies to nearly every Fear, and to nearly every potential solution. The first sentence:

- *What's the worst thing that can happen?*

If you don't know the "what the hell" speech from Terry Johnson's play *Insignificance*, I urge you to share it with your ensemble. The Actress (Marilyn Monroe) shows up at the Scientist's (Albert Einstein) hotel room at 2:00 A.M. to prove to him she understands the theory of relativity, which she successfully does. In the wonderful teacher/student moment that follows, the Actress describes why she took the risk:

> And I knew my last chance to see you before you left New York ... would be to wake you up in the middle of the night and I told myself go ahead, because if he doesn't understand how you have to wake people up in the middle of the night sometimes, nobody will. I thought What the Hell. Have you ever noticed how what the hell is always the right decision?

And if someone continues to say things like: "I'm afraid I'll go blank," or "I'm afraid I'm not giving my partner enough," go to the second sentence:

- *The well is never dry.*

And then proceed to point out all the things they've done to *prove* that your theory is correct. Keep it simple. It's less about praising them for good vs. bad things, but to help them realize how much they're *already* doing, despite their focus on the negatives. Draw their attention to strong, clear actions they've taken, and give them specific examples. Ask them "Did you freeze? No. Was your partner able to work with what you gave them? Yes. Did your pants catch on fire because you took an extra moment to honor your impulse? No." There is always water in the well, and the spring that feeds it is fed itself by everything that surrounds us; including the ensemble.

## Conclusion

Understanding and recognizing our historic relationship to Fear and its relationship to our need for community will help you create and maintain a stronger and healthier ensemble. "Those who do not study the past are destined to repeat it." That counts for our anthropological history too. Though we state in Chapter 3 that you're not a therapist destined to fix someone, neither should you *ignore* the fears when they arise. Remember the three A's: awareness, acknowledgment, and action. Don't simply identify their Fear once you've become aware of it and leave it at that. We've heard actors being told "You're tense; relax!" or "You're not allowing." Well no kidding – but saying those things alone doesn't help the actor confront the issue. You need to take *action*; action that will guide and support them to solutions that will diminish what blocks them.

### Rose

While discussing the exercise Kitty Wants a Corner in class, an actor shared the fact that as she sought to exchange places with someone in the circle, she felt her neck go stiff and she stopped breathing. After some gentle questioning, she realized that she was afraid of being "caught." Her real Fear though, was that that would mean she had failed and gotten it "wrong." I then told the ensemble that the only thing they could possibly do "wrong," was to do *nothing*; everything else was a *right* answer. I swear I saw ten sets of shoulders drop and relax. When I suggested to the actor that perhaps her Fear thought it was protecting her from something, she smiled and breathed deeply.

In modern society, unless we're in a supportive environment or are incredibly resilient, we struggle with what to do with our Fear once the danger has been removed, or we remove ourselves from the danger. We stay on alert; our Fear sees the danger embedded in a casual remark, in an unfamiliar school or theatre company, in a playful exercise that asks you to take a risk. "Where's the judgmental parent waiting to attack? Where is the harsh teacher waiting for us to fail? If you keep quiet, and don't share your ideas, you'll be safe. *I'll* protect you." What the heck do we do with something that big that promises safety?

And yet, something brought the ensemble members, and you, here. Something compelled you to create bonds with others and seek safety in community instead of safety within your Fear. We find ourselves in these scenarios again and again; we *must* want to conquer our Fear and choose a new way to work and live our lives. And instinctively, or consciously, we're drawn to the ensemble in the same way we were drawn to create community in pre-history; to defeat our Fears and draw strength from our bonds with other people. The Ensemble takes on the role of the Protector, and unlike our Fear that isolated us, it gives us the fellowship and support of a community. Fear created Ensemble; Ensemble destroys Fear, and replaces it with something much healthier and more rewarding. The tango between Fear and Trust becomes a waltz between Trust and Ensemble. And we not only survive, we thrive. Just like the owners of those bones …

# 3

# LEADING ENSEMBLE

Leadership is the art of accomplishing goals through other people.
You can be the most brilliant innovator, problem-solver or strategic
thinker, but if you can't inspire and motivate, build relationships, or
communicate powerfully, those talents will get you nowhere.
–Daniel Goleman, "The Must-Have Leadership Skill,"
as appeared in *Harvard Business Review*

## Ensembles need leadership

An ensemble may have all the right ingredients for success and still not succeed. Why? It's often because of poor leadership or no leadership at all. When we hear "leadership," what comes to mind? The military? Politics? Athletics? Corporate management? Do these associations raise any negative connotations for you? The term gets bandied about so much that it has become a buzzword. It seems there's an article about it in every issue of those in-flight magazines that airlines stick in the pouch in front of your seat. *10 Steps To Becoming a More Effective Leader! Secrets of Successful Business Leaders! Lead from the Front, Listen from Your Rear!* It can be difficult cutting through all the hooey and jargon out there.

Being a teacher or director is synonymous with being a leader; yet in real life, we know this isn't always the case. Leadership may be the most underestimated and overlooked ingredient in teaching and directing. Some teachers and directors may look upon their academic or creative goals for an ensemble as the extent of their involvement. *I am to direct a great production. I am to make sure that my students learn this material.* Yet in order to accomplish these goals, they have to lead a group of people. Not students, not actors: *people.* Human beings with feelings, agendas, fears, personality conflicts, bad days, and so on. Human beings who may or may not be happy about being *led.*

Yet for all of these issues, how much time in rehearsal or class is spent on leading the ensemble? Directors typically do research and text analysis; they cast, rehearse, and collaborate with designers, all in an effort to mount a successful production. Teachers lecture, conduct exercises, give tests, and offer feedback, all in an effort to train their students. In this sense, ensemble members can become viewed almost as commodities that are merely a part of the process. Whether student or actor, they're judged for their individual talent, or their potential as performers, or their learning ability. They're not always considered as people who have to work together effectively to enable each other's full potential.

So what does leadership mean to an *ensemble* leader? What do you need to be an effective ensemble leader? To begin, know what ensemble members typically need from you to succeed as a bonded group:

- inspiration
- motivation
- discipline
- connection
- good will
- praise
- honest feedback
- guidance
- problem resolution skills
- a trusted confidant
- a good listener
- a strong sense of who you are and why you are here.

So that's what the ensemble needs from you. What do *you* need from your*self* to be a more effective leader? Be willing to go where you're asking the ensemble to go; examine what your contribution is.

## What do you bring to the table, and is this the right table?

Why do you want to be an ensemble leader? Why do you want to lead a collaborative ensemble instead of a competitive group? How do you see your role as a leader? It's impossible to be clear on the ensemble's goal if you haven't yet identified your *personal* goals. And it's impossible to identify your personal goals without knowing who you are as an artist and a leader. We decided to put these questions to ourselves and here are our responses:

### Rose

There's something about the connection in an ensemble that's so essential, so primal for me. Call it search for family, for home, I have that desire to come together with people and make those bonds strong. Years ago a therapist asked me why I chose to be a director and I told her "I want to create a healthy family over and over again. I want to be a good parent to this family that only lasts a short time. Then, the show or class is over, and

I start a new one. Being a good parent to the ensemble is what I find so satisfying." It may sound selfish, but it's true. What I do IS who I am. Can that be love? I think it's that simple; creating something that's going to make a positive difference in the world. Feeling so much love that comes from current and former cast members and students. Not love for who I am, but for what I do; for what we created together. I feed off of that. I love doing it. Leadership? Being a good parent. Teaching, and not resenting when they've learned the material. Guiding, and celebrating when they no longer need the map. Directing, and embracing when the actors make the show their own. Bringing a group together for a common goal and enjoying that you are one component of the whole, you're not the whole thing.

## David

I have a hard time creating on my own. It's not fun for me, I find it lonely. Sitting at my computer writing this chapter is nothing compared to talking about it with Rose. I love the excitement that comes from creating something *together*. I love what becomes possible through collaboration. I want to make great collaborations happen. That's why I want to be a leader. I need collaborators; they bring out the best in me and I thrive on bringing out the best in them. And the way to do that, for me, is to lead them to a safe place where they're so trusting of each other (and me) that they are free to be their true selves and free to take risks. Then I get to watch them soar. That place is ensemble. And leading people to that place can inspire devotion and love from them in return. As Rose says, not for who I am, but for what I do. I, too, feed off of that. It makes me feel less lonely, and that's what family is all about.

In answering the questions we opened this section with, you've begun to deepen your self-awareness and illuminate why you're compelled to work with ensemble again and again. Your responses help clarify the skills and talent you bring to the table. Now let's look at some essential leadership traits you will need:

- The willingness to commit fully to the goal – no matter what.
- Heightened awareness. This means superior listening and observation skills. Use those skills to answer the question, "What is needed?"
- The ability to earn trust and inspire others to do the same.
- The ability to communicate clearly and consistently. Be sure you know yourself and your goals; otherwise you'll struggle to articulate your message.

- The ability to tune in to different "frequencies" and "languages."
- The ability to find the one frequency that will bring them all together.
- The willingness to fiercely protect what has been created.
- The ability to empower others and give them what they need to keep the ensemble healthy.
- The ability to identify who is/are the natural leader(s) among the members and develop a relationship.
- The ability to share or even let go of your ownership.
- The openness to listen when your mind is screaming, "NO!" You don't have to tolerate everything, but do try to listen to everyone.
- The willingness to make personal sacrifices.
- The willingness to allow the ensemble to evolve.

You may not possess all of these in equal measure, so determine which are your strengths and which you may need to develop. Throughout this book you'll find ways to develop your leadership skills, and by the time you've finished reading it, you'll have a clear idea of what you need to put into practice.

## What kind of leader are you?

Good leadership, like good direction, is usually characterized by *not* being able to see the fingerprints of the leader. Ask a strong ensemble leader how they made something terrific happen, and they may say, "I just do what I do" or "I didn't do anything special – I just made sure we focused on the goal." These self-effacing responses are great clues as to why someone with strong leadership skills chooses to apply them in artistic realms instead of, say, the corporate world or the military. As you've worked to identify why you do this work, what you bring to it, and what you want from it, you've been working toward understanding what kind of leader you are. So let's find out – and let's do it in a fun way …

Somewhere between Captain Kirk and Colonel Klink is a range of leadership types that can be successful. Virtually no one is a Captain Kirk (and if you are, you probably don't need this book), and we will assume that none of us are Colonel Klinks. And while there is only one Rose Bonczek and one David Storck, we both possess recognizable leadership styles that fall into broad categories with like-minded leaders. Once we come to recognize ourselves, we can hone our leadership skills and grow toward the unique, specific style that best suits us: The Rose Bonczek and The David Storck. We have assembled a short list of the more common styles that we've come across among ensemble leaders. You may recognize yourself in more than one of these, but which one is closest to you?

- Mr. Miyagi. You possess a balance of good teaching and guidance, and know how to encourage self-reliance in ensemble members. You join the ensemble on the trail, but you allow room for them to choose the direction you take together. You encourage teamwork, and stress a need for one another.
- Ferris Bueller/Auntie Mame. You adhere to a specific philosophy that you believe guides the ensemble, and you believe that there is only one path to the destination. Without your leadership in teaching this guiding principle, the ensemble would be lost. "They need me. And the principle."
- Lucy Ricardo. You want to lead, but lack the confidence to do so. You have enough strength and intelligence to put the ensemble together, but then you find yourself seeking reassurance from the ensemble for your own personal need. You sometimes find that you have missed the collective goal, or don't have enough energy for the goal, because you're directing too much energy to your personal needs or anxiety.
- Winnie the Pooh. You have a light leadership touch, and can be heard to excitedly say: "I don't know. Let's find out together!" You tend to be more flexible, thrive on living in the question, and you understand the value in process and discovery, sometimes to the detriment of the destination. You inspire the ensemble to discover together, and you excel at helping ensemble members distinguish fear of the unknown from the joy and wonder of new discoveries.
- HAL 9000. You keep very strict rules in the group, and you're more comfortable being an authority figure apart from the ensemble vs. leading from within the ensemble. You tend to lean on structure, and believe that the goal cannot be achieved without adherence. This can generate an ensemble that is capable of great achievements; however, if you're blinded by the regulations, it can foment an ensemble of "rebellion." That is, an ensemble united against a common enemy.

The bottom line: know who you are as a leader: your style, your strengths, and your weaknesses. You can't lead effectively without self-awareness. In that spirit, we offer our own self-assessments to help you get the ball rolling on yours.

### Rose

Though it's taken me a long time to get to Mr. Miyagi, I was definitely a Winnie the Pooh for a long time (and need to be mindful about being tempted in that direction). I used to get so turned on by the process; I'd forget that sooner or later we needed to get to the destination. Nothing was ever more exciting than the unknown.

**David**

Rose and I are so alike on this with our mutual love of the process, which is what started the conversations that led to this book. I too began as a Winnie the Pooh (with a dash of Ferris Bueller/Auntie Mame) and worked to find the balance between process and destination that led me to a Mr. Miyagi. And of course it's a never-ending challenge, so I keep looking for ways to become a better Mr. Miyagi.

So is Mr. Miyagi the ideal? In a sense, yes. But don't get caught up in trying to fulfill this model. Remember, we're doing this in a fun way – even HAL 9000 has desirable qualities. Recognize which desirable qualities you may be missing and work to add them. And look to diminish qualities that may be harmful to your leadership ability. The ideal is the *Your Name Here* leadership style. Be the best leader you can be while remaining true to yourself.

## Strengthening/adding to your skill set

There are specific challenges that come with "accomplishing goals through other people," and the more you know about those challenges, the stronger your leadership skills will become. Have you heard the saying, "a camel is a horse designed by a committee?" Without proper leadership, that's exactly what you'll get. Because when a group of people comes together (whether strangers waiting in line at the bank or fellow partygoers), they will be unavoidably human. It's virtually impossible for them to look at each other without making comparisons in their minds. We all have egos, we all compare, even judge, and that can lead to feelings of competitiveness within the ensemble, and in you personally. These are significant challenges to your leadership abilities. Let's examine the roles of ego, judgment, competition, and how you can use your "sniffer" (we'll explain) to be attuned to them, and balance them, in the ensemble and in your leadership approach.

### *The role of ego*

#### *Managing your ego*

Let's start with the Big Cheese. What kind of ego is best for the leader of an ensemble? A healthy one; confident, not arrogant or needy. Particularly useful is the ability to cast an objective eye and assess your own ego. As leader, you must observe yourself because you are, indeed, a member of the ensemble. Along with being able to evaluate your unique strengths, you need to recognize your mistakes and shortcomings. Acknowledging them and adjusting in appropriate measure is part of establishing and maintaining a healthy ensemble. No one wants to follow a hypocrite, a tyrant, or someone hopelessly lacking in self-awareness. It *is* possible to admit your mistakes to the ensemble without weakening your leadership. If handled well, it can even enhance your position. Try not to allow pride to stand in your way, hard as that is for all of us. Ask yourself the difficult questions:

* Am I too controlling?
* Do I talk too much?
* Am I imposing my own discoveries at the expense of being open to the discoveries of others? Or conversely, am I not looking closely enough?
* Am I not providing clear guidelines?
* Am I not offering inspiration?

We're all susceptible to overlooking ourselves as the source of a problem.

On the other hand, you can't be relentlessly obsessed with what you're doing and how you're doing it or it will render you ineffective. Don't spend a lot of time trying to anticipate mistakes and prevent them. This goes back to our discussion of failure in Chapter 2, as mistakes are often seen as failures. Remember, as a member of the ensemble, you have a right to fail. Have you given yourself permission to do this? Have you told the ensemble? (Do it on your first day.) They need to know you're allowed to fail. If you're a good leader, they'll follow you even though you make mistakes. Exercise your leadership by how you *handle* your mistakes. Would you follow someone who pretends they don't make mistakes, or handles them poorly? We're more likely to follow someone who acknowledges mistakes. Mistakes are natural and they'll come no matter what you do, so *incorporate* them. They can be useful learning opportunities. Or, deal with them. On very rare occasions, ignore them (at your peril). As a wise man named George Storck once said, "Don't spend so much time and effort trying to avoid mistakes. Spend it on trying to avoid *repeating* mistakes."

In Chapter 1, we mentioned the issues of holding the reins of the ensemble too tightly or too loosely. If you realize that you're holding too tightly or too loosely, ask yourself why. Why do you need to keep tight control? Or, why do you avoid taking control? The answers to these questions are often related to your ego.

If you sense the ensemble is consistently doing things that are counterproductive, or "testing" you, then you may be holding the reins too loosely. Your ego is avoiding responsibility, possibly out of fear. You may find yourself worrying about being liked, or that you want to participate and have fun ("be one of them") rather than be the outsider. The way to bring them back to a better focus on the work is through organized, positive, disciplined, rigorous, hands-on efforts from you. The way to bring your*self* back to the work is to identify why your ego was avoiding responsibility in the first place. You *and* the ensemble may be feeling restless, bored, or unsatisfied. In that case, issue challenges. You'll all gain confidence in the process.

### David

I once encountered this restlessness from a beginning acting class of non-majors working on contemporary monologues. After weeks of growing frustration with their behavior, I brought in Shakespearean sonnets and told them, "No Intro class of mine has ever been able to tackle Shakespeare successfully. My Acting II class is working on these same sonnets. If you perform these as well as they do, I'll let you present them in front of that class." They practically tore the sonnets out of my hand. Three weeks later, the two classes met and each performed for the other. The Acting II class gave the better performances, but the Intro class surprised both themselves and the others with how well they did. The Intro class was also humbled by how well the Acting II class did and kept asking, "How did they do that?" To my surprise, the Acting II class said the same thing about the Intro class, "How did they do that?" They were impressed and inspired by some of the unorthodox choices the Intro students made.

There is a distinction between maintaining an open, collaborative environment and being a pushover who indulges every whim and request. Being strong and open are not mutually exclusive qualities in a leader. Find a balance for yourself and your circumstances.

### Managing their egos

Once again, healthy egos are the ideal, but they're not always what you get, so be prepared to manage the needy ones. And watch out: needy egos can multiply. They have the potential to create divides within an ensemble or destroy them outright and they can be challenging for leaders because they tend to push our buttons. Big egos can be off-putting and small egos can suck us into the vortex of that person's low self-esteem. So try to step back, take a breath, and listen. What is the ego asking for? Can you supply it? Maybe the person just needs a little recognition or reassurance. Through awareness, you can address the needy ego and diminish the need. *Bob, you're a good performer, but I'm not sure you believe that, because you frequently seek out my reassurance. I'm here to tell you that you really are a good performer and I believe in you. That doesn't mean you won't have to suffer through ups and downs like the rest of us. Even good performers have struggles. I promise to keep an eye out for problems and let you know if I see anything, so that you can stop worrying and get on with the work.* Take note of the tone used here; your approach is important. Egos are sensitive and best handled gently at first, and usually in private.

Problem egos come in two forms: too big and too small. Big egos seem inherently antithetical to ensemble. But even big egos are capable of being productive ensemble members. Your ego must be secure enough to manage the big ego without crushing it. The key is to get the big ego to see the value in the others and in the goal. But first, big egos need acknowledgment. Acknowledge that person's value to them in private, and convey the benefits that value has on yourself and others. Point out the special contributions this person is capable of, along with the *responsibility* that comes with being an ensemble member. Often, this is enough to relax the big ego and open them up to what else and who else is in the room.

Small egos seem to be inherently concordant to ensemble, but even small egos are capable of presenting problems. The small ego may not simply be self-effacing, but actually suffer from lack of confidence and/or self-esteem (see Chapter 5). The key is to do the *opposite* of what is done with big egos: get the small ego to see the value in *themselves*, their contributions, and their role in pursuing the goal. Small egos also need acknowledgment and a sense of responsibility toward the ensemble.

What about stubborn egos? You've tried the gentle approach, but it's not working. Does the ego need a wake-up call? As awful as this is to say, some big egos can be shamed into change. This choice is not to be made lightly. Calling the big ego out in front of the others can be the equivalent of punching a bully in the nose. *Bob, you keep pulling the attention to yourself. This behavior is disruptive. There is a roomful of talented, hard-working people here and you're sending the message that you don't respect them. I need you to put your focus on supporting the actions of your partners.* As leader, sometimes you're called upon to instill discipline. You may fear that you're breaking the "warm bath" of ensemble that you've created, but you're actually *protecting* the warm bath. There may be a temporary tension in the room arising from your disciplinary statement, but by jumping right back into the work, you give the ensemble members an opportunity to "make it right."

In this example, Bob may feel that his behavior has been criticized. And if he was acting out in selfish ways, then the criticism was warranted. This was disciplinary in nature and it addressed behavior that needed to change. However, beware of using criticism as a way to handle egos; it's a mixed bag. Ask yourself, are you criticizing someone's bad behavior or their work? *Bob, stop mugging, you're not that funny.* Misplaced criticism can make a big ego defensive and a small ego fold. But used in proper measure and at the appropriate time, criticism can inspire positive change. When in doubt, try following the rule of threes when offering criticism. Offer two items of praise followed by one of constructive criticism. The ensemble member is less likely to feel embarrassed or get defensive, and they're more likely to listen and take the criticism to heart. Also, try not to call it criticism: *here are two things that you do well, and here's an area where you have potential to improve.*

For more specific symptoms, causes, and actions you can take, see Chapter 5.

### *The role of judgment*

With egos come the inevitable comparisons to others; and judgment of self and others. *Am I as good as she is? I'm funnier than he is, why did he get the lead?*

This is unhealthy for ensembles because judgment can cause members to shut down creatively. They stop taking risks, make safe choices and withdraw from collaboration. Some will rise to the occasion, but judgment usually becomes a cancer and can spur unhealthy competition.

You've probably witnessed an occasion where an ensemble member took a great creative risk and it flopped terribly. Then another member laughs or rolls their eyes in reaction. This is the kind of peer judgment that can kill risk-taking. When you see this, you have to deal with it immediately and forcefully. Don't allow this type of behavior to take hold or it will destroy any chance of a united ensemble. If you fail to act, at best, you will have cliques. At worst, you'll have a room full of people who don't trust each other.

Let's not be naïve, ensemble members secretly judge themselves and each other and this cannot be avoided. However, the degree of judgment tends to lessen in time as the bond grows. In the early stages of an ensemble's life, all members need to respect the *idea* that negative judgments can damage the creative environment. And in turn, they should redirect their judgments into shows of support.

Despite the negative impact that peer judgment can have, judgment should not be eliminated altogether. Judgment, when necessary, must come from you. As leader, you're called upon to judge the students/performers in your charge. *But*, the nature of your judgment is extremely important. Does your judgment undermine confidence? The members of the ensemble will all recognize the necessity of judgment and if you aren't handling it, they'll step in and start sharing their own. So when someone needs to be called out, make sure you're the one doing it. It's part of how you protect the ensemble and maintain an atmosphere that is conducive to risk-taking and creativity. See Chapter 6 for more on redirecting judgmental behavior into healthier choices.

What about your judgment of yourself? And the judgments you *perceive* from the ensemble members? It helps for you to separate your roles for this analysis. After all, you're wearing two hats: you're an ensemble member (albeit a special one) and you're the ensemble leader. As a member, don't judge yourself too harshly, or you risk shutting yourself down. As the leader, judge yourself in this context: "Are my actions good or bad for the ensemble?" Don't make this personal – you risk falling into self-pity, self doubt, or other "me-centered" thoughts. This is about you only insofar as what is best for the ensemble. Yes, it's tricky, but not impossible, and it's something you can develop over time.

### *The role of competition*

Competition. It challenges us to be at our best. It can toughen us and it can be fun – most games are competitions. It separates the winners from the losers, so we know where we stand. You wouldn't want to choose your surgeon from among those who hadn't survived a competitive medical school education, would you? We compete to get into the best schools, get the best jobs, earn the highest salaries, date the cutest guy/girl. We live in a society built on competition: capitalism, entrepreneurship, elections. We watch countless hours of competitive sports, reality shows, pageants, eating contests, and as young children we all became fascinated at some point with the Guinness Book of World Records. We associate competition with the highest possible achievement. In our own profession, virtually every production holds auditions, callbacks, and sometimes interviews. But as with all things powerful, its power can be both creative and destructive.

Your leadership will be defined, in part, by how you choose to incorporate competition. Be careful. The competition of auditions pits your potential ensemble members against one another. But what happens once the ensemble is formed? What becomes of the need to conquer, subdue, eliminate?

It's important to recognize the value of competition as well as its limitations and apply it in useful ways. We want the fun and inspiration, but not the impediment to collaboration. This distinction is important because we're writing this book for ensembles that create. If you were building an ensemble for the purpose of playing football successfully, you would probably adjust the balance between competition and collaboration. So let's assume that we want competition only inasmuch as it contributes to a creative, collaborative ensemble. What role can competition play, and how can we use it effectively?

Competition that pits members against one another can be dangerous to a healthy ensemble. If members feel that others are trying to "beat" them, they may stop cooperating and collaborating. They'll no longer be vested in the other members' success, but in their failure. You then have a collection of individuals rather than an ensemble.

Competition that is friendly and fun because the consequences are minor can be useful. On the other hand, games that feature elimination as a component can have a negative effect. *Go sit down, loser. Only people who are good at this are allowed to continue.* That's the message some members will take away. Elimination can be downright cruel, and that doesn't always change with age. Put yourself in the shoes of your ensemble members, especially those who may have confidence or self-esteem issues. How will this game or exercise affect them?

### Rose

I love the exercise Zing, and use it in every class, workshop, and rehearsal. The ensemble forms a circle: Zing is an invisible ball of energy that each member sends to another with a direct arm gesture, eye contact, and saying the word "Zing." As soon as a person receives it, they send it to someone else, and so on. It's immediately noticeable when someone "drops" the zing or loses focus. However, I never allow elimination, so everyone stays in the circle and they're able to work through whatever their blocks might be. And Zing can *really* get cookin'. I was told a story about an experienced director at another college who played a version of Zing at rehearsals for a particular show, but he included *elimination* as part of the structure. To make matters worse, the director included himself as a player each time (note: it's *fine* for a leader to participate in the non-elimination version). One by one, his students would be eliminated, and the director himself "won" *every time.* Can you imagine? After a while, the cast apparently no longer wanted to play, and the director seemed perplexed as to why; he thought everyone was having a whale of a time.

Similarly, scoring "points" can also have a negative impact. Save the scoring systems for auditions, not rehearsals. If you're in education, you know the impact that grades can have on an ensemble. When scoring is necessary, try to keep low-scoring people looking up, aiming for greater success, rather than dwelling on the pain of a low score. Turn it into motivation for the future, rather than a condemnation of results.

Remember, competition arises naturally and it isn't always a bad thing. Members of an ensemble don't necessarily have to be equal. Greater and lesser members are inevitable. Here are a few points to consider:

- Each member must feel they are a contributor and can see the benefits of their contributions to the whole.
- Each member must meet a minimum level of effort/commitment.
- Each member must "have the back" of the other members. Loyalty, commitment, and dependability are essential (not unlike families).
- Competition between individuals can be divisive. Competition pitting your ensemble against another ensemble can contribute to bonding.

Try this instead: rather than competitors, everyone is a *contributor.* They all contribute to creating something. If competition makes us better contributors and keeps us collaborating, then it is healthy.

### The role of the Sniffer

Okay, looking back at the three elements we just covered: *ego* can lead to *judgment,* which can lead to *competition.* We've talked about how to deal with egos and competition, but we haven't said much about judgment beyond why it can be bad for an ensemble. So how do you apply your judgment in a constructive way to build and maintain a healthy ensemble? Your most valuable assessment skill and leadership tool is: Tada! your "sniffer." What *is* the sniffer? It's your ability to be aware of and recognize things that are rarely visible or audible, but are nonetheless *real.* We're constantly receiving information through all our senses (sixth sense included). Our sniffer's awareness of that information, and our instinctual response to that information, is what makes us uniquely who we are. Identify what kind of sniffer you have in order to take full advantage of its strengths. Here are a top few:

### Hunting Dog Sniffer

A good beagle trusts the very first whiff of a scent, and refuses to stray from the trail until it has found what it's looking for. All the while, they bay loudly, alerting everyone that they're on the scent. This leads to other dogs following, trusting that the beagle knows what it's doing, and where it's going. The complete trust that the beagle has in its sniffer focuses everyone's effort. You most likely have a hunting dog sniffer if you:

- trust your instincts and listen to them without needing to know where they'll lead
- are confident about honoring your first impulses
- are sensitive to subtle changes in working relationships
- are sensitive to subtle changes in the physical environment
- trust your intuition, even if logic is telling you something different
- stumble upon "the scent" through a happy accident, and you trust and follow it with full commitment.

A wonderful group sensation emerges when you or the ensemble has picked up the trail. Remember, a beagle can emerge from *within* the ensemble too; recognize this and encourage it when it happens. Sometimes more than one beagle emerges; if you're lucky, several members pick up the scent simultaneously. Sometimes you won't even know who the beagle *is*, you just know that someone has picked up the scent, and you're all running headlong on the same trail toward the destination.

Now, what if you didn't recognize the moment when the scent was picked up, or you doubt that you've found the "right" trail? What can make you doubt your sniffer?

- If an ensemble member found the trail before you did, and you want to guide, not *be* guided on the trail (check your ego at the door).
- If you're imposing the "story," i.e., expecting the path to be found in a pre-conceived location. Try not to let logic get in the way; be open to the unexpected as a way to the goal.
- If you believe the path might immerse the ensemble in chaos before reaching the goal. The terrain might be ideally suited for holding a scent, but sometimes, it's not. Terrain changes; so in brambles or at a creek, you might momentarily lose the scent, running to and fro. You know the scent is near, and while you may be temporarily off the scent, you're not necessarily off the trail. Allow for the moment of *not* knowing, or you risk walking all the way back to the beginning.

- If the idea came from an unlikely source in the ensemble. You selected that person for a reason, and even if they're a slow grower, they're as capable of discoveries as anyone else.
- If the idea came from someone who has challenged you in the past. Don't deny the ensemble their success because of your ego. A good idea is a good idea, no matter where it comes from.

Become adept at distinguishing the joy of discovery from random action. Think of a beagle that picks up the scent and becomes wildly happy. Their happiness of the "find" can make them spin, twirl, and momentarily lose the scent. You might think that what you're seeing is self-indulgent, and that there isn't a scent at all. Trust, and give each member (and yourself!) the benefit of that moment of joyous discovery ("Have I found it? Woo hoo!!"). It's within that moment that we all learn to strengthen our ability to trust.

Sometimes an old scent is picked up, and it doesn't pan out. Remain positive, and use it as an example of a successful failure. You'll all learn from following a trail that (seemingly) leads nowhere. You took the risk together and the ensemble feels supported because you trusted them to discover things on their own. You're now closer to finding the real trail through the process of elimination. Remove judgment from failure, and the ensemble begins to redefine what failure truly means. Individuals take greater risks because they trust they'll be supported, and greater risk-taking fosters courage and leadership *within* the ensemble. So if you think you're on a cold trail:

- Allow the ensemble to follow their choice; it instills trust, it respects them and their creative process, and it encourages openness to new ideas. Even if you're under time pressures, or if something is a locomotive-stoppingly-bad idea, everyone must take risks together, even if (and especially) you have no idea where the trail may lead.
- Don't impose your choice immediately; it cuts off exploration. You risk the ensemble focusing on giving you "what *you* want" instead of what the *goal* needs.
- Remember: you only *believe* you're on a cold trail, you don't know for *sure*. Allow yourself to be proved wrong.
- Even if it is a cold trail, you might discover something that will help later.

### Watchdog Sniffer

Good watchdogs have a keenly developed awareness of everything around them. They know their house and property so well that they could patrol it blindfolded. They also intimately know the humans that they're charged to protect; and it isn't only a logical knowing (the child is three feet tall, etc.), it's a sensory knowing. Each living thing has a sound, a smell, something that distinguishes it in the home or landscape. The watchdog instinctually recognizes everyone and everything that calls this place home, and they don't doubt that they know what they know. They don't need to *hear* the school bus to know that the child has arrived home and will walk through the door momentarily, or *see* the father walking across the gravelly back yard to know that it's him. Otherwise, a watchdog would be barking incessantly all the time.

This hyper-awareness allows them to instantly recognize when something new has entered the environment. Thus, the watchdog must develop the ability to distinguish what presents a danger, and what doesn't. "Newness" alone doesn't make something dangerous to the ensemble (it doesn't mean that it's entirely safe either). Watchdogs must be able to evaluate the benefit or harm of something being introduced to the ensemble, whether a new person or a new idea. You have a watchdog sniffer if you are:

- confident about trusting your instincts
- fiercely protective of the ensemble
- protective of the creative space (do you bark if a stranger inadvertently walks into your studio?)
- quick to alert the ensemble to something you've observed in their work
- adept at evaluating a new element and its benefit to the ensemble.

Now, watchdogs can tend to want to do *too* much for the ensemble. Allow the rest of the ensemble to develop their sniffers too. Be sure to:

- take the time to introduce a new member with an open heart so that the ensemble will follow suit. If you even hint that they're an intrusion, the ensemble will be "on guard." You set the example at all times, no matter how humble you may be
- spend additional time with a new member, giving extra guidance, and know when to let go. Don't spend so much time with them that the ensemble thinks they're not trustworthy. How much "watching" is really needed?
- be honest about the depth of your desire to protect the ensemble. Are you so protective that you're barking at everything? Does your zeal for creating a safe environment end up creating an isolated one, where new stimulation isn't possible?
- beware your own ego and pride. You don't need to bark incessantly to show the ensemble you're doing a good job. You can be watchful without being threatening
- be alert, but allow the ensemble to make judgments for themselves as to what does/doesn't pose a danger to them.

Question: what if I'm not a dog?

*Sled Dog Musher*

Once in a rare while we encounter leaders who either don't trust their instincts, or may have a "blank spot" in their instinctual and artistic impulses. "I have instincts about casting, but not how to get to the goal." Or, "I have instincts about working moment to moment, but I'm not sure how to guide the ensemble to bring those threads together to tell the story."

You might be a better human being than a dog: which is absolutely fine, as long as you embrace your strengths and trust someone else to provide what you're missing. You might be the Iditarod leader who assembles a magnificent team of sled dogs, selects one to be the lead dog, then gets on the sled and shouts, "Mush!" In fact, your instincts for selecting the team are what *ensure* its success. We've known several directors who say, "I cast well; I make sure I have the actors *and* the personalities I need, and then I get out of the way." We know they're underestimating what they do, but you get the idea. Whether you like to step back and guide, or be in the thick of the action and lead from there, you also need to develop a sense of when to get out of the way. Especially if you have a great team and the snow is slick for travel.

A good team of sled dogs is only as strong as the lead dog. Lead dogs are usually stronger, trust their instincts, and throw themselves into the work with abandon. This inspires the rest of the team to want to experience that joy and self-assuredness as well. The team *learns* to be stronger leaders by *following*. If you've cast the ensemble and the lead dog well, you may only have to shout "Mush!" at the start, and steer here and there until you reach the destination. It's still your responsibility to make sure the team gets rest, reassurance, etc. You may end up with very little to do, but remain vigilant for what the team needs.

If this is how you work, don't fall prey to insecurities about how you "should" be working. Recognizing what your unique skills are is the most essential trait you can have. Even if you rarely lift a finger, you're always leading through your experience and perspective. You can see farther ahead than the lead dog; and your knowledge and readiness to take action is just as vital a form of leadership as any other. If you're a Musher, pay extra attention to Chapter 5, as the success of your project can hinge on selection more than any other choices you make.

## The role of balance

How do you use your sniffer and other skills to create and maintain a healthy ensemble? Keep things in balance. Just as you may look to keep your own life in balance (between work and play, etc.), keep the ensemble in balance. If you're a Musher, consider rotating your dogs. Who takes the lead today? Who sits back? Sometimes you contribute a lot or a little, but the group has to adjust. Find your balance as an ensemble first, and then look to keep it as you evolve.

What happens when someone is absent? In a sense, it's not the same ensemble; a unique voice is missing. The remaining members may try to fill that void, and growth will occur for some as they step up and accept new roles. (Is the Sparkplug missing? As a result, has someone else found his or her inner Sparkplug? (See Chapter 5, p. 117.)) Let the ensemble know that it will have a slightly different identity with that voice missing and instead of *necessarily* trying to make up for what's missing, stay open to new discoveries born of the absence. Limitation is a parent of discovery; you can turn obstacles into opportunities. Then what happens when the missing voice comes back? The new discoveries have to meld with the returning voice. If the absence was significant, you may have to allow for a period of adjustment until a new balance can be established. And as Heraclitus pointed out, "Nothing endures but change." So the balance will always be in a state of flux. It's your job to monitor it and offer adjustments when necessary. What does it need? Just ask your sniffer.

## Universal needs

If you're an early career ensemble leader, or you're a Musher, and you're not yet confident about your sniffer, don't worry. There are universal needs that *every* ensemble requires; start with those. While you're fulfilling these basic needs, you'll also be building relationships and developing your sniffer. In time, when you ask, "What does it need?" your answers will become more specific to the moment. Until then:

- Inspire them: do something fun! We've done everything from cryptogram hunts to karaoke in the name of ensemble building. Surprise your ensemble from time to time. Add a new element. Issue a challenge. Rearrange the space. This is mentioned in Chapter 4, but it's also an important part of your ongoing leadership. Routine can be good for stability, but don't get stuck in ruts – *lead* them out of ruts, slumps, and boredom. An inspired ensemble takes greater risks and discovers more together.
- Communicate: get a dialog going and make sure you're letting them talk. They may be reticent, so lead them to a friendly starting point. Start by posing a specific question that they'll be eager to talk about, and then later steer the conversation toward your ultimate destination. You need to hear from them, and to really listen. They know the difference between someone who cares about what they have to say and someone who doesn't. Who do you think they're more likely to follow? You don't always have to act on what you hear, but you better remember what they said. In doing so, you're also setting the example for how they need to listen to one another.
- Listen, and allow them to vent, even if you personally find it distasteful. This might sound strange, but it's part of keeping them motivated. If they've got complaints (and don't kid yourself, they do), the frustration will begin to take a toll on their motivation. You can't have daily bitch-and-moan sessions, but sometimes a bitch-and-moan session can be like opening a relief valve. The pressure is vented and the system returns to normal levels. Monitor these

occasional sessions. Look for the point where they stop being productive – usually when complaints are being repeated – and move on to something else. Keep in mind that this is different from our earlier discussion on the dangers of judgment. What we're talking about here are group issues, not singling out individuals.

- Connect them: early on, have each tell a story that is personal and true. This doesn't mean they have to reveal deep, dark secrets; it just gives them an opportunity to get to know each other better. This is different than the socializing and storytelling they do outside of class/rehearsal. It's a shared ritual that builds their sense of community. Your presence and guidance makes this a formal ritual, as opposed to the casual rituals that happen outside, and both contribute to strengthening the ensemble.

- Motivate them by helping them see the value in each other. They get praise from you, but they also need to hear praise from each other. Not just in a general sense, as in, "Hey, good job." You need to lead them to a more specific, coordinated effort. Review the specific process and the language of feedback and critique that you'll be using in your particular project. Review supportive terms as opposed to critical ones so that members feel supported even during feedback sessions. A specific exercise you can do is to go around the room and have each member say one thing they admire about "Joe's" work. Repeat for all members. (See Appendix V.) It breeds respect, confidence, and tolerance. By gaining a greater sense of how they're seen and valued, their risk-taking will soar. If they're new to each other, they may not need this yet (or have enough experience with each other to have something to say). If that's the case, try the previous suggestion (share something about themselves). Make sure you participate as well. It nurtures their trust in you if they see you not only as their leader, but also as the person who traveled across Europe on a motorcycle or fainted in the delivery room. You learn the most enjoyable, curious tidbits about people this way and it helps us to see each other in new ways.

- Have expectations of your ensemble and be clear as to what those expectations are, and how they relate to the goal. Routinely upgrade your expectations and acknowledge their progress. It helps them to know that you're observing how they meet expectations and that you'll continue to "raise the bar." They'll feel challenged and come to trust your belief that they can meet those challenges.

A story about expectations:

*The excruciating five minutes* (as told by Arthur Kriklivy)

I was in my Classical Cultures class. The teacher was very cool and very passionate about his subject; the whole class loved him. Yet one day, no one seemed to want to participate. The energy in the room was drained. Then the teacher asked us a question. Dead silence. A few seconds went by and he just sat there, leaning on his desk, staring at us. After about 30 seconds, I started to get fidgety and looked around. Everyone was getting uncomfortable and squirming in their seats. Then it hit us; this was a question that he was not going to answer for us. The silence must have lasted a solid five minutes. It was easily the most excruciating five minutes of my life. I thought somebody was going to cry, but then finally a student raised their hand and answered the question. It was like a weight had been lifted. It's really amazing to see what a direct challenge can do to a group of people. He taught us a very important lesson that day. It was up to us to take responsibility for our education. How can we expect to really learn anything if we don't actively participate in the process? He could have given us the answer but we would not have earned that knowledge if we hadn't taken the reins. He treated us as equals and demanded that we take responsibility for not only our learning, but each other. We all made a silent agreement that day to commit to something bigger.

Sometimes, leadership is about what you *don't* do.

## Adapting your leadership skills and style

You need to know your ensemble. Leading a group of strangers is virtually impossible. And not all ensembles are the same; different ensembles will require you to adapt your leadership skills and style to suit their needs. To return to our party-hosting analogy, you wouldn't lead a group of children the same way you would lead a group of senior citizens. You must meet them where they are. Engage your listening and observation skills to discover the group's identity and who the individual members are (or think they are), and what they need. Use your sniffer. Then you can begin to figure out how you might bring them what they need.

If you're entering a new environment, listen to everyone from the chairman to the janitor. You can't lead people if they won't follow, and listening to them will make them *want* to follow. Unless you've assembled them and they've shown up because of you (starting a new venture), you've got to get to know them.

Do your homework, plan accordingly, and exert your leadership in ways to suit the conditions. Keep in mind that those conditions may change or reveal themselves to be different from what you believed. However, surprising turns can be wonderful and don't always have to mean disaster. Stay open, alert, and *keep* listening.

### *Some examples of adaptation*

When working with theatre professionals who are highly trained, it's advisable to listen more and speak less than when you're working with less experienced personnel. Don't dominate, wear your leadership lightly, and be sure to treat your fellow professionals as the peers that they are. You are a leader not because you are superior, but because that is your role.

In an educational setting, you may wish to speak more, but remember the lesson of the Excruciating Five Minutes. Students require more guidance than professionals, so being more hands-on is appropriate. And of course, there is a range within the realm of education. You will work differently with pre-schoolers than you will with graduate students.

You may even find yourself applying your ensemble skills to a business environment. In that setting, you not only have to adapt what you will do and how *much* you will do it, but *how* you'll do it.

### David

When I was using modified improv training to help business executives enhance their communication skills, I found that in some ways, I had to be more hands-off (they are professionals, so peers of a sort). But in other ways, I had to be more hands-on (they were much less familiar with the subject matter and a lot less interested in it, at first).

Beware, when working with an ensemble that includes a former leader of that ensemble, or someone who simply sees himself as the unofficial leader. Handling this is largely the same as handling big egos. The primary difference between this situation and the big ego is to see whom the followers are following. If they're following you, then handling the unofficial (or ex) leader as a big ego will usually work. If the other members are following the unofficial (or ex) leader, then your days are probably numbered. You may be able to win them over, but it will likely be a long, bloody struggle that will do damage to you and the ensemble, and that will compromise the quality of the goal. It's better to get on with your life and find your tribe. Don't let your ego get in the way ("I'll show them – no matter what ..."); there's a difference between failure, and showing up to host the right party.

Adapt your leadership style to the level of commitment within the ensemble. Some ensembles are comprised of true believers, diehards who will do anything for each other. Others are composed of folks who may consider this work a fun, part-time hobby. They don't want to stay until 2:00 A.M. to finish tech – they want to go home. This is why there are professional theatres and community theatres, conservatories and local workshops. Each place, though, has a required level of commitment that is appropriate for that place. As long as everyone in the ensemble agrees upon that level of commitment, the ensemble can work. You need to enforce and protect whatever that level is. When you have mismatches in the level of commitment, an unfixable disharmony is going to exist. Certainly you can work to inspire greater commitment from your ensemble members, but beware of trying to change them beyond their essential nature.

Asking your ensemble members for major conflicts before assembling the rehearsal schedule usually helps, and don't cast people who won't be available when you need them. Of course, this isn't always possible, and there will be unexpected issues that no amount of planning can anticipate. And not all of these commitment conflicts are black and white – sometimes you have to make very difficult judgment calls. How should you handle these tough calls? Try to balance the needs we all have as individuals with the needs of the ensemble and your responsibility to protect the ensemble.

### David

I relentlessly preach the importance of commitment to the ensemble and push my ensemble members to honor this, lest they harm the special bond we have and risk losing what we've built. This is the philosophical basis of everything I believe in. Then, inevitably, an ensemble member will come to me in tears about having to miss a rehearsal because their dad is having an operation or something equally important. At times like this I say, "Some things are more important than our ensemble. You need to be there for your dad – he's your ensemble too. We'll support you."

When everyone *is* committed, the ensemble can easily survive these individual conflicts. If someone is lacking commitment to the ensemble, however, their individual conflict is not the problem, but a symptom of something larger.

Whenever you make the wrong call (and we all do), admit it, sincerely apologize, and move on. This is not one of those times where it's good to lower your status; stay in charge. The ensemble may see you as unfair, inconsistent, or even hypocritical. If you are, admit it, apologize and move on. We don't recommend trying to fix the problem unless it's an easy and obvious fix. Trying to fix the bad outcome of a tough call only digs you into a deeper hole. Accept that you can't climb out of this one. Your sincerity, combined with your commitment to making better decisions in the future, will help heal whatever damage may have occurred.

Part of adapting to each ensemble is sharing who you are, what you do, and why you're doing it. Let them into your world. As much as you need to find that connection with them, they need to find one with you and they can't do that if they don't know what you're about. Open up, share, take a risk, and find each other.

### David

During my first week working on the Broadway production of *The Lion King*, I was handed a copy of a speech given to the company on the occasion of the show's fifth anniversary. It contained a reference to one of the show's shadow puppets. The puppet was hand-made in Africa by a tribal craftsman from the hide of a local animal. It had also been hand-painted. Why would anyone go to such lengths for a shadow puppet? After all, it would be behind a screen and only the silhouette of the puppet would be visible to the audience. Because, it further explained, this puppet came from where the story came from. This puppet grew out of the land of Africa. The two artists who would be performing with this puppet at each show would see the incredible detail and devotion that went into the puppet. The intention was that they would see this and find themselves more deeply connected to the story and their role in telling it and would reflect that in their performance working with the puppet, which in turn would be received by the audience. You wouldn't get that from a piece of foam or cardboard made in New York. I was so inspired by that and thought to myself, "This is home for me. I want to be here more than ever. I want to work with people like this. I want to do work like this." I continue to be just as inspired by it as I write this as I was the day I first read it.

If you are passionate about what you do, share it. Followers follow not just because of how you lead, but also because of who you are and why you lead. You're the host of the party, not the caterer. It's about more than setting up, cleaning up, and supplying food and drinks. It's personal – it's about what you uniquely bring to the party.

# 4

# CREATING ENSEMBLE

You can discover more about a person in an hour of play than in a year of conversation.

–Plato

Ensemble doesn't begin with the people, ensemble begins with an objective: what is the purpose, the reason that this specific group of people must be assembled at this moment in time? What is the goal, the story, and the mission of this ensemble? Remember what we said in the Introduction: think of it like a party; you've decided to throw one, which means your role is the host. But what's the party for? Birthday? Retirement? Closing night of a show? When you know the purpose of the party, then you'll know whom to invite. Think about it: you wouldn't invite someone who has the potential to *ruin* that party. Would you invite someone who sees birthdays as another nail in the coffin to your Big Five-Oh celebration? Nope. You invite people who are going to serve the *purpose* of that party, and who will endeavor to make it a great event. Everyone has their roles; you invite people who are gregarious, who'll keep the conversation going, as well as "doers" who will put out more chips, help with the washing up, and won't leave until the garbage is bagged and taken outside.

Now, if you *don't* plan carefully, and you invite random people without much consideration, your birthday will still happen, and the party will go on. But, you leave the *success* of that party to Fate. It might be okay, or it could be the worst night of your life. As painful as this may be, think about the worst party you ever hosted, or attended for that matter. Could the outcome have been changed by being more careful with the invitation list? And when you *did* carefully plan the invitation list, how hard did you really have to work to make it a good party, besides serving the food and drinks? What did that group of people create *together* that would not have occurred without that specific mix, and what role did your planning play in that?

Consider the classic sit-com, *The Mary Tyler Moore Show*. Mary was known for throwing notoriously bad parties. Lou Grant refused to come to his own birthday celebration because he knew it would be awful before he walked through the door. Mary's famous "spunk" and good nature wouldn't let her *not* invite someone to her parties, so she invited *everybody*. The comedy deliciously came from a gathering of characters that couldn't stand working together, much less socializing together. Blend that with Mary's neighbors, the good and the bad, and any lost souls she had happened across, and you had the perfect mix for a nightmare party. It's an hysterical but all-too-possible cautionary tale for what can happen if you don't carefully plan your party.

So why would you consider doing anything less when bringing an ensemble together? Yes, the production will still happen if you cast every role. Your improv group will still create improvisations if you have the requisite number of people with the experience needed. Your cohort of acting students will still study, do scenes together, and graduate on time. Those are the facts, and the less-than-ideal conditions. How can we work toward an *idealized* version of our goal? Why should we consider the element of ensemble as essential to any of these ventures?

Because it makes for a better party.

If you're clear on the goal, and ensure that those who surround you share that clarity and commitment, everyone steps up their game. They're "yes and-ing," and the positive collaboration of "yes and ... " is also like that at the good party. That is, the collaboration focuses on "What does this party need from *me*?" not "How can I suck the attention toward me and away from the Birthday Girl?" When we're committed to serving the purpose of the party, we're functioning as an ensemble, instead of functioning as a collection of individuals doing tasks.

### David

"Yes and ... " is widely agreed to be the core concept of improvisation, wherein a player says, "yes" to everything presented by their partner(s), then "ands" by adding information that will propel the scene. To learn more about "yes and ... " I recommend *Truth in Comedy* by Halpern, Close, and Johnson.

We're at an interesting moment in history where our society is very star driven (individual) vs. being driven by achievements of the group (ensemble). Casting director Kevin Kennison calls it "The American-Idol-ization of our society." Nobody would watch a TV program called *So You Want To Be an Ensemble?* (Well, David and Rose would, but ... ) The inherent star system gears many artists toward a culture in which one joins a group to be "discovered" or to stand out as the star of that particular group. That belief system kills ensemble and is destructive to the very thing that ensures a healthy collaboration. The popularity of competitive reality shows reinforces the notion that a single star is the ideal, and we see them rewarded with money, record contracts, fame, and even wedding proposals. People tune in so they can put themselves in that starring role, living vicariously through the success of the winner. But let's not kid ourselves; the ratings are also high because folks want to see people "voted off" and witness the personal drama that comes from those emotional blows. It's a very clean version of gladiator games where the entertainment is in seeing people defeated and eliminated, with a single winner emerging victorious.

If you want to work in an ensemble, you need to sacrifice what you want in *your* shining moment in order to give the ensemble *its* shining moment. If you can get people to commit *to* the ensemble instead of to what they're going to personally get out of being a *part* of the ensemble, then you strengthen the likelihood of its success. The ensemble must be the star, and every member must trust that and agree to serve it (see Chapter 3).

Now, there will still be varying contributions made by each individual member. Not everyone will be "equal" in that they're all capable of exactly the same skills. A baseball team has someone hitting .343, and someone hitting .264, but if the catcher hitting .264 has a killer arm and can mow down the guy trying to steal second, he's fulfilling his role in that ensemble. Not everyone is a home run hitter, even though the home run hitter tends to get more publicity. Every player has something that they're good at, and they were selected to fulfill the needs of the *team*. They show up every day asking, "What does this team need from me? How can I serve the goal of being a successful ball club?" They're clear that they're serving the purpose, and that clarity makes it easy for them to know their roles. We love reading the sports pages because baseball players are loathe to accept high praise, or to agree with criticism about a player going through a slump. They win as a team, they lose as a team. This is why controversy tends to erupt when a player badmouths teammates in an interview. Baseball players accept that you don't divide the team through negative statements or actions.

A while back, a prominent Yankees pitcher slammed his hands against a glass door in frustration, resulting in minor scrapes and cuts to his million dollar fingers. He later apologized to the team for his "selfish actions." Any team can win a game; but have you noticed that those that have winning seasons have that amazing chemistry of supporting each other, which allows them to stay loose, take risks, make great plays, and truly win as a team? Several years ago when the Yankees were having a particularly bad season, team captain Derek Jeter reportedly said, "We have a lot of great players on our team, but we're not *playing* as a team."

If you're saying "But I'm *still* unsure how to select my ensemble," go back to the question "What does the goal need from me and from the ensemble?" This principle will always be your guide. For example, you're directing a production of *The Crucible,* and your goal is to tell a story about a person who stands up against fear and fights for humanity. The audience must be able to care for the central character of John Proctor and invest in his struggle with his community or the story falls apart. So to serve the goal of the story, that individual role demands an actor who is skilled, and who isn't a jackass. You can't have a production of *The Crucible* where both the ensemble and the audience breathe a sigh of relief as Proctor walks off to the gallows. If you've ever seen a production of this play where the actor playing Proctor strutted like a star as opposed to serving the story and the ensemble, you'll know what we mean. Consider what the individual will bring to the *team* as well as to the *goal* at the time of their selection, and if you do, you're well on your way to a better party. And with nobody cheering when Elizabeth says, "He has his goodness now."

## Selecting the ensemble

You've identified the purpose, and you're about to hold auditions or interviews, and you wonder if you'll know the "right" person when you meet them. Clarity about the roles that need to be literally filled is the first step, but being aware of the roles that need to be filled in the *ensemble* will strengthen the work in countless ways. This is our "must" list for any ensemble that you're creating. You want and need people who:

- are open and willing to change and grow
- value working as a team
- assume the best and not the worst of people and situations
- are dedicated to the process of collaboration with fellow artists
- are good listeners
- enjoy what they're doing (This is not as obvious as it should be!)
- are just as open to being inspired by one another as they are to being inspired by the leader
- have a sense of what their unique contribution is to the group
- believe in "yes and ... ."

If you can start with people who possess the fundamentals of self-awareness, listening, flexibility, and openness, then no matter the purpose of your ensemble, you've got a strong foundation. So how do we reveal these traits in the selection process? What questions can we ask to flush out what we need, and reveal what could be unhealthy for the ensemble?

Ask the following questions when interviewing potential ensemble members for a class, workshop, or production. Taking the time to carefully consider their responses will be one of the most important things you can do in your selection process. You'll notice similarities from question to question, and that's a conscious choice. As playwright Meron Langsner writes in his play *Lying Makes Me Feel Like a God*, "I create worlds with my words ... words unlock worlds ... " and certain phrases will allow (or compel) a potential ensemble member to offer particular information. Many of these questions are open enough so that they empower the responder to *choose* what they want to reveal, and their choice can give you as much information as the information itself. Be careful of phrasing things in such a way that you embed a desired response. For early career leaders, we strongly recommend *Critical Response Process: A Method for Getting Useful Feedback on Anything You Make from Dance to Dessert* by Liz Lerman and John

Borstel. The authors share their system of forming and asking neutral questions in a clear, playful manner. The questions are designed to elicit honest responses from artists through eliminating embedded judgment in the questions themselves.

Questions to reveal Fundamentals:

- What is it, specifically, about this project/play/class that makes you want to be a part of it?
- What makes you want to work in an ensemble setting overall?
- What do you feel you uniquely bring to each ensemble you work with?
- What role do you feel you play in an ensemble? The Rock? The Nurturer? The Glue? (See Chapter 5 for more on these archetypes. This is simply another way to phrase the previous question and is helpful if the person is shy about tooting their own horn. Being ascribed a "role" can make someone more comfortable speaking about their contributions.)
- Can you tell me about a meaningful experience you've had working in an ensemble setting?
- What do you feel is your greatest challenge working in an ensemble setting?
- What do you feel are some of your greatest strengths?
- What do you feel you most need to work on?
- If you couldn't do this work, which profession do you think you might be in?

Listen to all responses in context. Certain statements may not be red flags by themselves, but they may collectively add up to something. For example, their response to the fourth question might be "I see myself as a leader and I like supporting the director by providing leadership within the ensemble." Fair enough. But if in addition, their response to the fifth question is "Oh! Once when I went up on my line in performance, I said something that made the entire cast break. The audience died laughing. I loved it!" then just back away slowly. And if you're thinking "Oh, that's the sort of good natured thing that happens in school theatre all the time ... " Guess what? That story was related to us regarding an Equity production.

The combined responses to these questions will reveal behaviors and values that will tell you whether to invite them to your party, or whether you've just avoided an unhealthy guest. The deal-breaker question that you should ask all potential ensemble members, and *yourself*, every time you embark on a new venture is:

*Do you know why you're here?*

This may seem like a "duh" question, but it goes to the heart of why some people seek an ensemble – *any* ensemble – instead of seeking the tribe that they are actually meant for. Do they know why they have come to this specific audition, this interview at *this* college, this audition for *this* improvisation group? Do they have an awareness of who they are, what they want, and why your project is a good fit for them? As you continue to develop and strengthen your sniffer in the selection process, listen for some of the following responses as positive indicators:

- I want a career as an actor, and your program focuses on the kind of training that I feel is essential to me becoming a better storyteller.
- Your company is committed to working from ensemble-based principles when creating productions, and that's important to me personally and professionally.
- I want to make a difference in society through storytelling, and my research showed that your productions focus on socially responsible themes.
- I've seen your improv troupe in performance and the actors bring so much depth and support to their scenes. They're not in it for the laugh; they're in it to make the best scenes possible.

Whether or not these are answers you *want* to hear, each of these responses indicate someone who knows why they're in that room talking with you. And that is a response you *should* want to hear. They've expressed a desire to commit to your goals, which they feel are in harmony with their own. There's a strong self-awareness, clarity, and a sense of identity emerging in these statements, and that will give you a strong foundation for your selection process.

Now, if you don't hear statements this clear and considered, but you heard something interesting that makes you want to include them, use your judgment. Were they nervous? How clear was the casting director with them before submitting them to your call? Assume the best and work from there; they may have been given incorrect information, or they may be bad researchers (you can teach them those skills). Also, if you're dealing with young artists or putting together a college class, weigh their responses according to their age and maturity. Are they away from home for the first time? Are they fretting about trying to find the "right" thing to say? We shouldn't expect them to fully know who they are yet, but we *should* expect them to have thought enough about why they came to this room to begin with. Even if they lack clarity about their identity, they may have clarity about the thing they seek. Which of course, speaks volumes about who they are!

If someone truly doesn't know why they're "here," you could end up spending all your time guiding them to an answer to this question rather than toward the common goal. They may be talented and smart, but if their energy is going to be directed *inward* to discover their personal purpose instead of *outward* toward the ensemble, then the goal won't be served. You can reveal these behaviors in the interview/audition process, and become more adept at recognizing them over time.

As there are recognizable behaviors in archetypes within ensembles (see Chapter 5), there are recognizable behaviors among those who don't know why they're seeking ensemble-based work.

### *The Wounded Puppy*

This is someone who is in search of a home (any home) in the quest for some place to belong. They're not picky, and that's unfortunate, because some Wounded Puppies can actually be quite talented. They are needy, lonely, and draw energy away from the ensemble. If they identify themselves by their wound, then the wound will always come before the ensemble. If in your first meeting they reference a significant negative event that they feel *defines* them, be on alert.

In an early acting class Rose taught, a student revealed on the first day that a family member had recently been murdered. In every acting exercise, she focused on this unimaginable loss, and on her obvious pain. She was urged to drop the class and get the kind of support she really needed. The class activities were only keeping the wound open, even if it might have felt therapeutic to the student in the moment. Of course you should be compassionate, but that doesn't mean your ensemble is where the Wounded Puppy should be.

Questions from the fundamentals list that reveal the Wounded Puppy:

- What is it, specifically, about this project/class/play that makes you want to be a part of it?
- What makes you want to work in an ensemble setting overall?
- What do you feel you uniquely bring to each ensemble you work with?

The Wounded Puppy will likely respond by putting their desires in a self-centered context, or with the ubiquitous "I don't know." Other responses may include:

- I've been through some tough experiences lately and I just want to work with a group that's fun.
- Oh, I love working with groups. It doesn't matter what the play is. (This can also be a signal of Identity Crisis; see below.)
- I love working with ensembles because it makes me feel accepted. (This might be true of many, but it should never be their primary motivation.)
- I'm really hoping this experience will help me work through some things.
- What do I bring? Well, I work really hard ... not that my previous group ever noticed ...
- My last experience on a play was terrible. My self-esteem is pretty shattered, and I need to rebuild it. (Again, this might be true, but if this is their primary motivating force ... ?)

### *Identity Crisis*

This is someone who is struggling to accept who they are, or even discover who that is. If someone is still struggling with self-identity, an ensemble isn't the best place for them. They could spend all their time trying to figure out the answer with the support of the ensemble, instead of supporting the ensemble to help *it* claim its identity. Questions to reveal Identity Crisis:

- What do you feel you uniquely bring to each ensemble you work with?
- What role do you feel you played in past ensembles? The Rock? The Nurturer?
- What do you feel are some of your greatest strengths? (Compare the response to the first question.)

Responses made by Identity Crisis may include:

- I don't know. I'm hoping you'll tell me.
- What role? Just whatever anybody needed.
- Why do you ask? (Defensive, or afraid to be specific about defining themselves.)
- Greatest strengths? I take direction well. (This may be true, and a good thing, but if this is the first thing they say, be on alert. They've responded, "I'll do whatever you tell me," instead of being specific about who they are. They're trying to get you to identify what you want to hear. They avoid specifics, which can mean that they'll avoid being specific in their choices.)

### *"I Heard … "*

This person has "heard" that the way to get ahead is to join an ensemble, or they "heard" that somebody famous once worked in this ensemble, or … ? Similar to "Identity Crisis," they're insecure and allow others to define them instead of advocating for their own identity. This is dangerous; as it's possible they'll embrace the ensemble itself as their new personal identity. They might be productive contributors for a brief time, but their unwillingness to take responsibility for themselves will ultimately have a negative impact.

### Rose

I once directed a large cast comedy and offered a role to an actor. His response was, " … that character only has 22 lines." I didn't know whether to be impressed that he had counted all the lines or to feel sorry for him that he evaluated a role by mathematics. I thanked him for auditioning and called another actor who was thrilled to be a part of the ensemble. The first actor telephoned me a while later and said, "I just spoke to a friend, and heard you were a New York director! I didn't know that and I'd really like to do the role after all!" As politely as I could, I said that my home address shouldn't be the reason for him to do a show and that I had respected his decision, but had moved on to another actor. He fumfurred and fussed, and asked me to keep him in mind for future roles.

Hmm ... :

- Note to ensemble members: It's fine to want to work with a particular director, but for goodness sake, know why you want to work with them and what you hope to experience. Be an informed advocate for yourself and your work.
- Note to actors: Home address doesn't guarantee quality of a director, or that they have the kind of career that can help your career. Just because someone hails from New York or Los Angeles doesn't mean they're good. And even if they are talented and can help your career, don't be a chowderhead and tell them that's your main reason for accepting a role.

Questions to reveal "I Heard ... :"

- What is it specifically about this project/class/play that makes you want to be a part of it?
- What do you feel is your greatest challenge working in an ensemble setting?

Responses from "I Heard ... " can include:

- I heard this was an up and coming group and I'd like to be part of that.
- I heard great things about this group. *From who?* Oh, I don't remember. (We're trying to ban the phrase "I heard ... " from our students' vocabulary. If they can't identify the source of the information within two moves and haven't bothered to find out if it's true or not, then they're spreading rumor at worst, and gossiping at best.)
- Greatest challenge? Making sure my voice is heard. (Not necessarily a bad thing, but if it's what they lead with, be wary.)

### *The Scapegoat*

They were wronged in a past situation that they still believe they were 100 percent right about. Feeling that they were unfairly targeted in their previous group, they've joined this one to prove they were right about ... being right. They put their personal mission first and neglect the goal of the ensemble. Scapegoats may benefit from the ensemble, but will the ensemble benefit from them? If they *were* unfairly targeted, then yes, possibly. Their dedication to proving themselves to others will help drive the action. If, however, they only *believe* they were unfairly targeted and they're still seeking justice, it could harm the ensemble. You'll need to decide if it's worth taking a chance.

Questions to reveal the Scapegoat:

- Can you tell me about a meaningful experience you've had working in an ensemble setting?
- What do you feel is your greatest challenge working in an ensemble setting?
- What do you feel you uniquely bring to each ensemble you work with?

Responses from the Scapegoat can include:

- Why? What have you heard?
- Ha! I can tell you about a *negative* experience!
- Have you ever heard of – ? (Name of company/person they feel they were wronged by.) If you answer yes, they may ask, "Do you have friends in that company?" They're looking for an ally in their quest for justice.
- Well, it's complicated.
- Greatest challenge? Avoiding those people ( … who they feel are responsible for the injustice).
- My contribution to the ensemble? Making sure everyone is treated fairly. (This could mean they'll be looking for injustices under every bush. However, this statement alone may not indicate a Scapegoat; could be the Caretaker in hyper drive. (See Chapter 5.) Review their responses collectively.)

### *The Orphan*

Akin to the Wounded Puppy, they were either rejected by a previous ensemble, abandoned by a leader, or experienced rejection in their own family. They know who they are, but their goal is to seek approval from the ensemble itself. The Orphan can go one of two ways. They may emerge as a Caretaker, giving abundantly to others at the expense of their own needs ("accept me, love me"), constantly offering you help with setting up or cleaning up the room ("if I help you, you won't abandon me"), or becoming so focused on generosity that they're missing the needs of the goal. The second way the Orphan manifests is in the direction of the Black Hole (see Chapter 5). They desperately want acceptance from the ensemble, but fear they'll be rejected. So, they pull their energy back as if to say, "I know you're going to reject me. I'm going to beat you to the punch."

Questions to reveal the Orphan:

- Can you tell me about a meaningful experience you've had working in ensemble?
- What do you feel you uniquely bring to each ensemble you work with?
- What makes you want to work in an ensemble setting overall?

Responses from the Orphan may include:

- Is it okay if I just talk about my favorite experience? My least favorite is kind of personal. (They crave acceptance, but unlike The Scapegoat, they're reluctant to talk about their experience. The fact that they reference it at all indicates their desire for you to know about it. They hope the ensemble will protect and accept them. The statement by itself may not indicate an Orphan, but possibly someone who is still processing a bad experience.)
- My previous ensemble leader told me I made a huge difference in the success of our project.
- What do I bring? I'm very giving and I'll help others in every possible way so that they can do their best work. (Note that they don't include themselves or their work in that consideration.)
- I love seeing everybody do great! I love being a part of that ... (As they respond, take note of their body language. They'll make direct eye contact, or quick furtive eye contact repeatedly, as they look for your reaction to their response.)

Now, on rare occasions, you may have an unusual project that demands an ensemble be made up of some of these very characters we're advising you to leave off of the guest list.

## Rose

I was privileged to work with director Larry Sacharow on his revival of *The Concept* in 1986. Larry originally developed this idea when working with recovering drug addicts at Daytop Village in New York in 1967, as part of their group therapy. He created an ensemble of residents and they performed their personal stories in a devised theatre piece. Originally performed to great acclaim in 1967 at La Mama in New York, Larry formed a new ensemble with their own stories while he was artistic director of River Arts Repertory in Woodstock, New York. I had been Larry's assistant on other ensemble productions, but had never, ever met a group like this. They fought, cursed, and chain smoked, but they were absolutely clear and committed to the goal, which was telling their stories as a community. Though there were harrowing nights when a fight would break out in the company kitchen less than an hour before curtain, it was always resolved (or resolved enough) that they came together by 8:00 P.M. to tell those stories. These actors would not have thrived in any other ensemble, but they were perfect for this one.

You may say, "Doesn't that prove that someone with a problem could do alright in my ensemble?" The Orphan or the Wounded Puppy may find a place to thrive in *an* ensemble, just not necessarily *your* ensemble. As compassionate as you might feel in adding them to your group, if they're unable to serve the goal, it's doomed. Your first priority is to the goal and the health of your ensemble. Those who can't commit need to move on and find something that *is* the right fit for them. Don't fall prey to your late night worries ("Will they be okay?"). You're not being cruel; you're helping by guiding them towards a different ensemble that will be a healthier fit.

### Rose and David

Believe us, we know the strong pull that Wounded Puppies, Orphans, and the like, can have on your sympathies. Sometimes they break our hearts and we become convinced that we can, or at least *should*, help them. You just want to pull them into your ensemble and heal them. We've both succumbed to these urges in the past, and though there've been rare exceptions, our experiences have consistently been bad. Now perhaps you're better with these types than we are and you can make it work consistently. But be warned, that's what we thought too, and had to learn the hard way.

When you ask the primary question, "Do you know why you're here?" be prepared to accept the answer, even if it means they're in the wrong place and need to move on. You need to help those individuals as much as the ones you do accept (it's easier than you think). There is a tribe out there for everyone; help them find it, and discourage those who pursue the pointless exercise of trying to force a Birthday Party into becoming a Baby Shower.

Directors, teachers, and improv group leaders are specific in their focus and assemble similar kinds of parties again and again. Every wedding is different, but a wedding planner will tell you there are things that are needed for *every* wedding, whether it's held in a church or in a farmer's field. Since planning a wedding is nothing like planning a kid's birthday party, let's turn to strengthening your skills for specific parties.

## Ensemble in a class or program

Ensemble training is invaluable for every actor's education. How can educators teach their students to embrace what makes them uniquely the individual artists they are, while teaching them about their role in the ensemble? How can using ensemble in academic training support overall growth? How can you discover aspects of the individual in the audition/selection process to understand how they'll work with the ensemble?

Every college and university has its own curriculum, standards, and practices; the theatre curriculum at Brooklyn College is wildly different from that of the State University of New York at New Paltz. Which classes you offer doesn't matter in this discussion as much as your teaching philosophy for artists in training. Review your criteria for students that you want in your program. Seriously, go to whatever documents you've created for your application and selection process (and if you haven't, it's high time you articulated your mission and philosophy). Take a moment to review it, and have it nearby while reading the next section.

Do you have "strong ensemble player" listed anywhere?

"But I practice ensemble building in the classroom," you say, "that's a given." So why wouldn't you include it in your selection process? If not, why not? Do you consider ensemble as an essential value in your program? If so, what are you doing in the selection process to reveal the candidate's traits as they pertain to ensemble building? Selecting strong actors who are *also* strong ensemble members will enhance their education, teach them valuable skills for this collaborative profession, and will support their learning by their commitment to one another. So how can you revise your selection process to include ensemble building as criteria, in order to recognize that student who is a skilled actor *and* a dedicated team player?

## Rose

### *Selecting ensemble for a class/program*

I've been assembling the annual cohort of BFA acting students for about 12 years as of this writing. I've seen a gifted actor poison the efforts of others and I've seen less talented but more generous actors draw that ensemble together. I can't separate how I select a class from how I cast a play. In casting, if an actor has less ability but is a stellar ensemble member, I hire them over a more skilled, but selfish actor every time (don't be tempted by talent; it never outweighs the cost of high maintenance). In a college setting, the pressure to produce the next "name" actor can be interesting; the administration, parents, applicants, want to know "What famous people went here?" I tell them, "We're not training them to be *famous* actors, we're training them to be *working* actors." An essential part of that education is teaching them how to collaborate, and that strengthens their learning *and* makes them competitive in their field.

My standards for selecting incoming students are the same as for casting a play. The challenge is that I'm casting for a play that hasn't been written yet. Each ensemble will ultimately write and tell its own story, comprised of the adventures, misfortunes, and joys that befall them throughout the years. But my goal remains constant: to teach and nurture young actors to prepare them for the profession with the support of their ensemble. Their first artistic community will remain a part of them for their entire lives.

I once auditioned a prospective student who handed me a picture and resume, and presented two good monologues. When I tried giving him an adjustment, his resistance was remarkable. "My manager worked with me on these pieces." I noted that he wanted me to know that he already had representation; fair enough. But his subtext was, "Nothing needs to be changed." I reassured him that we were only trying to get to know him better by exploring different colors in his pieces. The resistance continued; though he certainly had ability, he wasn't listening. During our interview, I asked, "What do you feel you bring to an ensemble?" He replied, "Oh, professionalism. I don't let what other people do bother me, I just do my thing." Needless to say, I didn't accept him.

Each year I dig deeper to discover behaviors that will reveal a willingness to work as a team. If we don't assemble the best ingredients for this party, we are in for a looong four years. I know that my purpose is to assemble a group of actors who, besides having acting ability, are:

- hungry to learn
- filled with the beginnings of self-awareness
- generous listeners
- willing to take risks
- curious
- excited to collaborate with an ensemble on the same journey.

They can have bad habits (in fact, they *should* have bad habits at this early stage of their development), as long as they're willing to recognize and work on them. They can be shy, as long as they're willing to try to stop hiding their light and share it instead. They can have healthy egos (and *should*), so long as they recognize that generosity is one of the greatest gifts they can give to themselves and their partners.

When interviewing prospective students, listen carefully, observe their physical behavior, and try to get a sense of their self-awareness. Are they saying what they *think* the panel wants to hear or what they truly believe? Are they really *listening* to what's being asked? If I had one piece of advice to offer theatre teachers from high schools or two-year colleges, it would be to encourage their students to *listen* more. This will serve them in college interviews and in every audition of their career. If a candidate brings even a small slice of listening and self-awareness into their audition, then I'm interested. I don't care if they blew their lines or mispronounced the author's name. Sure, sometimes the nerves that come with the audition structure can fluster even a good listener. If you meet a prospective student that, despite your best efforts, is giving you responses that have nothing to do with the questions, how hard will you have to work to break that isolating habit? And what will happen to them in a group-learning environment?

Do give strong consideration (and a callback!) to prospective students who:

- are open and willing to play when you ask them to make adjustments in their audition pieces
- seem excited or intrigued about new discoveries
- are willing to admit they're nervous
- are more focused on revealing who they are vs. what they think you want to see
- take risks in their work
- give their energy to you instead of acting at you
- introduce themselves to the full panel, not just the person they think is in charge
- when given the opportunity, ask strong questions (i.e., for which the answers aren't found in the written literature).

The following are statements that we consider "red flags" as to who may not be healthy for the ensemble. Nerves and the desire to please in an interview can make young people say (and do) crazy things, so consider the sum, not just the parts.

General Red Flags:

- Are they using the words "my" and "me" repeatedly? Are they speaking as if they're better than anyone they've worked with?
- Do they avoid taking responsibility for something perceived as a negative? Worse, if you point out something they should change for future auditions (such as, "Face us, not the upstage wall ... ") do they blame their current teacher for steering them wrong?
- Do they become defensive when given an adjustment? "I don't know what you want!" or "Is how I rehearsed it not good enough?" How would they handle critique in a classroom? How open are they to growth and learning?

- Are they interested in being good vs. doing their best and exploring?
- Are they making eye contact with only you and not the other members of the selection panel? Have they decided that you're the only important one because you make the final decision?

*Potential* Red Flag statements:

- I love acting because I have complete control over the audience.
- I want to pursue acting because it helps me work out my own problems on stage.
- I don't know what I'd do if I couldn't escape into a character.
- I'm more comfortable playing a character than being myself.
- I played all the leads in my high school plays. (We consider this a red flag not simply because it's annoying, but because they're speaking of their individual experience only, vs. "I played some major roles in wonderful productions that our high school produced.")
- I'm very dedicated – even when I'm cast in a very small role. (Red flag because we wonder: why do they even mention the size of the role? It implies a judgment value. Another version:)
- I work hard – even if I only have a small part. (Those words "even if" and "only" speak volumes.)
- I want to be an actor because I like making people laugh. (This is usually followed by a story about how fabulous the result was. This is a red flag because it focuses on a result that has nothing to do with the role, the production, or the ensemble.)

Statements that can be *confused* as Red Flag statements:

- I'm nervous. (This is actually one of the healthiest statements a candidate can make. They're acknowledging where they are, they're being present, and they're trusting you with that information. Nervousness is something that will be your job to assist them with over time. Use this as an opportunity to teach them something that you do in your program. An exercise to help them breathe and focus.)
- I've forgotten the lines! (If they forget lines while you're giving them an adjustment, this is a *good* thing. They're trying to let go of the rehearsed way of doing it to allow something new to happen. Don't use memorization alone as a measure of someone's potential.)
- How many people do you accept? (This may be a genuine interest in what their class size will be; sometimes an applicant can appear as if they're fishing for how well they're doing. Assume the best and trust that they're interested in a good student/teacher ratio.)

We're not suggesting the interview become a therapy session; think of it like an archaeological expedition that digs down a few layers to find what lies below the surface. You need to know about their foundation, but you don't have to examine every single brick.

Ask your candidates questions (and in callbacks, do exercises) that will reveal their perception of themselves in an ensemble. The following questions are very useful in the interview process:

- Do you have siblings? Where are you in that order?

As we've written, family is the first ensemble we encounter and those experiences color how we approach and choose other groups. When creating ensembles where the ages might range from 18–25, we need insight into how they feel about their pecking order in the family. Parents can be tricky to ask about; but ask about *siblings*, and if they've got them, they spill their guts. We've been told harrowing stories of elaborate pranks played on a brother, terrifying schemes to sneak out with a sister's help (involving climbing out windows and over rooftops!), tales of fights, and great tales of love. Candidates seem much more relaxed when talking about brothers and sisters. We've seen great tenderness revealed, and in the same breath they may say "but I can't ever let her know I feel that way." Very complex relationships; but because this is their familial ensemble, they *have* to find a way to make it work. Hearing *how* they make it work gives insight into how they might work within the acting ensemble.

- When you're in an ensemble, what role do you play or fulfill? Are you the Rock, the Caretaker, the Glue … ?

Their answer reveals how they see themselves. Sometimes they're honest enough to differentiate how they'd *like* to see themselves, instead of who they actually *are*. They've taken a risk in sharing that and it shows they understand that being part of an ensemble means knowing what your contribution is.

- You're going down to the character store and you can pick any character you most want to play off the rack. They don't have to be from a published play or film, they should simply be the ideal character that you would most like to play at this moment in your life. What personality traits do they possess and what sort of adventures or situations do they find themselves in?

This reveals so much about the individual and who they'll be in the ensemble. Do they allow themselves to be imaginative? Do they suspect a trap (i.e., there's a "right" answer) or do they smile in wonderment at being asked a fun question? What does the choice of character reveal about how they see themselves and how they would *like* to be seen?

- A playwright has written a new play and the lead character is you; the play is about you and your life. The director has cast an actor to play you, what would be essential for that actor to know about playing you that might not be apparent on the page?

If the candidate struggled with the character store question, this version sometimes frees up their responses. Young actors typically struggle to say positive things about themselves. This question gives them permission to say nice things about who they are without worrying that it may come across as being egotistical.

Questions *from* the Candidate:

We've sometimes had our hearts broken when an interview/audition is going well, and we ask "Do you have any questions for *us*?" You hope that the question they choose to ask will reveal another aspect of their creativity, or reveal the prepared and thoughtful student that you hope they'll be.

Red Flag questions:

- Can you tell me about what classes I'd get to take? (This one always kills us; they've done little or no research into what the program offers. They may be casting a wide net for many schools but not researching what differentiates each program. How can they care so little for their future? A second piece of advice we'd give to advisors: encourage your students to apply only to those schools where they can actually see themselves training and living. Otherwise, it's a waste of their money and resources.)
- How did I do? (They're asking for a review instead of using the time to ask about:
  - The program they're considering committing four years of their life to.
  - These strangers [faculty] and their background.
  - Teaching philosophy.
  They're result-oriented, or worse, may want approval more than they want to learn.)
- Has anybody famous ever gone here? (They're more interested in the destination than the journey.)
- How many shows will I get to be in? (If your production season and audition policy is clearly posted on your website, this reveals a lack of preparation. Or, it can reveal a tendency to be more interested in performing than in receiving an education. Productions should exist as opportunities for students to apply what they're learning, not a reward in and of themselves.)

No matter how overwhelmed you feel by time, hold callbacks. Some things are revealed in group exercises that you simply can't get to at individual auditions.

The candidate may be more relaxed, feel more supported by the group, and give themselves greater permission to play. In group work, you can get a clearer sense of how they listen and play, and what kind of ensemble member they will be. Group exercises such as Come Join Me, West Side Story, and What Are You Doing (see Appendix C) reveal their connection to impulses, how they respond to being challenged, and what their fear level may be.

## Wait lists, or reconfiguring your first ensemble

In a perfect world, after auditions, you create your dream list for the ensemble. However, the students may receive a better offer from another school and say "no thanks." They may also say "yes" initially, then crunch the numbers and realize they can't afford college. In the long run it's better for the ensemble for these people to decline, but it still plays hell with your dream guest list for the party.

So now you go to your Wait List. Be careful with this new alchemy of mixing people from the original list with those who may not have the same abilities or maturity. You risk alienating ensemble members who could feel held back, and the Wait Listed folks might feel others are racing too far ahead. So who *must* you have in order for it to succeed? If you have the following, you can make almost anything work (see Chapter 5 for full descriptions):

- The Glue: the one who literally holds it together. Their steadiness, grounded nature, and unwavering commitment make them irreplaceable.
- The Nurturer: derives strength and joy from witnessing the growth and achievements of others. Universal donors with a seemingly endless supply of generosity of spirit.
- The Rock: an excellent listener, dependable, steady, strong, grounded. Their reliability makes them an internal leader who guides through setting personal examples.
- The Sparkplug: the initiator, the one to get things going.

If we have a Nurturer to help as a surrogate mother to the ensemble, a Rock to rely on, a Glue to hold things together when the center hasn't held, and a Sparkplug to initiate a new idea with joy and abandon, then we have a strong mix of internal leadership that will help negotiate the sometimes choppy waters that may occur in a re-configured group.

## Getting the ensemble started for a class/program

Creating an ensemble for a class has some interesting challenges: the goal of each ensemble member is to get a strong education to prepare them for a career in acting. They may ask, "Isn't getting a good education an *individual* goal? Why do I need an ensemble for my education?" The fact remains they're choosing a collaborative profession. There is no course listed anywhere in our curriculum titled Collaboration 101. Collaboration must be taught in each class through experience, exploration, and creative play together. Collaboration is the foundation of theatre and of the theatre artist's training. The student's goal, and ours, is that they develop skills that will enable them to succeed. They must also work together throughout their training to learn the essential role that ensemble plays in the creative process. They must develop collaborative skills, and an understanding of the sacrifice it takes to meet common goals together. As we've written elsewhere, good technique may get a young artist their first job; poor collaborative skills will deny them their second.

There is no single model that will result in the ensemble achieving their group *identity*; otherwise we might have a six volume set. However, the following guidelines will always apply no matter what model you ascribe to:

- No elimination exercises in classroom. As we wrote in Chapter 3, elimination creates insecurities that are brutal to untangle. Without elimination, they learn that they will have multiple opportunities to try again and that the ensemble will support them no matter what. The consequences of not doing something well are to simply do it again.

- Sitting out is not an option. This way the ensemble knows that everyone has the same expectations, considerations, and opportunities. This helps those who are initially reluctant to participate to know that they must eventually participate, and it allows the ensemble to support them in that effort.

- During discussions, don't permit students to "review" themselves or others. *That was good. This was terrible.* Give them specific, constructive vocabulary: "What seemed to work? What was a strong or clear choice?" And as they become aware of their individual differences, remind them that those differences make them the actor they uniquely are and define what they uniquely bring to the ensemble.

- Consider doing physical instead of verbal exercises in the first few sessions. With new people, verbal work tends to ignite feelings of unproductive comparison and bad cases of "the enoughs:" *That wasn't clever enough, that wasn't funny enough* or worse, *That was the wrong thing to say* or *Listen to how smart Maureen is; I sound so stupid* or *Listen to how funny Manny is – I'll never be that quick or witty.* Words kick the analytical mind into high gear in new situations and instincts and listening go into the back seat. If students are focused on harsh self-comparisons, there's no room for listening or getting to know one another. Physical exercises encourage a greater sense of play and seem to ignite the intuitive rather than the intellectual.

## Rose

I once taught a group of graduate improv students who were incredibly smart, mature, and experienced. In our first class I noticed that they wanted to talk, a lot. They were brilliant analyzers, but they were (perhaps unconsciously) using their life experiences as security blankets in conversation. They were discussing things that "elevated" them from one another. I felt they were trying to prove to themselves that they "belonged in the room" with these strangers that they perceived (or feared?) were more talented, more experienced, smarter, etc.

For the second class, I made sure every exercise was non-verbal (sound and movement only). I introduced West Side Story (see Appendix E), which asks for two groups of people to be lined up "against" one another. Alternating leaders initiate a structured six-beat sound and movement that their "team" must quickly emulate while moving forward, "pushing" the other team back with their energy. Then someone on the other team leads, and so forth.

I observed a few panicky moments of them trying to sort out how they might preconceive something – and realizing they couldn't. Many hands shot up, asking for additional clarification (granted, WSS does take longer to explain than to do!), and they were clearly stalling. I ended the conversation with, "Let's dive in!" Because of the structure, everyone noticed the difference between when they were *thinking* about a sound and gesture, and when they were *responding* with a sound and gesture. They recognized that stopping and thinking was actually *counterproductive* and an individual "stop" was a stop for the whole group. No one could proceed until that leader committed to a choice. Once the group accepted responsibility for maintaining a continuous rhythm, they didn't have the option of stopping and thinking. Even better, there was no desire to stop and think. They were responding instead of making a considered choice. The more trust they gained in themselves, the more trust they had with one another. They realized that whatever response they had would be embraced by the group. In turn, they felt more accepted and their physical choices became riskier as the exercise progressed.

When I called, "Go to neutral," they collapsed in an exhausted pile of laughter. Someone shouted, "That was so hard! But so fun!" *What was fun about it?* "Well, I was trying so hard to come up with an idea that would be good, but there was no time to do that." *What did you do instead?* "I had to follow my impulse." *Where did that come from?* "Oh, from my partners!

Everybody gave so much!" Someone said, "I was so busy trying to think of something that would be really clever to give my partner, I suddenly heard silence and realized, 'Oh shit, I'm not giving them *anything* right now.'" "Yeah, I had to let go of thinking and trust that my impulsive choice would be enough for my partner to work with." *And was it?* Everyone in the room shouted, "Yes!" Someone else said, "At first I felt I must look ridiculous. Then I realized everyone was doing it. More importantly, it felt good to be that physical and silly! And I learned a lot about each person from how they moved." *What did that make you want to do?* "It made me want to reveal more of myself."

The magic really happened when someone said, "It became a real conversation. We were communicating entire stories to one another as *a group*. I didn't need all those words that I thought I needed. And, I couldn't do it alone. I needed everyone with me. It was hard at first to trust that whatever I led with would be enough, but everyone said 'yes and ... ' no matter what choice we made." At that point he turned to the entire class and said, "Thank you. That's something I haven't felt in a long, long time." Then he paused, smiled, and said, "I want more!" Everyone laughed, but the expressions on their faces told me that they *all* wanted more of this. "This" was the bond and support of ensemble, trusting that they were enough, that the ensemble would support them and their choices no matter what, and letting go of intellectual separation as a means of identity. It was the first moment the group discovered that individual identity wasn't consumed by an ensemble, but rather that individuals collaborating together *are* the ensemble.

- Include exercises that focus on building trust, particularly blindfold work. Blindfolds seem to erase the imaginary Judge, from inside and outside. Somehow, if a student or actor can't see the potential judger, they cease to exist. Even if that Judge is imaginary, that tangible blindfold seems to protect the wearer from the harsh power the Judge wields.

### Rose

I taught a class that was struggling with harsh comparisons. They told me privately they were worried what others thought of their choices, but actually *they* were being brutal with themselves (their weekly journals made this clear: "I'm the worst in the class. Everyone must wonder how I got accepted into this program."). One day I introduced the exercise "The Cobra" to them (see Appendix G). The group members stand in a tight circle, put on blindfolds, turn to their right and place their hands on the shoulders of the person now directly in front of them. They explore the back of the head, etc., of the person they're touching. They break the circle, move out into the space, and then are asked to silently *reform* the circle in its exact order.

As you can imagine, this was met with "Are you kidding? That's impossible!" and then their worst fear revealed, "I'm going to be the last one, I know it." But, they were game and dutifully put on their brightly colored bandanas after fighting to get their favorite color. I can't tell you why, but letting them pick their favorite colors seems to give them a starting moment of confidence. I think it simply gives them comfort to have control over *some*thing. Now blindfolded, they turned and explored the person in front of them in the now-connected circle. I saw their fingertips trying to "memorize" a necklace chain or pony tail and I observed in their bodies that most were feeling pretty hopeless; slumped shoulders, slouched backs, all low status positions. I called for them to break the circle and they moved away and out into the space. After allowing time to mix up the order, I called for them to reform the circle.

After a few moments of zombie shuffling, they began to tentatively seek the shoulders of the person that had been in front of them. When the first student found the person they sought, their physicality changed instantly. Their fingertips stopped abruptly as if to say, "Wait, can it really be you?" They searched furtively to confirm what their senses had already told them, and then a physical signal (a tiny pat to the back of the head) communicated their joy of, "I found you!" Their chest opened, their head lifted higher, and everything in their physical being changed. I saw this joyful transformation occur as each link was formed; when a seeker found a chain, they expressed physical elation. Ultimately, one long line shuffled until the last one still seeking found the final person needed to reform the circle. I saw everyone *hear* the sound of the collective movement change from "still searching" to "we are here!" I called for them to pause, remove blindfolds, and see if they were where they began in the circle. Everyone quickly removed their blindfolds; the moment when they realized they had succeeded was glorious, and they let out a collective cheer.

When I asked them to share, one said, "I was so afraid and felt so alone in the dark. I thought that the sounds I heard was everyone finding each other and that I'd be all by myself. But in that moment, I realized that I wasn't moving. It was *me* stopping me. I wasn't even bothering to search for my partner. And then I realized oh my god, that sound is somebody looking for you, so you better move!" *What happened next?* "The minute I took action and started moving, like almost immediately, my partner found me! That inspired me to find who I was looking for." *So how does this relate to acting and ensemble?* "I never realized how much I imagined eyes watching me, judging me, and how that stops me all the time. It's weird, but the blindfold erased them. I explored some risky tactics to find my partner that I don't think I would have if I didn't have the blindfold." Another student said, "I don't know why, but the blindfold helped me see (!!) how much I really, really need my partners." Then the student who had been most hard on herself said, "Wow. If we can do this, we can do anything together."

## Ensemble in production

Take a moment right now to think about a favorite ensemble that you worked with. Stop reading and close your eyes, just for a second. What images and faces come immediately to you? What's the first feeling you get? What's happening in that image or memory? There is likely a joy, a sense of satisfaction, and we'll wager you've caught yourself smiling. Most of you just recalled a show or a rehearsal for a show, whether a professional setting, college or even high school. There was something about the group you worked with that made you run to rehearsals and drag your feet as you headed home. If you were an actor in that group, what did the director do to nurture or encourage those ensemble bonds? If you were the director, what actions did you take to create that "favorite ensemble?" How did having the bonds of ensemble make that production and its rehearsal process such a great party? What were you able to do *because* of having that ensemble that you might not have been able to do without them?

Now, if your response was, "I don't remember that we did anything special to make it happen; it just happened," you might be a lucky beneficiary of stars aligning. However, we would venture to say that you were part of a group of strong "yes and-ers." There's a terrific quote from Ringo Starr: "I've never really done anything to create what has happened. It creates itself. I'm here because it happened. But I didn't do anything to make it happen apart from saying 'Yes.'" Can you imagine what you can create every time you embark on a production if you consciously take actions to build a strong ensemble?

### *Selecting ensemble for productions*

The first criteria for selection are obviously determined by the needs of the script, followed by your vision of the story. By the time you're ready to cast, you've

86

explored the text and you understand the needs of the play. Each role has particular demands, but the ensemble will require specific contributions from each cast member as well. Remember our earlier example of casting a selfish actor in the role of John Proctor? *The Crucible* needs ensemble members who honor the themes, are willing to commit to the story's truth, commit fully to their character's part in the story no matter what size the role (no focus-stealing Cheevers, please), and who are willing to support every member of this 20+ size cast. The ensemble for this show would benefit from several Sparkplugs, a Cheerleader, several Rocks, and at least one Ox to move things forward when the going gets tough (see Chapter 5). The material is emotionally draining, and often there are 12 to 15 people on stage. You need an ensemble comprised of excellent listeners, who play well with others and who constantly ask, "What does this need from me?" Good productions, especially if they have longer runs, need an ensemble to create self-sustaining energy and support, which provides ongoing life in the storytelling itself. A strong ensemble makes for a stronger production.

After you've drafted your wish list of actors, make a list of what the special demands will be for the ensemble. If you're directing *Take Me Out* by Richard Greenberg, do they need to be physically playful, emotionally mature, and have a good understanding of baseball and the meaning of "team?" If *The Rimers of Eldritch* by Lanford Wilson, should they be excellent listeners, have strong kinesthetic awareness, a sense of musicality either in their bodies or voices? Just as each role determines a set of needs, each production has specific demands for its ensemble. Consider this as much a part of your preparation work as anything else.

### *Getting started: creating the bonds (no matter the length of the rehearsal period)*

We acknowledge that rehearsal schedules don't always allow time to be set aside for building ensemble. Likewise, not every director thinks ensemble is of particular value, or that it's their job to create ensemble in the cast. Some directors like to encourage healthy (and unhealthy) competition among their actors, others focus on the story and leave ensemble to the actors. Still others say, "Well, that's fine for educational productions or community theatre, but I direct in the real world." In a *New York Times* article on a Broadway production of Arthur Miller's *All My Sons*, cast members John Lithgow and Patrick Wilson discussed various ensemble exercises that the director, Simon McBurney, had them do in early rehearsals. Their rehearsal schedule was nearly double what a traditional Broadway schedule is, and it included workshops, status exercises, and improvisations. The article stated that the " ... award-winning actors readily admit that Mr. McBurney's unconventional process worked. The exercises helped build up ' ... the trust we have in each other,' said Mr. Wilson." Rather than feeling that their time was wasted, the actors credited Mr. McBurney's process for " ... the depth and richness of their performances." There's no reason why including ensemble work has to label your process "unconventional" – what a shame that is.

If you find yourself saying, "But ensemble isn't always necessary for a great production," we're happy to debate it on our blog (see Conclusion: Last Call). We aren't saying that lack of ensemble makes for a poor show, but creating ensemble in your production will make for a *stronger* show. The following suggestions are simple and involve very little time; make room in your rehearsal schedule to include them.

### First, create a supportive atmosphere

- When preparing for the first read-through, make the seating "equal." Set up chairs in a circle, rather than the typical classroom style of rows where a hierarchy could be implied. Be sure everyone can easily see each other.
- Next, infuse the space with the kind of energy you want it to have. Rearrange things, if necessary, and make sure the space is clean (the garbage has been taken out, the windows open, the room airy). Clear the room of anything undesirable so it can be filled by the positive energy of those about to arrive. You don't want to start your work by fighting the stink from someone's lunch left in the garbage pail since Tuesday.

### Rose

However, I once directed a group that bonded over a horrific rat problem; the smell of dead critter was *reeking* throughout the theatre. We tried to joke about it, but when we saw the *artistic director himself* crawl under the stage to nose out the offender, we knew that everyone was doing all they could to solve the problem. So no one complained (much), the artistic director embodied ensemble in every way (not asking anyone to go somewhere he wasn't willing to go himself), and the ensemble united against a common enemy!

- When everyone has assembled for the read-through, begin promptly; show respect for everyone's time. We don't mean launching right into page one, but beginning the process itself, in whatever form you've designed.
- Give ample time for personal introductions. In your eagerness to get started on the play, don't discount how much can be achieved by people getting to know each other.
- Always introduce yourself and answer the same questions that you ask the cast to respond to (you should go first!). This portion should be separate from your opening remarks (e.g., Rose never identifies herself as The Director, she says "I'm Rose Bonczek and I'll be your host for the next five weeks"). Find something light in that introductory moment that works for you. For students and early career actors, the word "director" has so much weight to it. Find a

way to make the cast know that you consider yourself the leader and a part of this ensemble.

### *Your opening remarks*

Remember when we were kids and we all got together to play in someone's yard at the end of the day? Unless someone took charge of spelling out the rules of the game, you could be there all night arguing. You didn't want to look stupid by doing something that wasn't "allowed," and you certainly didn't want to let your team down by doing the wrong thing like running to the birdbath for home base when you should have run to the butternut tree. Spelling out the rules isn't an imposition, it *frees* us to play. The structure of the game doesn't limit players, it gives an equal understanding of expectations and *how* to play so that everyone can do their best. As someone once said, "You need the cauldron to make the alchemy." Your brain can then let go of trying to figure out what comes next; instead, you have all this room inside you to create and play and get a hit. And hope that the big white fossil rock you're running toward really is first base.

What you share in your opening remarks is an opportunity for you to consider your own process too. What are your expectations? What should the company know about how you work? What can you encourage the cast to do that will plant healthy seeds for ensemble? You can all unite through shared expectations and the goal. We list a few examples of what you might say at a first read-through. These apply whether directing for a college production, a community theatre, or Off Broadway:

- We will work together to create an environment that is safe and supportive, so that creative play and risk-taking can flourish. I will do everything in my power to create that with you and I need your help to protect what we create together.
- Failure is a necessary part of the creative process. We won't feel comfortable trying things unless we feel free to fail, to learn from that and to try again. If we play it safe, our choices will be safe. So let's create an environment that supports risk-taking.
- Be patient with one another, cheer each other on; each failure leads us further and further from a safe choice. And remember, I need room to fail too, so I ask for your support in that as well.
- I expect everyone to have respect for themselves, the work, their partners, and for the ensemble. We don't have to love one another, but mutual respect is essential. NOTE: If working with younger students, consider adding the following clarification:
  - Respect yourself and the work by being on time, warmed up and ready at the stated start time, not running in the door on the dot with coffee and snacks.
- Support one another's choices, but please try not to direct each other. Let me do my job and trust that I'm encouraging your partner to follow a particular path for a reason.

- Assume the best, not the worst, of one another. Assuming the worst is disrespectful to yourself, the work, and ultimately blocks you from taking responsibility for your choices.
- I ask a lot from the actors I work with; I need you all to bring everything to the table. Don't ask permission to make a choice, just do it. NOTE: freedom to explore should always be a part of your rehearsal process, no matter the length of time you have. Nurturing instinctual choices from the beginning will *save* time, not waste it.
- Try to say "yes and … " instead of "no, but … " Try not to judge a choice or an action before it's had the chance to live and breathe. Try to trust that your impulse may be the source of your next discoveries. NOTE: using the word "try" vs. "do" allows for a more open consideration of the person's abilities. And if you have a cast member who is result-oriented, it helps them focus on the exploration vs. obtaining the result.
- Our commitment is to tell this story in the strongest way possible. For that, we need this unique group of actors, designers, and stage managers to bring all that you have to this production. Only this group can tell this story in their unique way. What does this story mean to you, why are you telling this story at this moment in your life? Try to allow that to inform your choices.
- The structure of the story, and of this company assembled here, gives us our cauldron, and within that, we'll be making some magic.

By establishing specific expectations, you give clear guidance for rehearsals and performance. Everyone has permission to play and discover, and they understand that together you will protect the environment. By emphasizing the goal of storytelling, actors consider their role in the story, not the role they possess. We know it's obvious that we're here to produce a play, but saying out loud that you're here to tell the story makes a difference. We're often surprised when actors tell us, "I never hear a director speak about us as storytellers."

You've also stated expectations for everyone to personalize the story for themselves, to seek meaning in this event happening at this moment in their lives. This deepens their investment in the story and in each other. The actors know that they're all sharing something personal in their work. Deeper investment in the story brings a deeper commitment to one another and the probability of them bonding because of this is vastly increased.

After clarifying goals and expectations, use your ensemble criteria list to guide you in additional activities. Do a group warm-up that supports the rehearsal plan for the night. For example, if you're rehearsing one of the ballpark scenes from *Take Me Out*, have the cast play five minutes of catch (yes, with real gloves and a ball!). If rehearsing the big confrontation scene in *Savage in Limbo*, have the cast do five minutes of physical status work on the set as they vie for one another's "territory." Each of these examples are fun exercises that foster the trust actors need to do their individual work, nurture deeper connections to support the relationships between characters, and support the bonds of ensemble itself.

### David

I was discussing ensemble with my friend and grad school classmate, Tim Fannon. Tim has spent many years performing regionally and in New York, in addition to creating ensemble-based work with his own theatre company that, as he says, "is extremely rewarding." In our conversation, Tim was lamenting the lack of ensemble that he encounters in his freelance work, where he is hired strictly as an actor. Theatre is expensive to produce, so rehearsal periods are short and there is little time for ensemble building or exploration. He related working on an intimate scene with an actress that he had met "the day before yesterday." They had exchanged pleasantries, but not even a full conversation had passed between them due to the intense schedule. I asked him if he felt that our ensemble work in graduate school had been for naught, given the circumstances in the "real world." "To the contrary," he replied. "It's more valuable than ever. I need that level of trust and am forced to find it very quickly. My past experience with ensemble helps make that possible. Let's face it, I *will* be working in an ensemble, whether it is planned for or not, and whether it is a good one or not. I do everything I can to promote the strong bonds of ensemble because it makes the work so much better."

## Ensemble in improvisation

Creating ensemble for improv groups is very similar to what you've read in the first part of this chapter. The questions, red flags, audition and interview tips provided apply here as well. What we'll focus on in this section is not improv ensembles, per se, but any ensemble that will be creating its own material. Of course, improvisers create new material on each occasion, but if your ensemble is creating material that will eventually be memorized and repeated, this section applies because your process is bound to encounter many of the same issues.

The big difference, obviously, is the relationship that the ensemble has to the material, and this affects the relationships among the ensemble members and with you. For instance, if your ensemble is performing *The Crucible*, all of the performers have been assigned a role(s). The actor playing Ezekiel Cheever knows what his role is, and consequently, what his relationship is to the other roles and within the story. He won't show up one night and suddenly start playing the role of John Proctor or deliver a long speech revealing Cheever's thoughts (as much as he may want to). A very large part of his definition within the ensemble has been made clear and is unchanging. Without the structure that the material provides, the ensemble is much more adrift and therefore reliant upon each other and the strength of their collaboration. You require an even stronger and more nuanced ensemble because there is more to be shared, negotiated, discovered, and agreed upon.

And while the performers may be more adrift, they're simultaneously more empowered. They're not just performers, but also writers, directors, choreographers, and sometimes more. They *are* the material. They create their own structure. Their ability to work with each other is paramount.

The initial lack of material that comes with improvising can be frightening and liberating at the same time, and it comes with greater responsibility and greater risk. One performer can easily decide to hog the stage or disrupt fellow performers. This can happen even when intentions are good. There is nothing to fall back on, except each other. As one of David's student improvisers, Dylan Travers, once said, "There's no place to hide."

When a performer has an unlimited number of choices to make at every moment, having performers who can stay together is imperative to keep things coherent.

### *Selecting ensemble for improvisation*

We begin the same way as before, by identifying our purpose. With improvisation, though, it's as if you have to plan a party, but you can't tell the invitees what the occasion is, what to wear, what will be served, if they need to bring something, or what to expect. So whom do you invite? You invite people who are flexible, helpful, positive, and diplomatic. People who love surprises, aren't easily embarrassed and make friends quickly. People who aren't control freaks or who have an agenda, but are willing to go with the flow. People who are equally good at talking and listening. Imagine that you're planning a pool party, but you can't tell your guests this important detail; none of them are likely to show up with swimsuits. One option would be to invite people who you know would be comfortable swimming in makeshift swimwear (like shorts or underwear) or those who love to skinny-dip!

When selecting ensemble members for improv, you might expect that only those comfortable with taking risks would show up for auditions. Surprisingly, we've found this not to be the case. We encounter people who are shy, reluctant, or downright petrified. When we ask why they're auditioning, they cite reasons such as, "I thought it would be good for me," or "I'm forcing myself to do something adventurous," or the dreaded "I was told I had to." Just as before, try to understand why a person wants to be in this ensemble and ask the questions we outlined earlier.

The first thing to look for when selecting improvisers is the level and nature of risk they're willing to take. Keep this in mind: there's a difference between foolish risks and brave risks. We're looking for the latter and willing to tolerate a certain amount of the former. In auditions, look for people who have a willingness to:

- jump in when they have no idea what to do
- jump in to help someone who is flailing

- play a moment straight rather than forcing it to be funny
- work with anyone in the room, not just "good" people
- commit to a scene no matter how badly it's going, rather than bailing out.

The ultimate risk, though, is willingness to give up control. The items listed here are examples of that. A performer who unhesitatingly accepts what their partner gives them is willing to give up control and go wherever the scene (and their partner) may take them. Thus, they're inherently relying on others to create, rather than trying to get others to go along with them.

Some red flags to watch for in auditions:

- Ignoring, correcting, or denying an offer by a partner or from you.
- Lots of talking, not much listening.
- Consistently aggressive behavior and/or violent character choices.
- Always playing the highest status in a scene.
- Frequently judging others or self.
- Trying to be funny and/or ensure that the scene is funny at all costs.

## David

Here's the one "comedy" consideration I make when looking for members of an improv ensemble. As far back as Aristotle (and undoubtedly before him) we've known that most comedy is about surprise, and the easiest way to surprise people is to shock them. Yet it takes no particular skill or talent to shock people. Any idiot can easily invent something shocking to say. Shock comedy, therefore, is the easiest form of comedy to achieve. Some might say *lowest* form, but I prefer easiest. Shock comedy has its place in the comedy pantheon and I'm not above using it myself. However, if that's all you do, then you're not working hard enough; you're taking the easy way out. Watch out for those who rely too heavily on shock comedy and when you encounter them, request that they do a "no laugh" scene. That is, to just play it straight and not go for any jokes. Assure them that it's okay to be dramatic or even boring, just don't go for any laughs. See if they can do it. If they can't resist, beware.

The second thing to look for in auditions are listening skills, and this is closely related to willingness to give up control. Players who connect with their partners, listen, and incorporate what they hear make strong ensemble members. It's not all about them; they look to collaborate, thrive on inspiration, and enjoy feeding off of others.

### David

On occasion, I've had to create an improv show with college students who had little or no previous experience. The first time, I only had five weeks to put it together, so I felt pressure to find performers who would naturally gravitate toward ensemble work. In auditions, the students continually encountered moments of not having the faintest idea of what to do. Most responses fell into one of two categories: seeking comfort by trying to control the action or seeking comfort through connection with their partner. The latter group's default condition was to listen, observe, and try to stay together. By identifying those students, I was able to select a cast that would survive when things weren't going well (which in improv is inevitable).

A simple way to think of this is to remember what it's like to observe children at a playground. You can tell which ones play well with others and which ones don't. In a basic sense, improv is just another form of playground behavior: everything is a series of games and make-believe scenarios created on the spot. Look for the people who play well together.

When auditioning improvisers, see them in large groups (ideally, 8–12 at a time) to observe how they interact within an ensemble. When you want to see them perform in pairs, have the others sit and watch. You should not only observe the pair performing, but also look at their audience of fellow auditioners to see what they're doing. Are they watching intently or drifting off? Are they staying in the moment by listening to this scene, or are they calculating what they'll do when it's their turn? How is their posture: open and accepting, or defensive, such as arms folded tightly? Do they make comments after a pair has finished (often phrasing it in a question, such as "Do you want us to do it like THAT?"). Once they've caught on to this system, do they try to align themselves with a specific partner or avoid a specific partner vs. working with anyone? Watching the watcher can reveal a lot.

In improv, the performers *are* the script. So once you've identified who the best ensemble players are likely to be, choose the most diverse selection from among them. This will give you more variety in the material that is generated.

### David

I was once a member of an improv group made up of recent college grads whose primary preoccupations in life (outside of improv) were contemporary blockbuster movies, comic books, and science fiction. (I was the lone exception.) I would estimate that three-fourths of our material was in some way connected to one of those three topics. I've since found that the more diversity there is among the performers, the more diversity there will be in the material that is improvised. If I were casting an improv group at a high school, I'd hope for a group that resembled *The Breakfast Club*. But remember, this idea of diversity is secondary to finding players who share and play well together.

### Getting the ensemble started

Regardless of how well you cast your improv group, those cast members will surprise you as you get to know them and they get to know each other. Again, your cast members *are* the script, and what comes out of them will change depending on who they're working with, what inspiration they're drawing upon, and even what day it is. You want to keep them doing what they do best at this party, and they will do that most effectively, *if they are working well together*. A successful improv show is one where all the members are so in sync that they can finish each other's thoughts, because then they're collectively creating a coherent script for the audience.

Your cast members, if they bond well, will not only be a group with a collective name ("The Improvadudes" or whatever), but they will have a group identity and aesthetic, even if they don't consciously choose one. A true sense of who "The Improvadudes" are is just as clear as the identity of a single human being. People have personalities and so do ensembles. Some of this identity will be recognizable to you as part of your goal and what you hoped to achieve through casting, but some of it will be unknown, waiting for you to discover. Over time, the ensemble's identity will reveal different sides of itself, just like people do.

If the improv group is a long-term venture, expect that the identity will evolve. In six months, it may be somewhat different, just as our human identities change over time.

### First rehearsals

The same things apply here as stated for other ensembles. Create a supportive environment, introduce yourself, and establish expectations. In these early days, it is your job to establish yourself as both enforcer and protector of the ensemble. Once the members trust that you will enforce the safe environment and protect them from destructive behavior, they will begin to fly. And, just as before, start with non-verbal exercises.

95

## Conclusion

We started this chapter by telling you why you should want to create ensemble (it makes for a better party!) and how to do it both in general and in particular circumstances. When speaking with sports writer Pat Ruff of *The Post-Bulletin* in Rochester, Minnesota, we asked him if, in our current sociological climate that emphasizes individual achievement, he felt that people were less likely to want to be part of a group. He emphatically said, "No. Now more than ever, I see young people and people in sports want to be part of something bigger. They want to forget about playing for themselves, they want to play for a common goal, do whatever they can. They're selfless enough in the hope that they can make something happen for their team. Instead of asking 'What are my stats?' they ask 'What can I do to make us better? To make our group better? I can't worry about being a shining star, I have to make this *group* the shining star.' People are fulfilled when they're on a team, it's exhilarating. Even individual sports players (like tennis players) look for ways to make it a team sport; they play doubles, etc. It *feels* better. You can win as a team. You get to celebrate together. There's a feeling of accomplishment when you're in a group, everybody in the sports realm hungers for that. People love being a part of a group; it's another level of experience than just winning by yourself. They want to raise a trophy *together.* When you're jumping into that pile at the end of the game, you're celebrating as a group instead of celebrating by yourself. It's *better.* People want to be with people, it's not enough to be by yourself. You want love, and to be loved. If you can accomplish something with a group, it's another level of happiness. It's just better."

# 5

# ARCHETYPES WITHIN ENSEMBLE

The larger concern is to be able to tastefully explore the stereotypes, and still move past them to see the core of people.

–Forest Whitaker

Who's coming to the party? Wallflowers? Party animals? Raconteurs? Our potential invite list includes some familiar types, some we might or might not like to have at our party. How we choose to define and categorize these types is important. We want to acknowledge recognizable patterns of behavior, without lumping people into characterizations that are a disservice to our understanding. So let's consider archetypes ...

Archetypes exist in mythology, in literature, and in our personal and collective psyches. These characters connect to identities that we instinctively recognize, and often represent someone we strive to be, or someone we try to avoid. Just as our myths tell stories of heroes and villains, tricksters and lovers, we find archetypes in our everyday lives, and in our art. Jung would argue that these archetypes are already embedded in our genetic memories. Ever have the feeling that someone "looks familiar," or *seems* so familiar? We recognize people and qualities that, intellectually, have no business being familiar to us; and yet they are. Whether you consider these moments of recognition as connected to primal instincts, or to the treasure chest of our collective unconsciousness, we recognize, seek, and avoid people in life based on this internal knowledge. Who is the hero/warrior who will protect us? Who is the caretaker/mother figure that will nurture us? Who is the physical or emotional predator/villain who may harm us?

One definition of an archetype is, "an original model or type after which other similar things are patterned; a prototype." Or in Jungian psychology, "an inherited pattern of thought or symbolic imagery derived from the past collective experience and present in the individual unconscious." Examples of some archetypes include the Superman (the Omnipotent), the Hero (Beowulf or Harry Potter), the Wise Old Man (such as Obi-Wan Kenobi or Gandalf), the Trickster or Ape (such as Brer Rabbit or Bugs Bunny). We differentiate an archetype from a stereotype, which the *American Heritage Dictionary* defines as, "a conventional, formulaic, and oversimplified conception. In modern usage, a stereotype is a simplified mental picture of an individual or group of people who share certain characteristic (or stereotypical) qualities." The term is often used in a negative sense, and stereotypes are seen by many as undesirable beliefs that can be altered through education and/ or familiarization. Throughout history, storytellers have drawn from recognizable characters and stereotypical situations, in order to quickly connect the audience with new tales. Archetypes are "original models" that are complex, stereotypes are "formulaic and oversimplified." We can sometimes observe an archetype in a story slide into a stereotype. Thus, we see Harry Potter, the archetypal Hero, who in the stereotypical Hollywood way, is played by a photogenic young man who is much better looking than the image of Harry we had in our heads after reading the first few books.

Over decades of work, we've seen similar recurring behaviors emerge in every production we've directed, and every class we've taught. With each new group, individuals displayed behavior that we recognized immediately, and it created a kind of shorthand that allowed us to predict dynamics, and identify potential conflicts far in advance. Because of the consistency with which these behaviors recurred, just like our myths and stories, we had to accept that ensemble had its own archetypes. Once we trusted this, we were able to identify Ensemble Archetypes early in the process, which enabled us to be proactive with care and maintenance, and to guide the ensemble more effectively toward the goal. After familiarizing ourselves with the behaviors, and after identifying the needs of a specific project, our search for the people to *fill* those needs became easier and more successful. Of course, each ensemble is not comprised *solely* of recognized behaviors, and most members are actually an amalgam of traits. Every individual is unique, and anyone who says "there's nothing new under the sun" hasn't worked with the wonder that is Human Behavior for very long. There is *always* something new in each human being, something unrecognizable, confounding, or surprising that adds to the excitement of creating that ensemble. Our discussion here is less about *one* specific prescription and more about what *may* be occurring in your group dynamic, and how to guide that behavior for the benefit of the ensemble and its goal.

Group settings can amplify certain traits – usually to the good of the ensemble – sometimes to the not so good. As directors, during the audition process we recognize that seemingly ephemeral connection between the individual before us and the needs of the singular character that we've already analyzed. We sense that this individual is the one who can bring great things to what the role needs. But what will the individual bring to the ensemble itself, and what role will they fulfill there? If we devote more time to consider that, and how their contribution will ensure the success of the collaborative goal, we can increase the chances of the project's success. Knowing what role each person will fulfill in the *ensemble* can and should be just as important as finding the "right" person for the role.

So how do you approach fulfilling this dual need of role within the ensemble and role defined by a script? Moreover, when there is no scripted role to speak of (such as in an improv troupe or a class), what exactly are you looking for? There's always the old standby, "I'll know it when I see it." But can you create a flexible human blueprint for the foundation of the project, which is the ensemble itself? Yes; by developing deeper awareness, you can recognize archetypes of the ensemble. And in developing those deeper recognition skills early on, you can strengthen your ability to predict the needed outcome for the group.

Try not to fear that too much knowledge about the nature of ensemble will somehow suck the life and creativity out of it. Something we've discovered through the years is that human beings are wonderfully and maddeningly, well, human. They're unpredictable, willful, squirrelly, and surprising. No matter how much analysis, preparation, or investigation we do prior to starting a rehearsal period or teaching a handpicked class of actors, the chemistry created when these individuals come together will always create a single entity with its own amazing life force. Try to trust that the Magic and Mystery won't be killed by preparation and deeper observation; in fact, preparation, awareness, and action will help you build a stronger foundation for the ensemble. The more awareness and knowledge you have of all aspects of your project, including your ensemble members and their behaviors, the better the ensemble's chances at succeeding.

We've assembled the following list of archetypes that we've identified in our work, and at the urging of several colleagues, organized them in order of which ones need the most attention to the least attention, from you the leader. You'll undoubtedly recognize most, if not all, from your own experiences. You may come to define your own set of recognized behaviors that differ from ours. You may combine two archetypes into a broader category or break one down into two or more. The important thing is to watch, listen, and learn so that your experiences better support creating and maintaining ensembles. It's fair to say that a majority of actors exhibit a combination of these elements: someone who is a Sparkplug can also have traits of the Nurturer. The Rock can also be a Trail Master at times. We're all amalgams of a range of traits. The observations listed here can help us get closer to a person's *perceived* identity. This, in turn, will help during casting as you search to fulfill the needs you've defined. Remember that this isn't about putting people into convenient categories as a shortcut or substitute for getting to know each person as fully as possible. It's about recognizing patterns of behavior within each unique individual so that you may better guide the ensemble once it's assembled.

## Categories of behaviors

Forest Fire Danger Index: *High, Medium, Low.* (As Smokey the Bear says, "Remember: only *you* can prevent forest fires.")

## *Category 5: Destroyers, Lex Luthors, Draco Malfoys*

Forest Fire Danger Index: *High*

Alert: remember that fire is both good *and* bad. Those of us who remember the horrific fires in Yellowstone National Park some years ago wept when we saw the photographs of charred devastation. Then we listened as park rangers noted that some of these fires occur naturally from lightning strikes, and that many of the trees can't reproduce and revitalize the forest *without* the fire burning away old growth and releasing seeds from cones. Then again, sometimes some idiot throws their lit cigarette on the ground, and there goes ...

### *The Black Hole*

Black Holes are the ones who draw energy toward them with little or no energy returned to the group. They can bring action to a halt, make ensemble members feel guilty about not giving enough, *and* make *you* feel guilty about putting the ensemble's goals before individual needs. Black Holes are bad news. Their individual needs overwhelm their ability to see the greater need of the ensemble and they fall into patterns of, "If I can just get the ensemble to acknowledge me and how much pain I'm in, I'll feel better and then I'll be able to do my job." For many Black Holes, there is no bottom to the well of that need. They're often well intentioned and see the project/ensemble as an opportunity to heal from something, or see it as a place where they will belong and finally be able to function. Though this is true of some individuals, it's not true for the pure Black Holes. Black Holes are almost incomprehensibly drawn to ensembles and may first manifest as Nurturers. They seek home, but a home where they can lock the doors and hear everyone knocking outside wanting to be let in. To them, that knocking equals love. But if they answer the door, they have to take responsibility for their feelings, and be ready to let them go. We've rarely met a Black Hole who was able to open that door and risk giving energy instead of feeding on it.

Recognizing a Black Hole:

- They sit apart from the group.
- They arrive exactly on time, or 1–3 minutes late. Never enough time to warm up early.
- They start side conversations with other members when you're addressing the group. The conversation is nearly always about a personal problem they're experiencing. When you stop everything to ask what's going on, the response is either, "Oh, nothing," or "Nothing, I've just got something going on and Lynn was consoling me." Of course, this makes everyone want to ask, "Consoling about *what?*" and the energy is then directed at the Black Hole.

- They'll leave the classroom or rehearsal room without permission. When asked why, their response tends to be, "I had to get out, I'm sorry. I've got some personal things going on," or "Louise was making me so furious, I couldn't stay." Their statements require a follow-up question or meeting, and additional attention.
- In production, they're often last to be off book. If reprimanded for this, it gives them an opportunity to:
  - throw something in frustration;
  - cry;
  - tell a story as to why they weren't off book. (Trust us, this story will involve a bad break-up, a death [fictional or real], or an anniversary of something bad [fictional or real]);
  - rant about how incompetent they are, leading others to reach out and console them in their pain.
- They tend to exaggerate when something truly *is* going on in their lives. A parent going in for bunion surgery will be portrayed as being on Death's Door.
- They sometimes outright lie. Rose once had an acting student who was repeatedly late with assignments and was a minor Black Hole in class. When asked about her lateness, she began to tell a tall tale about her parents, and "problems" they were having. Rose purposely asked follow-up questions with "embedded" details; e.g., instead of, "What's your relationship with your parents?" she asked, "Do your parents have unreasonable expectations of you?" The student clung to every detail, took each embedded statement and spun it wildly, and the reasons for the lateness and poor study habits grew more outlandish. She seemed to grow taller with each "suggestion." Cruel? Maybe. Did it confirm diagnosis? You bet.
- When telling stories, they portray themselves as the victim. Things happen *to* them; they act as if they have no power to take action to change anything. This is what makes us most sympathetic to Black Holes; and that's dangerous in an ensemble.

Pros:

- Though the most dangerous to the ensemble, they're endlessly fascinating. Take a moment to think about conversations you've had with colleagues or friends about a Black Hole in your project. How many hours did you devote to analyzing, speculating, and theorizing? These discussions will sharpen your analytic and observation skills in fantastic ways.

Cons:

- Go back to your undergraduate Astronomy class and read what happens to a universe when a Black Hole gains power.

If you've cast a Black Hole, you have no choice but to address the behavior immediately. Otherwise, you'll eventually lose the ensemble. The Universe will, quite literally, go flat from the space being sucked away. We've tried several methods in positively re-directing Black Holes:

- Honest conversation about their behavior. If you're fortunate, you won't be the first person who has told them that they're sucking the air out of the room. Having that recognition and acknowledgment, they will hopefully make an effort to change.
- Exercises that focus on a positive return of partner generosity and responsibility. For example, Blind Offers, West Side Story, Blindfold Freeze Tag (see Appendices A, E, J).
- Trickery. Black Holes lack self-awareness, so we might say, "I need your help with something ... Vera has been struggling with this particular scene. Can I ask you – as a great favor to me – to try the following that might help her, and help me?" (Depending on the situation, you can enlist Vera to help in this effort.) This has worked more times than we care to admit. The Black Hole perks up immeasurably; they feel acknowledged and needed, and they're free of having to take responsibility for their actions because you asked them to do something, so there is no need to fear judgment. They also feel respected, and this can temporarily – or permanently – give them the confidence to reconnect with the ensemble. If you're an actor who we've done this with, we may have had another reason for asking for your help. Please don't wake up in the dead of night thinking, "Oh crap, am I a Black Hole? Is that what she was doing?" It's never a bad thing for us to take a moment and ask ourselves, "Am I being as generous as I can in rehearsal and performance?"
- In improv, if the above suggestions don't work, we'll force the hand of the Black Hole. For instance, we might say, "Joe, you can only play positive, enthusiastic characters today." As Joe slips back into Black Hole behavior, he is side-coached to "stay positive" or "start jumping for joy in reaction to your partner's offer." This unexpected behavior tends to get a good response from the others, including laughs, which can set off a light bulb for the Black Hole. Positive choices within the work can lead to more positive behavior from them, but diligent reinforcement from you is a continuing need.

As mentioned, ensemble members may exhibit the qualities of more than one archetype. Similarly, many ensemble members can be a Black Hole when they're having a bad day. This is different from the relentless Black Hole and can be handled easily or even ignored, as it's likely to be gone by the next rehearsal or class.

## The Complainer

The Complainer can be more benign than the Black Hole, but this is the one who'll complain outwardly, and their body language will reflect dissatisfaction in the clearest possible terms. Rather than suck energy toward them, Complainers thrive on putting negative energy *into* the ensemble, which in turn draws the attention to them and to their complaint of the moment. The cool part for the Complainers in doing this is they get to dodge taking responsibility for putting forth negativity, and they hide behind what they consider a viable complaint. They don't have the same force as the Skeptic ("I don't see the value in why we're doing this. Can you explain?" instead of, "I don't feel like doing this ... can't we do that other exercise?"). They rarely take responsibility for their opinions. This usually manifests in a victim mentality in which their complaint is measured by how neglected or misunderstood they feel. If there is a passive/aggressive in the ensemble, it will be in the persona of the Complainer. When confronted about what their actual concern may be, they can become defensive, and blame others. Blame the leader, blame the ensemble, blame the author of the play ...

Complainers are generally easier to identify at an initial audition than most. However, their capacity to make you feel guilty for judging them can be unsettling. Everyone on the planet has survival gifts; theirs is the ability to be accepted when common sense tells you to take a pass.

Recognizing the Complainer:

- At an audition: if you ask if they have another monologue, their response is, "My acting coach made me pick the one I did."
- At an audition, they apologize on their entrance: "I just got here and they told me I had to come in, so I didn't even get to warm up." (Invariably, we find out from the monitor that this isn't remotely true.)
- In class: "I couldn't do the assignment; they didn't have the book I needed."
- They use words like "they" (not being specific about their oppressor), "everybody" (as if the world is against them), "never" (to make something an impossible task before it's tried), and "I heard ... " when asked to support a statement of persecution that they may have just uttered. For example, "I didn't go to the callback because I heard it was cancelled. How am I supposed to know?" *Who did you hear that from?* "Somebody. I don't remember."
- They blame, and blame some more. Subways are why they're late, lovers or parents are why they're unable to focus, teachers play favorites so why bother trying, directors are mean and play favorites, so if the favorite is going to get the good review why should they bother?
- Complainers usually avoid improv, but if that's your project, or part of your rehearsal process or curriculum, you're going to have your work cut out for you. Two core values of improv (say "yes and ... " and commit) are antithetical to the Complainer. The good news is that improv will be good

for them, if they let it. The bad news is that they tend to resist with all their might.

Pros:

- They're predictable.

Cons:

- Are you kidding?

It's rare that the Complainer's energy can be redirected, but it's possible. We have to believe that we see something in them to begin with, so depending on the circumstances, you can:

- ask them to be specific about the thing they're complaining about. If they can get specific as to the truth of the matter, they either see that they've been avoiding the work, or that it's not such an overwhelming issue, or that a solution *does* indeed exist;
- ask about their personal passion for the work; if their answers aren't connected to the goal, find out what drew them to the group to begin with. If you get any answer related to the work itself, there's hope. If you get a vague, "I just want to do this," then you need to start thinking of your goodbye words to them;
- recommend additional physical training. Sometimes Complainers simply suffer from poor physical health and complain because they feel listless. Without the energy or reserves to do anything about the problems they face, they dump it on the ensemble. Complainers can transform once they begin to feel physically stronger and healthier. Complainers who must ultimately be removed will also go more readily if given an easy "out" (i.e., something to blame);
- recommend therapy, if appropriate to your situation. In Chapter 6, we clearly state that it's not your job to heal or fix anyone, and you may do more harm than good if you try. It *is* your job to try to guide them toward what they actually need.

### The Ensemble Killer

What if you have someone with the potential and desire to sabotage the ensemble? Do the very skills that make you want to accept someone sometimes develop into traits that can damage it? Have they exhibited leadership skills, been a major contributor to the group, gained everyone's respect – then something changes and they begin to lead the ensemble away from the goal, retreat from collaboration, and find ways to disrespect the ensemble, the goal, and you?

Recognizing an Ensemble Killer, they:

- shut out people they had previously been close to
- take actions that are willfully hurtful
- betray another member's confidence
- disrespect you
- make statements that diminish the value and worth of the goal ("I don't know why we bothered with this production season; nobody's coming to the shows")
- play war, and seek allies within the ensemble against a perceived (or fabricated) enemy
- make disparaging comments about the ensemble's past work.

Pros:

- Their presence or emergence will help you clarify your own commitment to the ensemble.
- They help you hone your observation skills.

Cons:

- They're in the ensemble.

If you've just had a flash of recognition and said, "Uh oh":

GUIDANCE

- "Invite" the Ensemble Killer to leave.

The Ensemble Killer gets satisfaction from destroying an ensemble. Sometimes they don't recognize anything wrong in killing the ensemble; they see it as something that *should* be killed. They see themselves as righting a wrong, that it's a mercy killing, or that the group has somehow become "infected" and needs to be destroyed and then reformed. Sometimes the Ensemble Killer recognizes that it's wrong to kill the ensemble, but they do it anyway. Funny enough, we've met more leaders who are Ensemble Killers than ensemble members, and they tend to be in a class or workshop more so than in a production (see Chapter 3). There's often a strong intellectual component to their behavior, and we suspect they observe an ensemble like a science experiment, by viewing it as a personal challenge to see if they can dismantle this carefully built ensemble. They destroy it just to see if they can.

Once in a while, we have a Random Ensemble Killer. This is usually someone who starts out having an interpersonal conflict with another member and believes the rest of the ensemble has sided with their rival. It can also be someone who has recently been through a difficult personal situation with a family member (usually a parent) or romantic partner. They don't feel they can take out their anger on the person in their personal life, and instead direct their rage toward the ensemble. This Ensemble Killer is easily spotted and is often defused by a private and honest discussion. But if that doesn't work, they need to go.

### Category 4: Doubting Thomases, Rebels With or Without Causes

Forest Fire Danger Index: *Medium to High*

### The Skeptic

Everyone has moments of doubt; the Skeptic has them daily and hourly. Skeptics are drawn to ensembles because they long to be part of a collective, but that's so they have a forum to be heard. They question you about new exercises, they balk at trying something before a thorough explanation is given, and they doubt partners and their intentions. If something goes awry, the Skeptic will often assume the worst instead of assuming the best. Skeptics can be wonderful in discussions because they're fearless in expressing a doubt that others may be too shy to express. However, the level of their internal fear of everything else can be overwhelming. They fear taking risks, they fear judgment from you and the group, and they fear the Unknown; especially in themselves. A Skeptic can sometimes be converted if things are carefully explained, but the ensemble gets impatient and they groan when the doubt is repeatedly raised. There comes a threshold when the ensemble loses their temper with the Skeptic's insecurities and the Skeptic can present that as proof that they were right to be skeptical to begin with!

Recognizing the Skeptic, they:

- are often last to volunteer
- may tell you they're "unprepared," but really they doubt the value of the assignment or task itself
- are anxious about "doing it right"
- love discussion periods because it lets them off the hook from "doing"
- are most confident in their intellectual vs. physical or any other skills
- make statements such as, "But *last* time, you said that we would … "
- quibble about particulars, which prevents action from moving forward, which delays their fear of being "enough."

Pros:

- Have strong analytical skills.
- Help create lively discussions.
- Are usually articulate and clear.

Cons:

- Have doubts that can be contagious in the ensemble.
- Lack awareness of how their fear and doubt is affecting the ensemble, which can make them appear selfish to the group.
- Ask questions they already know the answers to.
- Fear making mistakes more than they desire to grow.

### GUIDANCE

If you convert the Skeptic, you're a pretty damn good leader. The best approach is to limit the time for verbal discussion, as the Skeptic will want to extend the discussion in order to avoid doing the exercise or scene. If you take away the time they (or anyone fearful) use to obsess about the fear, they use the time for "doing" instead. If they take action, and prove their fears wrong, it lessens their anxieties and makes them more productive members of the ensemble. Skeptics rarely respond to intellectual proof (private discussions in which their concerns are addressed), but we've seen a lot of Skeptics become Believers in the goal after experiencing it through action. *Don't talk about the scene (again!), do it.* When they're not allowed to hang back and intellectualize, they experience the difference between releasing impulses, and intellectual preplanning that *blocks* those impulses.

The Skeptic's behavior can come from a fear of making mistakes or fear of being wrong (know any perfectionists?). It can be helpful, when they fail, to cheer the risk-taking and applaud the failure as "bold"; anything to help lessen the stigma they've attached to making mistakes. What they often want is to make it clear that whatever is proposed "won't work," so that when they fail, they can say, "I told you so," rather than experience the failure. We like to tell them that most proposals end in failure, but if you keep trying, you will eventually find successes. If you don't try proposals, you're guaranteeing failure, or at best, stagnation. This quote from Michael Jordan is a favorite of ours on this subject:

> I've missed more than 9,000 shots in my career. I've lost almost 300 games. Twenty-six times, I've been trusted to take the game winning shot and missed. I've failed over and over and over again in my life. And that is why I succeed.

Identifying the Skeptic early and taking swift action can make a difference. As the ensemble environment and attitude develops, the Skeptic begins to feel free to risk and make mistakes, feels safe from judgment by the others, develops trust and gains confidence, and their need to show skepticism can subside.

## *The Rebel*

Rebels differ from the Skeptic in that they're invested in making the ensemble agree with them; the Skeptic is more interested in proving you wrong. Rebels see subjugation, authoritarianism, and spirit-stifling oppression under every rock, and are quick to question motives rather than question ideas. Though they consider themselves honest, they're dishonest with themselves about their motives for leading a rebellion in the ensemble. Rebels fear being controlled and losing their individuality, and they see the collaboration of the ensemble as a threat to both of those concerns.

You might wonder why Rebels are drawn to ensembles to begin with; seems counterintuitive, doesn't it? Part of the reason is because they thrive on the drama of the rebellion itself. It's hard to rebel when you're alone in a room. Rebels stop listening early on because they fear being turned into "a sheep." They can be isolated until they see an opportunity to challenge you, or challenge a partner, simply for the sake of not conforming. They see themselves as brave and intimidating, but their fear is very, very palpable. The louder they are, the more they tend to lose the respect of the ensemble, which they sense (but don't necessarily admit), and this only increases their anxiety.

Recognizing a Rebel:

- In group exercises, moves more slowly because they're busy observing what others may be doing.
- Sits apart from others during talkbacks, but observes everyone.
- Body language is often crossed arms when at rest, slumped to one side vs. a physical readiness.
- Asks questions not for clarity or guidance, but to challenge the premise itself.
- Purposely resists instructions or adhering to the structure of an exercise or improv.
- Is suspicious of a partner's intentions, even when that partner has never exhibited anything but commitment to the work.
- Is an expert passive/aggressive.

Pros:

- If the ensemble itself is threatened, the Rebel takes the lead in defending it. They unite and inspire the ensemble against the Common Enemy; budget cuts, evil landlords evicting the theatre company from its space, etc.

Cons:

- When the Rebel believes *you're* the Common Enemy, it will end in tears – for somebody.
- Is insensitive to the rhythm or flow of the rehearsal or class, and they gain power by disrupting the task at hand with a frivolous concern.
- Can be manipulative if they feel you or the group disagrees with them.
- In improv, audiences often reward rebellious behavior. Yet good improv requires a discipline that coexists with the spontaneity and irreverence that makes it so much fun. Rebels get laughs and are loved by audiences, but they achieve this in a way that tends to alienate their fellow performers. One notable exception to this is an ensemble entirely of Rebels – in David's early days with the Upright Citizens Brigade Theatre in New York, he saw it happen regularly. It can be a brutal environment, but it works.

GUIDANCE

A Rebel can be redirected, often with some difficulty and a great deal of status work. If their behavior becomes destructive, seek a private meeting with them. If you're fortunate, Rebels may have a desire to lead themselves. Ask them to clarify why they joined this ensemble. If they believe in the goal, then ask them to lead *with* you.

- Honest Approach. "Do you see how we're really working toward the same thing, but simply speaking a different language? Would you like to help me, work with me, and be a leader in the ensemble? You can lead by your actions, by picking someone up when they fall. You can also challenge me if you feel I'm leading us away from the goal. But, if you simply don't like the route that your partner or I might be choosing, then suggest another route instead of simply telling me or your partner that we're wrong."
- Indirect Status Approach (can work with Big Egos). "You seem as passionate about the goal as I am. I think I must have misspoken early on, as you give the impression that we disagree about the goal. I apologize if I made it sound as if the goal was X and not Y – I'm sure that must have been frustrating to you. Thank you for caring so much about the purpose."
- If Indirect doesn't work, meet with them again and say: "Thank you for your passion on this project. Clearly, you have a very specific idea about how this should be accomplished. Do you think this ensemble is the best place for you, or might you be happier leading a group of your own? I know it must be frustrating to you that we somehow can't seem to see eye to eye on this." If the Rebel says, "I want to stay," then give them a dose of tough love, insist upon respect and cooperation, and if they can't do that, they will be asked to leave. If the Rebel says, "You're right, I really want to lead a group of my own," you've illuminated something huge for them.

If the Rebel has reasons for joining the ensemble that have nothing to do with the goals, then your decision is an easy one. The remaining ensemble members will quickly come together and dissipate the energy left behind by the departing Rebel.

---

### Rose

I recall a Rebel in a long ago improv class who was asked to participate in a classic commedia Master/Servant status exercise (see *Impro* by Keith Johnstone). The Master creates a task for the Servant, but if the Servant displeases the Master, the Master can kill the Servant with a snap of the fingers. We were doing the One Snap version and having a great time, but when the Rebel's turn to serve the Master came, he slammed his fist against the wall and declared, "I'm nobody's slave!" Fortunately, the ensemble saw his fear and didn't allow themselves to be intimidated. Rebels are often neutralized by a combination of the Rock, the Glue, and the Sparkplug. The Rebel's best friends are the Complainer and the Skeptic. They become excellent allies, but an Unholy Trio for you.

---

### *The Controller*

The Controller tends to have deep-rooted fears that manifest in the need to steer, always. Their energy is turned inward, and they resist moving forward with the ensemble unless they feel they have a very specific road map. Unlike the Skeptic, they don't always outwardly question, but their panic and anxiety vibrates in the air. They take copious notes, and will be among the last to volunteer every time. Their internal need to "get it right" is connected to the specter of harsh judgment: from their peers, their past, and themselves. They're extremely rule conscious, and quick to point out when someone has deviated from instructions. Coloring outside the lines is not an option for the Controller, and the honest listen/response process constitutes the greatest risk of all. Controllers realize at some point that they can't control their partner's response, although they may try to. "Hey, I said X to Eugene, and he was supposed to say Z, but he didn't!" They desperately want to let go of their anxiety, but the process of being affected by their partners makes them keenly aware of how little control they actually have. Until they learn that the release of control actually *frees* their impulses, they won't evolve in the collaboration process.

Controllers can devolve into Ensemble Killers if they sense their lack of control increasing ("If I can't control it, I will destroy it"). The destruction is something that they *can* control. Controllers also tend to judge other ensemble members, and they don't hide those judgments. They point out bad habits and mistakes, pounce on errors, and are unforgiving of perceived slights. This is incredibly destructive if it spreads. Judgment needs to remain in your objective hands so that the members can trust one another.

Recognizing a Controller, they:

- Write in a notebook, not on an electronic device or scrap paper.
- Are always five minutes (or more) early.
- Instead of taking a partner aside when something goes awry, they will have the conversation very publicly.
- Can react poorly to change. When working on a new play, they can become apoplectic when the playwright brings in new pages. In the classroom, when a project on the syllabus is changed, they'll let you know they're unhappy about it. In production, if they call for line and you don't give it to them word for word, beware.
- Can be physically tense and held.
- If a rehearsed moment doesn't "happen," there may be tears, a thrown prop, or a kicked garbage can.
- Can sometimes express their frustration physically (script thrown on table, door slam, needing to "walk down the hall").
- Tend to dislike others touching their things.
- Can sometimes dislike being physically touched, period. Touch can feel like someone else trying to control them.
- In improvisation, where few rules *always* apply, they ask for hard and fast rules and definitions. Controllers tend to avoid improv, but when they show up, give them as much structure as possible and try to partner them with another Controller (if you have one). Surprisingly, they don't reinforce controlling behavior in each other as much as they find comfort.
- Will frequently direct their gaze to you when they should be working (to see if they're getting approval, or worse, to see if you've noticed and are going to correct a "rule" that's just been broken).

Pros:

- Has a steel-trap memory.
- Is consistent.
- This is terrible, but: in rare instances when you need a "spy" to help root out a problem you've struggled to identify the source of, the Controller is delighted to be that spy. They happily share every detail they've noticed about everyone else ...

Cons:

- ... However, the Controller is sometimes a rat. They tattletale on people even when you *don't* want to know about internal dynamics. It's hard to convince them of someone's innocence.
- Is resistant to change.
- Can kill a mood in a room almost as fast as the Skeptic.

- In improv, will only want to work on forms or exercises that "are successful" or "audiences like" which translates to "things that I'm consistently good at and feel comfortable with." These are often the games that are most formulaic or can withstand the Controller successfully preplanning in their head.

GUIDANCE

To redirect a Controller, it can be as simple as acknowledging their concerns and empowering them by thanking them for bringing up a point. Controllers respond well to positive reinforcement. Be sure to acknowledge something that the Controller is doing *well*. Be specific, as it helps them eliminate things from their list of "what I'm good at/what I'm not good at." Their internal Manual of Operation that lists "How Things Should Work" also includes several lists of personal assessment. Their list of what they're bad at will far exceed what they believe they're good at. This is one reason why they fight so hard to be right. They don't actually believe they're right about many things. This can be deceptive, as their egos seem to be pretty healthy, but that's rarely the case. As our mothers used to say when someone on the playground bossed us around, "They're just insecure, dear." Don't you hate it when mothers are right?

Seriously, a Controller can be converted to a positive force. Point out their strengths and acknowledge their concerns. As their understanding of their abilities expands, they'll become much more trusting, and open to taking actions without having to know exactly where they'll lead.

### Category 3: Masked Crusaders: Batman, Zorro

Forest Fire Danger Index: *Medium*

### Class Clown

We hesitated to put the Class Clown in here, but our students encouraged us otherwise. The Class Clown is someone who is a laughter junkie; they'll do anything to hear the immediate response of chortles, guffaws, and full-throated roaring from their "audience." At some point they made the direct connection that laughter equals approval; and it was a love/hate relationship from then on. Laughter lets them know they're doing something "right." If they *don't* get the laughter, they don't trust their choices, and what may seem like a strong and healthy ego quickly turns to insecurity. Their reasons for joining the ensemble can range from wanting daily reinforcement to wanting to learn how to trust themselves more – whether the laughter comes or not. Ensemble can be a safe place for them to work out this emotional math equation.

Class Clowns can also be incredible allies during tough times. Their desire to joke is rarely intended to undermine you. In fact, they often feel badly when it's

112

pointed out to them that indeed, they're undermining the goal by cracking wise. But on a dark day or in challenging circumstances, they can place a well-timed joke that will earn them the gratitude of the whole ensemble.

### Rose

I had a student in an improv class in 2001, Sabrina Cataudella, who was going through a brief Class Clown phase, and I brought to her attention that she sometimes made jokes when she was avoiding going deeper in her process. Sabrina had excellent timing, was a good listener, but simply a bit insecure at that time. She acknowledged the note and worked to address it. On September 11, 2001, we watched events unfold from Brooklyn College, and many of us were stranded when the subways stopped. Sabrina was one of a few people who had a car and she offered to ferry people home. Me, and approximately eight graduate students, piled into her mid-sized car. Since I'm short, I sat across the laps of some of the long-legged male students in the back seat. As we drove down Fourth Avenue in Brooklyn, we rounded a corner and had a clear view of the massive smoke plume in lower Manhattan. In the silence, just when we thought we would all crack, Sabrina looked in her rearview mirror and said, "Hey! What's goin' on back there? If he gets an A in class, I'm complaining!" We broke into the kind of gut busting laughter that overrides all tension, and she continued making jokes to distract us until every one of us had been delivered safely to our homes. I will always be grateful to her for her actions that day, and so much more.

Recognizing the Class Clown:

- Self-deprecating humor ...
- ... but an *excellent* sense of humor.
- Their mood can swing from confident to insecure.
- Can be observed watching the room to "take the temperature" before delivering a well-placed joke.

Pros:

- Is sensitive to timing and moments.
- Is an excellent listener (they just don't always follow through on it).
- Means well, and is a giving partner.

Cons:

- Don't always trust their first impulse, and default to "entertaining the troops."
- They equate laughter with success and become nervous when the laughter isn't present. In improv, this translates to going for easy laughs (sometimes at the expense of other players) rather than committing to the scene or game and being patient enough to allow the payoff of more honest laughter from having touched a deeper place.

### GUIDANCE

Class Clowns respond well to honest and supportive communication, and positive reinforcement. Have a private discussion as to why they default to a joke and ask what's behind it. Assure them that you're not trying to squelch their positive spirit, but trying to help them gain confidence with their choices that *don't* elicit laughter. You're not trying to take *away* their ability to make a joke, but to encourage expansion of the many other abilities they're capable of contributing to the ensemble.

### The Cheerleader

Cheerleaders come in several shapes and sizes. Most often, they're more comfortable in verbal vs. physical work. They outwardly encourage everyone to participate, to take risks, and they're generous with compliments and support (statements or clapping or literal cheering). They make great partners to Sparkplugs, and when trepidation is present, they're the first to say, "C'mon, we can do this!" Different from Springboards, they don't necessarily volunteer first – in fact, quite the opposite. They tend to hang back while others initiate and often are the last to go in an exercise or Round Robin improv. You may have to remind the Cheerleader that it's their turn. The reply is often "Oh man! I was so mesmerized by all the great things everyone was doing, I forgot to go myself."
Hmm.
Their outward enthusiasm can be a mask for their own insecurities and they struggle to give themselves the support they're able to so freely offer to others. In their desire to keep the positive feelings and confidence levels high, they end up cheering *everything*, and the ensemble loses trust in the validity of the Cheerleader's observations and remarks. Still, they can be indispensable, especially in home stretches of productions, and during "goodbyes" for a show, a company, or graduating class. This can also be part of the reason why they seek to join the ensemble in the first place. They enjoy providing energy and positive support, and the overt nature of how they express themselves can make them feel responsible for the successes of the ensemble.

Recognizing the Cheerleader:

- Is enthusiastic.
- Struggles with silence in scenes or in the room in general. The Cheerleader mistakes silence for "we're not doing enough" or "someone must be feeling bad, they're not talking."
- Hangs back from the primary action or primary discussion.

Pros:

- Is supportive.
- Is always the first to reach out to a new ensemble member.
- Works to keep the mood positive and upbeat.

Cons:

- Sometimes makes ensemble members uncomfortable when they single others out for compliments or praise. "Elaine! That was fantastic! You were the best of us all in that exercise!"
- Is not a good listener; not because of selfishness, but because they want to keep everything "up." Whether it wants to be or not.

GUIDANCE

Cheerleaders respond well to private discussion. As with the Class Clown, you don't want to diminish their enthusiasm for the work, you want them to become more specific in what they're responding *to* in order to nurture specific elements. If you're in a class or improv setting, ask the Cheerleader to start volunteering to go first. Tell them that you'd like them to experience supporting the ensemble through leading the way, not solely through cheering those who *have* been initiating. If they're shy about this, remind them that their generosity must extend to themselves, and that they'll end up giving *more* to the ensemble by being more generous with themselves. This self-generosity must extend to time (taking the time they need instead of considering it as time taken *away* from others), willingness to risk failure so that they can re-define what failure means to them, and willingness to explore the power of silence. Exploring silence will also help them experience the power of actions that can occur without words and begin to sensitize themselves to times when encouragement may actually be needed, vs. giving it at all times.

Exercises that can specifically help the Cheerleader include the Blindfold Series (which is silent), Blind Offers, and Sound and Movement (see Appendices G, A, D).

## The Competitor

Competitors tend to have an incredibly healthy ego and much of their identity is tied to being first, being fastest, enduring the longest, and/or being the *best*. They're invested in being "better than" someone, or something. Competition in ensemble can, of course, be healthy and conducive to strong collaboration. However, Competitors compare their achievements with those of others. They're quick to point out something they did differently, *very* quick to point out what they did that elicited laughter, and quick to announce any "firsts" they achieved. Not as personal bests, but "firsts" compared to the ensemble. "Hey, I'm the first one who wasn't conquered in Steal the Flag! Eat my dust!"

They're great record keepers; they can tell you, to the minute, the last time you picked them to initiate something – or more importantly, *didn't* pick them. Let's face it: we don't remember whom we asked to initiate what or when. The Competitor takes it personally, and then works doubly hard to prove why you should acknowledge them more.

Recognizing the Competitor:

- Is hardwired to seek recognition and seek out individuals that they see as *personal* competition. They try to partner with those they see as rivals.
- Once partnered with that "competition," they point out that person's shortcomings and offer "help." Look for warning signs and try to neutralize it early on.
- Makes statements such as, "Cristina took what *I* was going to do," or "Hey, I think mine was the first improv we've ever done about hedgehogs," or "I'm so glad I'm off book and it's only the second day of rehearsal." And they say it loudly so everyone can hear.
- Makes self-deprecating statements such as, "I wasn't quick enough on that," or "I didn't give Nick a strong enough choice," or "I can't believe I did X, *everybody* does X" (when talking about a specific choice of character or action in an improv).
- Suffers terribly from the "enoughs," which feeds their sense of competition (e.g., I'm not smart enough, creative enough, original enough, strong enough, etc.). The Complainer would simply complain; the Competitor takes action and becomes focused on doing it "better."

Pros:

- Is a keen observer.
- Is hyper-aware of surroundings and what might be useful to the task at hand.
- Can stimulate healthy competition in certain exercises.

Cons:

- Not always present or in the moment. If the Competitor is always rushing ahead, wanting to be the first to cross the finish line, how can they be present with their partner and the story? Or be connected to their own choices?

GUIDANCE

Because the Competitor has a healthy ego, they're often easier to reason with than other Category Threes. Take the Competitor aside and give them "special tasks." Tell them that their energy and commitment is admirable (and it is) but that they're running so far ahead of the group that it makes it challenging for everyone to reach the goal together. Rather than telling them to "slow down," ask them to give more to their partners to help bring *them* further along in the process. Again, this has worked more times than we can count. Eventually, the Competitor starts to get lonely setting themselves apart, but after a certain point, their ego doesn't give them a way back to the ensemble. You can facilitate the way back for them.

And if you're an actor that we've ever said this to, didn't you have more fun after you started focusing on staying with your partners instead of running ahead?

### Category 2: The Flash, Energizer Bunny, and Road Runners

Forest Fire Danger Index: *Low to Medium*

#### The Sparkplug

Sparkplugs are the electric generators for every ensemble. When energy is flagging, they're the one you can plug into for extra resources. They insert themselves into the center of the activities and try to ignite positive combustion to get everyone going, and most of the time they succeed. Their energy is infectious, and they can be honest and direct to a fault. But they're always forgiven because their willingness to put themselves on the line is undeniable. Their gifts in the energy department can lend themselves to unfocused "Kapow!" moments, so be especially vigilant in teaching Sparkplugs how to focus, and how to be sensitive to time and place for energy infusions. They also have the potential to become addicted to the concept of "energy equals progress," whether that energy is focused or not. Sparkplugs can, at times, become Teddy Roosevelts or Springboards. Always try to cast at least one in every ensemble. They're worth their weight in gold.

Recognizing Sparkplugs, they:

- arrive early and begin their physical warm-up (and offer to lead the group warm up for you!)

- bring in an article or book that they thought you or an ensemble member would find useful
- usually have a great sense of humor
- can have trouble sitting still and will literally vault up into the playing area when it's time to work
- sense when someone has started a challenging improv and will hurtle themselves into it early so that they can have "dibs" on the most challenging choices
- are heard to say:
  - "Do you need help with that?"
  - "Next time we do this, can I go first?"
  - "If you need anybody to do an extra scene with anyone, let me know."
  - "It's Wayne's birthday today – do you mind if I play a trick on him during our scene?" (Said with great love and a beaming smile.)
  - "Do you mind if I bring cupcakes for us to have after rehearsal?"

Pros:

- Are you kidding?
- You can always ask a Sparkplug to help you with something and they'll consider it an additional treat, not a burden. This has the double-positive of getting additional time to teach them to focus their considerable energy and skills.
- When directing a large cast production, tech weekends can be murder, so Rose secretly "deputizes" several ensemble members to be Morale Officers during the long stop-and-go of tech. Responsibilities include looking for someone who is tired or frustrated, and to do anything from telling them a joke to getting them to help play a joke on someone else. There are profound benefits in letting the ensemble create a prank, so long as it doesn't inhibit what the designers or crew need in the moment, and of course, no one gets hurt. Ensemble members creating their own fun is a step toward their ownership of the show and we've seen fantastic benefits come from long and potentially draining tech days. Always ask your Sparkplug to be Tech Day Morale Officer. You can trust them to keep things responsible, but fun and lively. After the fact, they'll share with you that the ubiquitous "page of porn" (well, ubiquitous where we come from) has been inserted into a book that is opened by someone in a scene – tech rehearsal only, never performance. One of Rose's favorite stories from a Sparkplug happened during a tech day in a 400-seat theatre, and she and the designers were way back in the house. Apparently, during a lengthy discussion about a series of light cues, her very mature and responsible actors were holding a farting contest on the stage. Initiated, of course, by the Sparkplug. (And won by – who else – the Competitor!)

Cons:

- Can become addicted to the energy they generate and they risk losing focus.
- Their energy can feel overwhelming to some ensemble members.
- Very important: Sparkplugs can burn out quickly without guidance from you. Your gut may tell you to stay out of their way, but this can be to the detriment of the Sparkplug's shelf life.

### GUIDANCE

A Sparkplug's high energy can prevent them from listening effectively. In improv, energy needs to have a natural ebb and flow (within a reasonable range). In scripted theatre, this flow is often apparent in the script or story, but in improv, the performers need to listen and develop a sense of when to pick things up and when to take it easy. This is learned through experience, trial and error, and with guidance from the leader. Sparkplugs can be slow to develop this sense and are apt to deliver high energy at all times. David will often give a note that he heard from an old acting coach years ago, "Don't just do something – *stand there*," encouraging them to explore silence and stillness in their work. After a time, they come to him and say, "Now I realize what I'm doing when I'm silent and still: I'm listening!"

### The Springboard

The Springboard is brave, outwardly enthusiastic, and eager to try anything. They're the first to volunteer, the first to say, "Let's try something else" when the group is stuck, and are often physically expressive to a fault. Their body language is generally the easiest to read: they're the racehorse in the starting gate (who can also break the gate!). They're excellent in discussions about new ideas or challenges and they'll offer their opinion with little thought to the right or wrong of it. Springboards make it safe for others to come out of the shadows, proving that something isn't so "dangerous" after all. They're opinionated in a positive way, clear in expression, and have very thick skin. Because they get used to "going first," they're also used to processing ideas through discovery or discussion, so they're open to being transformed, or having their opinion changed by new information or new direction.

Recognizing a Springboard:

- Physically antsy.
- Can sometimes interrupt you or their partners (because of their enthusiasm, not disrespect; but it can become a problem).
- In an educational setting, will raise their hand. A lot!
- May interrupt a lecture portion of an acting class to ask, "Can we just try it and see what happens?"

- Seek constructive criticism, but don't always absorb it the first time. Because of their desire to "do," they can get ahead of themselves. They can struggle with listening, but they're very receptive to observations and quick to adjust.
- Start the exercise when the instructions haven't yet been fully given. Usually, we don't stop them. We may laugh when we see Springboards realize they've dashed into the circle without knowing what the hell they're supposed to do when they get there, but the ensemble has witnessed a great lesson in risk-taking.
- Don't reach out to individuals as much as Sparkplugs, but can be heard to say "C'mon everybody!"

Pros:

- Their fearlessness is invaluable in a classroom or educational production. In those settings, they'll do half of your work for you in encouraging others to bring out their best. Particularly with improvisation, where risk-taking is highly valued and can sometimes get inhibited, Springboards are the first ones to "jump off the cliff". Every improv ensemble needs a Springboard, and ideally, has more than one.
- Their fearlessness, coupled with their joy, can inspire ensemble members to jump off that cliff as well!

Cons:

- Sometimes Springboards start thinking (and acting) ahead of the beat they're actually supposed to be *in*.
- Ensemble members may perceive them as hogging time because of their desire to go first, and frequently. This can have the adverse effect of others withdrawing.

GUIDANCE

In rehearsals or classes, Springboards need additional guidance regarding listening, being present, and being in the moment. In improv, Springboards must take their turns going second, third, and so on, even last. Let them go first frequently, as is their desire, but for their own good, as well as everyone else's, they need to make discoveries as followers, not just leaders.

### Charge! (or Teddy Roosevelts)

Sibling to the Springboard, Teddy Roosevelts (Teddys) throw themselves into every exercise and every moment of a rehearsal with a force and momentum that is thrilling to see and frightening to be in the path of. Teddys are passionate, courageous, playful, determined, and willing to do absolutely anything you ask of them. They honor every impulse and they thrill at the very thing that many shy from: the Great Unknown of the First Moment.

A potential danger of Teddys is that they're so enthusiastic, they lack awareness of the world around them. This can include sharp objects, and partners. We've seen partners get knocked down, pushed aside, and conked in the head by the whirlwind of a Teddy. We've witnessed Teddys take mighty falls into large and dangerous objects, and because they were flying at such speed there was no time to stop them or redirect their energy. Ensembles love this person and appreciate them for their daring, but these same dynamic feats can make partners nervous about working with them. They can feel blocked by the Teddy, and if they feel they won't be allowed to contribute, they quickly drop out and the scene becomes a solo performance. Teddys seem to lack the awareness that a Springboard has. If a Springboard is diving into a rock quarry pool, they make sure the path is clear, run towards the cliff edge, dive off, and after they've come up for air, they shout up to the ensemble above them, "C'mon in! The water's great!" Teddys see the cliff edge, are oblivious to the people between them and that edge, and scream "AAAHHHH!" as they run, knock someone over, hurtle themselves off the edge, and cannonball into the pool below. After they've come up for air, they may say to nobody in particular, "Wow, man! That was awesome!" Think Chris Farley from Saturday Night Live. (In *Truth in Comedy* by Halpern, Close, and Johnson, Chris Farley shares how Del Close cautioned him to harness his Teddy into a Springboard.)

Teddys need to learn the difference between a bold, creative risk and a dangerous one. The difference is in the consequences. If a bold risk fails, the result may be foolish or inappropriate. If a dangerous risk fails, the result may be injurious (physical or otherwise) and impede trust, encouragement, and further risk-taking. Ask your ensemble to try not to subsidize their choices with random energy rather than specific choices. If they're a Springboard or a Sparkplug, they will nod and say, "Thank you." If they're a Teddy Roosevelt, they'll smile, say, "Okay!" and may still get up and do the same thing again. It's possible to transform a Teddy into a Sparkplug, but it can take a few tries ...

Recognizing a Teddy Roosevelt:

- Is enthusiastic almost to the point of spontaneous combustion.
- Physically antsy.
- Is passionate about a task, any task.
- Bumps into other people – a lot. Teddys can often be heard saying, "Sorry!" after inadvertently bumping someone, stepping on a toe, or knocking over books.
- A Teddy Roosevelt smiles – a lot.
- Despite the name Teddy and some common associations with this type of behavior, we've seen our fair share of female Teddys.

Pros:

• Is pure in heart, completely committed to the goal of the ensemble.
• Is a fearless risk-taker.
• Gives the ensemble someone to look after (like, well, a well-worn Teddy Bear). A Teddy Roosevelt will always need some TLC.

Cons:

• Sometimes takes *dangerous* risks.
• Can equate sheer exertion with creativity and can lack trust of simpler, quieter choices.
• Not always a great listener.
• Has an underdeveloped sense of physical awareness.

GUIDANCE

In improv, if you ever pair a Teddy with a Controller, you're probably going to have an ugly – or amusing – incident. Beware!

### Category 1: Hero, Wonder Woman, and Superman

Forest Fire Danger Index: *Very Low*

### The Caretaker

Close to the Nurturer in behavior, Caretakers give endlessly to the ensemble, but sometimes to their own detriment. Their desire to be good partners can cloud their ability to meet their own needs, and their own growth may be stifled because of a desire to see the ensemble meet its full potential. Always with the ensemble's best interest at heart, their impulses lead them to "parent" a scene or situation to the extent that it can feel controlling. Caretakers are helpful during challenging times and their motives are always pure. However, they may have learned in their past that focus on the self means "being selfish." Ironically, this leads to an inability to listen, respond, and be affected honestly *because* of the desire to be a "good parent."

Caution: Caretakers can become defensive when their behavior is pointed out to them. They're often unaware that they're deflecting their own needs for others and they can feel "punished" for doing exactly what an ensemble calls for: sacrifice.

Recognizing the Caretaker:

• Focused on taking care of scene or partner vs. allowing scene to happen *with* their partner.

122

- Devotes a lot of energy to complimenting and reaching out to others, believing the act of generosity is more important than being generous within the work.
- Physically expressive (hugs, back rubs, etc.).
- Fears being seen as egotistical or self-involved.
- May have suffered a traumatic loss in their past. Over-giving to ensemble can be connected with trying to fill the void from the loss.
- Struggles to ask for help.
- Needs more guidance from the leader than they're willing to admit.

Pros:

- Is passionate about the ensemble's goal.
- Is very giving and can provide an injection of maternal/paternal energy, giving the ensemble comfort.
- Loves to be relied upon.

Cons:

- That maternal/paternal energy can feel smothering after a time, and the ensemble wants to break away from the too-tight hug.

GUIDANCE

If the Caretakers' behavior starts to inhibit their own growth, remind them to be as generous with themselves as they are to the ensemble. Be careful that you don't take advantage of having the Caretaker in your ensemble. You might be tempted to let them handle some of the ensemble issues that need attending to. It's not that you shouldn't rely on them, just don't let it be at the expense of their growth and full participation.

*The Enforcer*

Personally, we love Enforcers, even if they drive us a little crazy in a moment. Enforcers are hungry, wildly enthusiastic, and *so* focused on the ensemble doing its best, they ingrain the rules and criteria into their mind/body/spirit. It's almost like a psychic tattoo; they instantly recognize when someone isn't playing by the rules or is holding back. And when they recognize this, they have *no* problem saying so out loud. Think of a Reverse Controller: Controllers are anxious about the outcome and results, and want everyone to follow the same prescribed instructions each time or they fear the result will be ruined. The Enforcer isn't focused on the *results,* but *is* focused on the creation in the *moment.* Is everyone listening? Are they being as open and receptive as they should be? Is everyone supporting each other as much as they can? The Controller may say, "You didn't give me the choice that we planned!" The Enforcer will say, "Hey! You rejected

Eric's offer! I saw you!" The Controller may observe, "Hey, you didn't give me the same choice you gave me before. I can't do my job!" The Enforcer may say, "Hey! You gave me the same old choice as before; you didn't take in or respond to what I gave you. I can't do my job if you're not listening!"

Recognizing the Enforcer:

- Is like the Conscience Police, and recognizes and calls out anyone who isn't working to their fullest ability *in the moment.*
- Is honest and outspoken; sometimes tact is not their strong suit.
- Has a recognizable thrill when the work is really cooking.
- Is very perceptive and sensitive to what the ensemble needs in a given moment.
- Is playful in a fierce sort of way.
- Gives a thousand percent and expects everyone around them to do the same.

Pros:

- Is a wonderful partner to have, once they've been made aware of how to positively express their observations.
- The rest of the ensemble gets so shit-scared of the wrath of the Enforcer as a Trust Tyrant, it makes them step up their efforts.
- In improv, Enforcers are worth their weight in gold. Someday, we'd love to see an improv group made entirely of Enforcers, just to see where they go with the work.

Cons:

- Has absolute faith in the potential of the ensemble to create something wonderful together, but can't abide someone who lacks that same faith. When you hear the Enforcer say, "You're not sending the impulse around fast like we're supposed to!" try to realize that what they're really saying is, "C'mon, *trust* already!! We're all here for you! When you don't trust, it affects us all!" Of course, you will still need to say, "Andy, you need to let me do my job so that you can do yours."

GUIDANCE

Enforcers can miss the fact that everyone works at a different pace and sometimes they take it personally if someone is a little slower to trust the ensemble than they are. Remind the Enforcer that everyone's differences can enrich the ensemble. This can have the added benefit of slowing them down a bit and they'll get more out of their work too.

### The Trail Master

Trail Masters are akin to the Rock and Nurturer, but tend to have more leadership capabilities and are more likely to put themselves out in front to lead the way. Trail Masters also volunteer first, but not with the same outward (and sometimes wacky) energy as the Sparkplug. After they initiate, they tend to keep an eye on "the Herd" to see how things are developing, and they often adjust their own choices accordingly. Steady and nurturing, they often have the best objective eye of the ensemble as to what the ultimate goals are, and they're sensitive to the collective energy. They sense when focus has shifted, when the pace has slowed, and when they're in danger of not reaching the destination.

Trail Masters are essential; however, they can also be the member of the ensemble who challenges you. "We know where we're going; get out of our way." This can be valuable, or frustrating, in the ongoing challenge of status.

Recognizing the Trail Master:

- Is usually physically strong, don't ask us why.
- When they decide to take the lead, they're much more obvious than the Glue (who likes to be unobtrusive). Trail Masters don't have the same personal ease as the Glue, and in their desire to make sure everyone is on the same page, will announce, "Okay, here's what we'll do!"
- Can lose a little focus on their own actions because they're observing and taking in the actions of the ensemble.
- Is very sensitive to energy shifts and perceptive as to the causes of those shifts.

Pros:

- Courageous; unafraid to take leadership roles.
- Keenly aware when the ensemble has started down an unproductive trail and eager to lead them in a stronger direction.

Cons:

- Can sometimes overwhelm another ensemble member with their sense of conviction about the direction that should be taken. "Gee, they seem so certain, they must be right."
- Can sometimes be so focused on the goal, they risk becoming result-oriented and may rush themselves or ensemble members to "get there."

GUIDANCE

The Trail Master is important to have in your group; try not to be overly sensitive when they may seek to take the reins. Often, they're right. Trust what can happen if you *do* step out of the way. Remember, it's not about you, don't take it personally. Let the Trail Master know you appreciate their leadership, and acknowledge when they've steered the ensemble in a more productive direction. Trail Masters don't have a stake in "being right" like the Rebel or Controller, they simply want what's best for the ensemble and the goal. They're likely to respond, "Oh. I'm just glad it's working out. Thanks." And then they'll go back to work.

### *The Ox*

Similar to the Trail Master, the Ox is the person who, when energy is flagging, will put the traces on and say, "Let's pull this thing forward!" They possess incredible strength and have been known to pull the entire wagon train by themselves. They're invaluable in large ensembles or in long runs of shows. The Ox won't be the first to volunteer, but if something is amiss and reluctance is all around, they will eventually say, "Oh, for goodness sake!" grab someone's hand and get something going. They don't enjoy attention like the Sparkplug, and though they possess some of the same qualities as the Trail Master, they're often uncomfortable being a leader for very long. They yearn to be the strength and heart of the ensemble, not the one choosing the direction.

Recognizing the Ox:

- Willingness to dig in and do whatever it takes to get something going.
- Sensitive to energy shifts, perceptive of connections and disconnects.
- Particularly sensitive to when things are going wrong in the ensemble.
- Willingness to carry the entire ensemble on their back during a challenging moment or scene.
- Self-sufficient, rarely ask for anything.
- Not always comfortable when the focus is on them individually, but they're supremely comfortable in the ensemble structure.

Pros:

- Always reliable.
- Can't bear to let something "die" onstage and will always step up to fill a void.
- Always humble about the work.

Cons:

- The Ox can get so used to putting the traces on to pull the group forward, they may put their own needs dead last.
- The Ox can also get so used to doing things on their own that they may forget to allow themselves to be affected by their partners, or to allow their energy to be replenished by others.

GUIDANCE

Be careful of exploiting the Ox. If a project isn't going well, we can be so grateful for the Ox that we don't stop them from sacrificing their own needs for the good of the whole. In productions, make sure you're not ignoring the Ox in the "Squeaky Wheel" scenario (the Ox's work is solid, they're prepared, working hard, growing steadily, etc.). Have you given them any notes in the past few days? Have you been spending all of your time with the Squeaky Wheels? Even if you only have a small note for the Ox, give it to them. Giving them significantly less input than other ensemble members can reinforce unhealthy habits of "going it alone." This might feel as if you're manufacturing something, but trust me, as directors and teachers we can always find something for the Ox to work on, even if it's: "That thing you're doing in that moment? Go further with that."

## The Rock

The Rock is dependable, steady, strong, grounded, realistic, and an excellent listener. Though they'll often defer to others, they're indispensable for their dedication to the ensemble and to the goal. Their noticeable enthusiasm can vary, but it's deeply focused on the work at all times. Rocks recognize when things are going awry, and they try to fix it by remaining consistent in the work. Rocks can momentarily become a Trail Master, Sparkplug, or Ox. Unlike the Nurturer, Rocks give back to the ensemble through their dependability and commitment to the goal, not necessarily through actions expressed toward individuals. Unlike the Glue, they don't have the same focus on both the work and the people with the same ease.

Recognizing the Rock:

- Their level of work is always consistent. Rocks rarely have bad days.
- Has strong self-trust, is an excellent risk-taker, never takes things personally.
- May seem to be "cooler" emotionally and harder to read than the Glue, but cares deeply about the ensemble. Think of Irina's speech from *Three Sisters* by Chekhov, "What we must do is work, and work, and work."
- Is the catcher of the team. They'll rarely miss catching the ball as it comes over the plate. The trade off is they'll rarely have a .300 batting average. They're dependable and consistent, not overtly sparkly.

Pros:

- Is your barometer for how the journey to the goal is going.
- Lead by their focus on the work, so they remain non-threatening to ensemble members.
- Is dependable, dependable, dependable. Their cooler emotional status helps you trust that "what you see is what you get."

Cons:

- Can be hard to read at times, which makes it challenging for you to keep a pulse on their individual needs.
- Can inadvertently be insensitive to a moment because of the intensity of their focus.

Try not to underestimate the Rock's contribution, ever. Their humbleness to the work can (as with the Ox) make you overlook their needs and move on to a Squeaky Wheel. Though they're fairly self-sufficient, their reliability and consistency should never be taken for granted. Make sure you always have at least one Rock in every group. They will be the heart of the ensemble.

### The Nurturer

Nurturers derive strength from experiencing the growth of others (while never taking their own growth for granted – different from the Caretaker). They're universal donors, with a seemingly endless generosity of spirit and an intuition for what's needed in the moment. They focus more energy on individuals than the Glue does, while maintaining commitment to the goal. Glues rely on their focus toward the goal to inspire others; the Nurturer does that, *and* devotes additional time to reaching out. Nurturers provide leadership within the ensemble, with a quiet hand at the wheel, gently steering and supporting those around them. Unlike the Trail Master, they're natural leaders who would never actually volunteer to lead. They like to guide others through examples of generosity and openness. They're the gardeners who sense when a plant needs water instead of mulch, and their reward is the strength they gain from helping others achieve their full potential. Like the Glue, they're adept at keeping everyone focused on the goal, and they do so by giving to others. The difference tends to be that Nurturers extend their generosity beyond the "work time."

Recognizing the Nurturer:

- Is keenly perceptive, acknowledges others, and innately understands what will benefit everyone most.
- Is an excellent listener, truthful in response, makes their partners look great.
- Share the joy in their work more openly.
- Finds it easy to offer subtle compliments to partners (not effusive or potentially cringe-making like the Cheerleader).
- When a group has newly formed, they're the ones who announce they're having a party for everyone to get to know each other better.
- During breaks, they're the ones asking others, "Did you bring a cereal bar? I have an extra if you want."

- When a member has an emotionally tough moment, Nurturers will have tissues, offer them silently, sit quietly with that person, and if they sense it appropriate, will place a gentle hand on their shoulder or back.
- Note: the Nurturer can be male *or* female. We're talking archetypes, not stereotypes.

Pros:

- Excellent internal leader.
- Provides individual acknowledgment of ensemble members that you may not always have time for.
- Their generosity costs them nothing, because they gain strength from doing for others. You will never have an "overdue bill" from the Nurturer. They expect nothing in return.
- Offers a much needed space for the ensemble *away* from you and the work structure, if the ensemble decides that they would like that.

Cons:

- Members who struggle with intimacy may find the generosity of the Nurturer smothering, or perceive it as something to distrust. Oddly, generosity or kindness can make another actor temporarily close down because they suspect something behind it. When directing a production for Synergy Ensemble, Rose had cast a wonderful Nurturer named Lloyd Cameron. Another actor took her aside and said: "Lloyd is so *nice*. What does he want?"
- When they hit their own roadblock in the work, their ability to focus on others can mask their own issue.

GUIDANCE

Be careful not to take advantage of the Nurturer's seemingly endless supply of selflessness. They could become Caretakers (losing sight of the goal), or Rebels if they feel taken advantage of.

### *The Glue*

The Glue is the ensemble member who literally "holds it together" – not just for themselves, but also for the ensemble as a whole. They are the blood type that is the universal receiver and donor. Uniquely equipped to handle a wide range of personalities, they're easy in spirit and able to allow things to roll off their backs and move forward. This enables them to also serve as Rocks, Nurturers, and to be accepting and supportive of Sparkplugs and Enforcers. They have the ability to put their individual needs into the back seat for the sake of the ensemble's need in the moment, and yet they never turn into the Complainer. Out of everyone, they inherently have the most trust in the process, the members, and in you. They're secure, and they have complete faith that their needs will be met by you and the group. They never expect anything in return for being the Glue, and they draw strength and personal fulfillment from providing that cohesion. If their needs are not met, they generally have a positive way to bring that fact to your attention. Having members who easily demonstrate the value of sacrifice to the others can be invaluable (see the Caretaker).

The Glue tends to be the most grounded person in the room and in production is the one who never loses sight that the goal is to tell the story. If the Rock is the heart of the ensemble, the Glue is the conscience. The Glue is also the role that most members would like to see themselves as, but it's a rare person who truly fulfills it. It's the most rewarding, most demanding, and the most essential role in the ensemble.

Recognizing the Glue:

- Is an excellent listener; present, truthful, trust their instincts.
- Is dependable, never showy.
- Offers assistance to a struggling ensemble member and makes it appear as if it was that person's idea.
- Is sensitive to knowing what is/isn't needed in a moment.
- Excels at making their partners look good.
- Their reward is in the work, not in individual recognition.
- Can be quieter than others, may seem to be less "active." But when you check in, they've absorbed everything.

Pros:

- If you have the Glue, you have an internal leader in the ensemble that will provide great support for the goals and for you.
- Organically heads off potential conflict before it begins. Someone with a propensity for "acting out" tends to be too embarrassed to do so in the presence of someone who is committed, focused, and mature during positive discoveries as well as in frustrating moments.
- Instills confidence in an ensemble member who is struggling (they make their partners look, and feel, good!).

Cons:

- The only one we've ever seen is jealousy. An ensemble member may think they're jealous of the popularity of the Glue; they're actually jealous of the Glue's confidence and their ability to commit and "let go of the small stuff."

Make sure you always have the Glue in your ensemble. If not, try to nurture one to emerge within the group. Don't leave home without your Fabulous Four: the Rock, the Glue, the Nurturer, the Sparkplug, or some combination therein.

## A special note for new or emerging ensemble leaders

If you're an early career ensemble leader, remember that taking immediate action when you feel you've recognized a certain behavior may not always be the best option. A Sparkplug shares a few traits with the Cheerleader, but they're ultimately quite different. The Nurturer may simply be having a bad day and may momentarily act like the Rebel. With experience comes greater awareness and greater confidence in guiding behaviors, so be patient with yourself. Be careful not to label someone too quickly, especially if you're only now gaining experience with ensemble work. Some people will push your buttons and you might be prone to push back. Ask yourself (on a case by case basis):

- "Is identifying and monitoring this individual more useful than taking immediate action?"
- "Am I *acting* on what I've learned or am I *reacting* to this person?"

## Conclusion

At the risk of this chapter reading a bit like looking for one's astrological sign, we ask you the following: did you skip ahead, looking for yourself in these descriptions? Did you feel that the one you actually *are* was different from the one you *hoped* you would be? It's neither bad nor good, it simply gives you information about how you work, and how you see yourself. What are the traits that your hoped-for archetype possesses, that you feel you want to obtain? What are the positive traits in the archetype that you felt closest to, that you had been denying ("Oh, I don't want people to think I'm full of myself … ")? Why might we be denying what our current strengths actually are, while looking over the fence at another's greener grass?

We strongly encourage all directors and teachers to make the time to hold group callbacks when auditioning for ensemble-based projects. Taking this time at the beginning to explore and identify behaviors that may/may not support the goal will strengthen the ensemble in the long run. Select specific exercises that will illuminate behaviors that are essential to your project, and will highlight behaviors that could harm it. For example, in an exercise that demands leaders "trade off" leading at different moments: do you notice one person who resists giving up the steering wheel? Or one who doesn't seem to ever want the wheel? What would those details mean to the goals of the ensemble you're creating? (See Appendix X for suggestions.)

Empowering yourself to recognize archetypes will give you the invaluable skill of predicting and redirecting behaviors in the ensemble. It may seem like magic, but as we wrote in Chapter 1, it's all based on specific observations, actions, and choices. Your ability to forecast ensemble dynamics in advance will be based in your awareness, trust, experience, support, and commitment – and the bonds created from that will be solid so that the magic *can* happen.

# 6

# CARING FOR AND
# MAINTAINING ENSEMBLE

We realize that this is the chapter you might be skipping ahead to. Trust us, we get it; but please be sure you've read Chapter 3 before going any further. In it, we discussed the essential skills needed for leading an ensemble. It's an important primer for what lies ahead.

## How long can a party last?

Let's begin by acknowledging that everything grows, and everything eventually dies, including ensemble. If you've been clear on the goal, thorough in selection, and created a good bond that is elastic, an ensemble can survive a full lifespan with proper attention and maintenance. This can mean anything from allowing it to evolve and change, to asking someone to leave the group. In this chapter we examine your role as Doctor, Intuitive, Diagnostician, and sometimes even the Psychic (there's that sniffer again). Your objectivity allows you to see what the nature of the ensemble is, and what it isn't. You can recognize the difference between a growing pain and a fracture, or a healthy and an unhealthy change. Once you've attuned yourself to your observations, you'll be able to make a diagnosis and determine a course of action to keep the ensemble healthy. But. The one thing you *must* do is take action; there is no such thing as an "inevitable" outcome.

Now, is it possible to achieve the goal with a group that's falling apart? Sure. But who wants to work that way if you don't have to? Making the ensemble's health a priority will strengthen your ability to achieve the goal, and you'll all be a lot happier along the way.

### *Before you begin*

There are no magic silver bullets, but the good news is that there are no werewolves either. Most of us have seen a skilled mechanic take a good look at the engine and begin to operate like a skilled surgeon. We've also seen bad mechanics open the hood, and begin to tentatively "tink, tink, tink" with a random tool, hoping they look like they know what they're doing. *You* need to be clear about what you already have in your *own* tool kit, and what you need to develop (see Chapter 3). So before you even reach for that tool bag, consider the following for every ensemble that you lead:

- Trust the ensemble to help you with any care and maintenance. *You are not alone and you need the ensemble's help to make any solution work.* Please re-read that before moving on.

- Assume the best, not the worst, of the ensemble. Try not to look for problems that aren't there, and don't let another ensemble leader's war stories make you see goblins where none exist. Remember, no werewolves.

- Know when to get out of the way. Try not to equate the ensemble's independent choices to something "wrong." They will learn more from being allowed to crash the car, and from your trust in them *after* they've crashed the car, than if you inhibit their independence.

- Take action when needed, but don't micro-manage. Your desire to make the ensemble "perfect" can create too much pressure and pressure causes fractures.

- Once you've taken an action, allow appropriate time for it to take effect before trying something else. You wouldn't take a week's worth of a prescription in one sitting to get well faster, would you?

- Be open to the possibility that the repair may not be within your power to achieve; it may lie solely in that of an ensemble member(s).

- Trust your instincts and consider them carefully instead of acting on them impulsively. Observe, intuit, and then decide on a course of action. Impulsive responses can make things worse before they get better.

- On the other hand, don't be too slow to act on something you've observed; try not to doubt that you know what you know. Have you ever told a friend, "I sensed something the minute I walked in the room? I knew it; I knew it in my bones. But I told myself, 'you're crazy ... that can't be true.'" There's always *something* that makes you doubt that you know what you know. Tell it "thanks for sharing," then flick it away.

- It's all about the goal; it's not about you. Try not to take things personally.

- Listen for what is needed and be willing to *ask*, "What is needed?" again and again, especially with long-established groups.

- Anyone can have a bad day: including, and especially, you. Try not to panic; the only thing worse than allowing a hairline fracture to grow into a full break is to *create* a break by assuming the worst. Keep breathing, and come in fresh tomorrow. The second day will tell you if there's an actual problem or if the ensemble collectively got up on the wrong side of the bed the previous day. It happens.

- Observe the ensemble by observing the individuals. You may not always feel comfortable focusing so intently on their moment-to-moment behavior, but remember: you're not seeking a problem. You're being a good shepherd, keeping watch.

- Taking an action isn't punitive toward the ensemble (unless you make it so); action promotes health and growth.
- Most important – and Rose will forever thank Dr. Beverly Brumm of SUNY New Paltz for making her mentally write this 100 times on her imaginary blackboard – there is *always* something you can do. There *is* always *something* you can do. If you find yourself saying, "It's out of my hands" or "It's not my fault," please start writing on your *own* imaginary blackboard. It may mean accepting responsibility for having created the problem, but it also means accepting responsibility for trying to make it better. We've become a society that blames others, a lot. This leads to inaction, which stops progress. There is always an action you can take. That alone can build your confidence, and that of the ensemble, and empower you all to return to the goal.

### *When is it time to get the tool box out?*

Recognizing a healthy ensemble is fairly easy. You see everyone's commitment through their listening, creating, exploring, and playing with one another. Folks are diving into the deep end without dipping their toes in first. Even if they're exhausted at the beginning of your class or rehearsal, they're honest about acknowledging the fatigue, and are eager to shake it off. You can feel their connection and commitment, even before the work begins.

Recognizing a problem can be more challenging. Have you ever walked into a rehearsal, class, or meeting and felt that something has shifted, but you can't put your finger on it? You feel the room vibrating when you enter, much the same way as the air itself starts to crackle from ionization because of an impending thunderstorm? We all know what a bad day or a bad mood feels like; this is different. You sense a deeper change; your instincts are telling the artistic hairs on the back of your neck to stand at attention. Just because you can't see it, doesn't mean it isn't true. And sometimes, you *will* see it: you observe delays in response time, or the listening skills are noticeably poorer. Fewer risks are being taken, and the caution becomes contagious.

To answer the $64,000 question, "How do I tell the difference between behavior indicating a problem, or being a fleeting anomaly?" go back to Chapter 3: how developed is your sniffer? Are you an early career instructor who is only beginning to experience ensemble or are you a seasoned artistic director who has a keen eye? A developed awareness of your instinctual responses and observational skills helps you tell the difference between simple growing pains and real trouble. Add that to our advice and over time your confidence and skill set will grow.

Below, we list the most common behaviors that we've observed as signs of something amiss. You will observe every one of these behaviors *at some point in your process*. Don't run to the toolbox just yet; they may be happening simply because it's early in your collaborative process. We're not talking about behaviors that naturally occur in beginning stages, but those that are chronic and happen after the ensemble has established its identity. Early on, someone might be late because they don't know the route yet; they might be holding back because it's the first week and they're getting to know new people. *Ensembles aren't formed overnight*; allow for a reasonable amount of time before you consider something to be a symptom of anything other than a natural course of events. It takes time for the ensemble to coalesce; only after the ensemble has bonded is there anything *to* care for and maintain. In fact, the ensemble can *benefit* from simple errors being allowed to occur without making a fuss (remember: let them crash the car). Don't make a big deal of a one-time occurrence, and the ensemble will realize that you trust them to recognize and self-correct the errors themselves. So observe, and get ready for when you do notice a recurring pattern of behavior.

## Behavior 1: Lateness

Potentially the most innocent of the behaviors, but it can be the most frustrating. Sometimes the subway just won't move between stations; sometimes for all the pleas to St. Anthony, we just can't find our keys. It happens. Most of the time, ensemble members are late for innocent reasons, and they're beating themselves up as they rush through the door brimming with apologies. We're talking about chronic and/or uncharacteristic lateness. Is an ensemble member with a strong track record of being on time suddenly showing up late? Repeatedly? Observe them when they enter the room; are they creating a tall tale about why they're late? Are they dead quiet? Do they make eye contact with anyone else? Observations give you clues to root causes; learn the root cause and you'll be able to redirect the behavior positively.

### *Possible causes?*

They may be:

- simply overextended. They've overbooked their time, haven't prioritized, and may have been reluctant to tell you about their other commitments
- reluctant to enter what they may perceive as an increasingly unsafe or frustrating environment
- consciously or subconsciously "punishing" the ensemble for having let them down somehow
- feeling neglected by you or the ensemble and drawing attention to themselves
- reluctant to tackle increasingly challenging material. A scene may be hitting too close to home, compelling them to confront something they don't want to
- having an interpersonal conflict with another ensemble member. Being late helps them avoid any personal time for casual conversation
- having a personal conflict at home
- experiencing drug or alcohol abuse. This is a viable possibility for *all* the behaviors we list here, but we'll discuss it fully later on in its own section.

*Potential actions*

1. Address the group.

Sometimes the best way to tackle a budding issue is to address the group with a single theme. This has the double advantage of the individual having their behavior brought to their attention without being singled out and the group is reminded of its commitment. Everyone examines their actions, and it supports a re-commitment to the goal and to the ensemble.

Pros:

- The individuals recognize themselves in the announcement, realize they need to adjust their behavior, and correct it. They renew their responsibilities to the work and the ensemble, and appreciate not being singled out.
- You've opened the door for them to start a dialog as to why the lateness is occurring. When they tell you about the three other projects they're committed to, try not to blow a gasket. They may want *you* to be the one to decide for them, but of course, they need to make that choice for themselves.
- The ensemble feels their time and commitment is acknowledged and respected, and appreciates you taking the time to address the unhelpful behavior.
- The public announcement is quick, allows everyone to get back to work fast, and the ensemble sees that you're willing to take decisive action on their behalf.

Cons:

- The individuals do NOT recognize themselves in the announcement and the behavior continues.
- They DO recognize themselves in the announcement, but they get angry that more is being asked of them than they feel they can give, and the behavior worsens.
- They recognize themselves in the announcement and feel disrespected because you didn't speak to them privately.
- The ensemble feels that you've acknowledged the behavior, but that addressing the group vs. the individual is the "chicken shit" way out. They may feel their time and effort is being disrespected.

2. Speak privately to the individual.

Pros:

- They realize that you're observant, they're reminded of their commitment to the ensemble, and they correct their behavior.

- The individuals were unaware of the behavior (we know, we know … ), and it compels them to examine their actions and consider why it's occurring.
- The one-on-one time gives you the opportunity to offer specific guidance regarding why they're late. If they're in conflict with someone, are they ready to solve it themselves? Or do they need your guidance? If they're experiencing personal problems, do they need additional support? If they admit to being confused about a direction that the ensemble is taking, this is an opportunity for you to articulate your vision of the goal, or dispel fears they have. You may also discover that the ensemble member is concerned for good reason. You may be in error about something and the latecomer is sensitive to it. Don't underestimate your *own* need for care and maintenance.
- The one-on-one gives you time to reassure them about their positive contributions. It never killed anyone to include praise along with critique.
- You simply get to know an ensemble member better; more info is always good.

Cons:

- They may be embarrassed by being singled out, grudgingly correct the behavior, but will announce their on-time entrance thereafter! The first time this happens, welcome them with a smile and ignore their wounded pride, even if it kills you. If it happens a second or third time, ask them (seriously) why they want to work with this ensemble, what their perception of the goal is, and what they feel their responsibilities are to the ensemble and goal. Accountability is a major issue in ensemble, especially where Big Ego is concerned.
- They may feel you're nitpicking ("Don't you know how far I have to commute by subway to be here?") and that you're unappreciative of their personal sacrifices.
- They may not recognize themselves at all in what you're saying, but realize that they've let the ensemble down (without understanding why). Their insecurities may grow, along with increasingly unproductive behavior. This most often happens when someone is so focused on judging themselves that they miss when they actually *do* something that negatively impacts the ensemble. Self-fulfilling prophecies are no joke.

3. Acknowledge the behavior publicly and purposefully.

We also call this the "Three Strikes" rule. Sometimes you have an ensemble member who claims to be committed, but they continue to arrive late, armed with excuses. The one thing they don't do is apologize to the ensemble or to you.

This isn't our favorite approach, but if someone has been given every opportunity and still tries to make the ensemble feel grateful that they've showed up at all, then all bets are off. When they arrive, stop the work and address them in front of the group. Note their lateness and state what the consequences will be if it recurs. Don't listen to the excuse, don't get engaged in a conversation, make a statement, period. And if they arrive late once more, stick to the stated consequences, no matter what.

Pros:

- The group's frustration will be channeled (and hopefully vented) through your public address, and they'll be better able to positively engage with the offender.
- The need for total commitment is reinforced.
- The ensemble feels their efforts acknowledged and protected by your unwillingness to accept the latecomer's behavior.
- No one will be late again. They won't want to risk being called out publicly for their behavior.

Cons:

- The ensemble might be shocked by this rare public admonishment and begin to wonder if things are changing, which could impact the safety of the environment.
- The ensemble could sympathize with the self-same offender who they were just kvetching about in the green room the day before. Drama is drama.

4. Acknowledge the behavior publicly and let the ensemble decide consequences.

Once in a very rare while you have someone who is committed to the goal, the work, and the ensemble, but all the clocks in the world won't help them be on time for anything. They're the person the phrase "he's gonna be late to his own funeral" was created for. It's as if they have a genetic misunderstanding of time; they're late for *everything*, and in these rare instances, people in their lives have simply come to accept them as they are. Funny enough, we've found it most often in a Sparkplug (see Chapter 5). To save yourself countless meetings and their recurring apologies, ask the ensemble itself to decide on the consequences. You have to walk a fine line between their genuine fondness for the person and the need for everyone to abide by the same structure. The ensemble will likely decide on a personal "in" joke ("next time you're late, you're doing the coffee run at break"), and the latecomer is delighted because they truly want to make up for the failing. It keeps things light and the ensemble feels empowered and respected. It also makes for a hilarious running joke as the person comes flying breathlessly into the room, sees that they're the last one to arrive, and they get out their notepad to get ready to take coffee orders.

### Rose

I had a student whose commute to Brooklyn College was nearly two hours by subway and he was chronically late in the first few weeks. He was a dedicated Sparkplug, hard worker and a sweetheart (whose mom attended every production – whether he was in it or not). He became so fearful of the humorous "punishments," that he started coming to school ridiculously early and then going back to sleep again on the mangy sofa we used in the acting studio. We would wake him up when we arrived; he gained the ability to fall asleep anywhere, anytime, and he earned the nickname "Couch."

## Behavior 2: Lack of Preparation

This rightfully has a louder warning bell. Lack of preparation is willful, conscious, and the person enters the room *knowing* that they've failed to keep their commitment. Rarely is it accidental ("I was in the bathroom when you asked us to bring a new monologue to the next class"); a specific decision has been made *not* to do something required of them. If they've previously been committed and prepared, what may have triggered the change?

### *Possible causes?*

They may:

- be over-extended and their very comfort with the ensemble may make them feel that if they have to let something go, then the group will be more forgiving. Every year we see acting students, when their science and math classes start to overwhelm them, stop doing their requirements for their acting classes. It's like the family analogy in Chapter 1; we know on some level we can get away with more at "home." Until we can't;
- no longer want to be a part of the ensemble and they're laying the groundwork for being asked to leave so that they don't have to quit;
- have an issue with something they've been requested to do, so they begin to pull back from the work. They realize that you'll have to speak up at some point to acknowledge their failing;
- wish the ensemble were moving in a different direction. By neglecting to do the required work, they make a statement about what they feel the value is – or isn't – about where the ensemble is going;
- be feeling neglected by you, and like the chronic latecomer, seek negative attention.

140

### *Potential actions*

1. Address the group (see Behavior 1).

This more willful behavior can grate on the ensemble's nerves more than lateness. If you're addressing it early, this approach is best. However, if the ensemble has already reached a breaking point with the behavior, you risk frustrating them further with this choice. Rose was once observing another teacher's acting class who, throughout the semester, had used the metaphor of "Peter pays for Paul" to mean that when one person didn't contribute fully to the ensemble or to the work, someone else (and sometimes *everybody* else) would pay for it. The teacher began to admonish some students who were unprepared. Again. It took up class time and disrupted the momentum of the work. One of the *very* prepared students sighed and said, "I *hate* Paul … "

2. Address the individual (see Behavior 1).

3. Ask them privately: "Why do you want to be a part of this ensemble?"

If their answers are focused on the goal ("I love this play, I believe in this company's mission," etc.), then redirecting their behavior will be easy. Discuss the lack of preparation itself; are they fearful of getting something "wrong?" If so, why, and what can you do together to solve it? Are they suddenly doubting their contribution and by not being prepared, they self-fulfill the rejection that their fear is manufacturing?

   If their response is ego based ("I thought this would be a good career move," or "I wanted to play the lead"), then redirecting can be more challenging. Re-clarify the goal as the central purpose; their initial reason for joining may have been ego based, but they may still have the potential to commit to the goal. Point out the impact of their behavior on the ensemble; if they seem concerned, then they still have an investment that you can work with. If they seem offended, or they tell you that they can't give more than they already are, then you need to make some tough decisions. More on that later.

## Behavior 3: Holding Back

This is the behavior that has the most potential to be misidentified. Sometimes we momentarily hold back in our process because we're figuring something out, or we're working to break through. Other times, the withholding is willful, conscious, and planned. The person has the impulses, but they're hugging the ball instead of passing it. You'll need to be very specific in your observations. Is a previously generous ensemble member suddenly:

• lacking commitment to choices, partners, and the ensemble itself?

- becoming a poor listener?
- preplanning to stay with safe choices?
- apologizing for their choices/judging them as poor?
- negatively commenting on something their partner has done?
- claiming not to understand the exercise or scene after it's been carefully discussed?
- uncharacteristically quiet during discussions?
- doing the minimum required in the work vs. exploring and playing fully?
- engaging in delaying activities that have nothing to do with the work (drinking out of water bottle, looking around the room, drinking out of bottle again, readjusting belt, etc.)?
- being more physically aggressive with partners in a way that makes others keep their distance?

This behavior has the potential to be destructive; it's easy for someone to help their partner when they're struggling to find their way. However, ensembles have great sniffers for someone who is *choosing* not to contribute. It's like Midas sitting on his gold; everyone sees the gold, Midas sees everyone notice the gold, but he ain't sharing. In fact, Midas *enjoys* knowing that everyone sees his big behind sitting on that pile of gold so they can't get to it. So, one of the first questions we ask is, "Why are you sitting on your gold?" Most obvious answer: to guard and protect it. From what? Ah *ha* ...

### *Possible causes?*

They may be:

- in an interpersonal conflict with another member. Are they withholding in every instance, or only when it involves a particular person? They may be protecting their "gold" from the judgment of that one person. If in an improv group or class, they may also be introducing thinly veiled scenarios that serve as surrogates for the real issue;
- involved in a romantic relationship with another ensemble member. They avoid working with one another so that they don't give away their secret. If this is the case, just tell them to stop it; the ensemble already knows, and unless they have a former lover in the group, they won't care;
- having personal breakthroughs in the material. This can feel different, frightening, and make them avoid the work because it feels "wrong." They retreat to something that feels familiar, but which has nothing to do with the breakthrough;
- going through a difficult personal time. They don't want to burden the ensemble with it, but of course they struggle to *not* think about it during work. So much societal conditioning asks us to muscle through problems, that someone can go into denial about the very real existence of the problem at hand.

### *Potential actions*

1. Address the individual (see Behavior 1).

Ask them open questions; don't impose your theory to their withholding immediately: e.g., "You've been holding back during table work. What makes you afraid? Nobody will think you're stupid for asking a question." You'll get much more useful information by seeing what they freely offer first. Instead, ask:

- I've noticed some changes in your approach to the work lately. Can you tell me what may be going on?
- You've been noticeably quieter in class. Is there anything you'd like to talk about, or any questions that I can help with?
- I've noticed that you and Alex have had some challenges working together. Can you tell me more about that?

Most of the time, someone struggling simply needs your help to open the door, and they'll happily walk through – usually relieved to get something off their chest. Never underestimate an ensemble member's fear of appearing weak. If they respond with the ever frustrating "I'm *fine*" to any of these questions (a favorite definition of "FINE," courtesy of Mickey Ryan: Fucked Up, Insecure, Neurotic, and Extraordinarily Fucked Up), then get more specific:

- You've been noticeably holding back where you were previously open and free. Something has changed. What is it?
- You've been harder on yourself lately, which is affecting your ability to be present. What's getting in your way?
- Your scenes with Rosa are dynamic; you're listening and playing freely with one another. Your scenes with Mack have recently become tentative, to the point where I can barely hear what you're saying. What can I help you with?

If they're still reluctant to offer details:

- You've been pulling back from the work, your partners, and your own choices; clearly you're not fine. Something is interfering with your ability to commit, and we need to solve this together. Everything that affects you, affects us all, and affects the goal.

## Behavior 4: Disconnect from the Ensemble Itself

Different from withholding, this is someone who is completely connected in the work, but the moment they're "off the clock," they disengage from social contact with the ensemble. Now, we endeavor to give everyone a break from scrutiny, but sometimes you can't help noticing the difference between their engagement while the work is occurring, and the detachment when it isn't. This can be an early warning sign or a companion behavior for one of the previous issues mentioned. During breaks, or before or after rehearsal/class, are they:

- not speaking to anyone?
- very obviously reading a book (head held low to the page) to keep others from approaching?
- very obviously checking phone messages so that they're left alone?
- immediately leaving the room to make phone calls when a break is announced?
- arriving in enough time to change clothes and leap into the work, but not enough time to engage in any conversation?
- looking at material that has nothing to do with the work at hand?

### *Possible causes?*

This behavior is much more personal and subtle. If you note the behavior, also note if it's impacting the ensemble at all. It may not be. But if it is, address it. It's not your job to get to the bottom of *why* the ensemble member may be disconnecting, but it *is* your job to recognize it when it happens and take measures to redirect their energy.

### *Potential actions*

1. Speak privately to the individual.

Remember: it isn't prying if their behavior is affecting the goal and others. Ensemble extends beyond the prescribed hours, especially with long-established groups. We're not suggesting you be on watch at a social gathering; but something may have *happened* at that gathering that the person is bringing into the workroom. Ask the open question:

- "I've noticed that you seem a bit preoccupied. Is there anything I might be able to help with?" If they respond, "Has my work been poor?" be honest and tell them what you've observed.

Only once in our combined 60+ years of teaching and directing have we ever heard an actor say, "You know, I'm just a private person. I know the ensemble wants me to hang out with them and be social, but that's just not me. I like them all a lot – I just have my own life on the outside and prefer to take that time for myself." Eventually the ensemble copped on to it without anything having to be said. Every *other* time we've had that conversation, however, responses have ranged from, "and Louise has been using personal information about me in some of our improvs, which I really resent. I don't want to give her anything to use against me." Or "I'm having some health issues and I just don't want to talk about it. I know that everyone here will want to help, but I'm just not ready to share this."

Assume the best, not the worst, of their intentions. We've had actors tell us that a parent had died, that they were sexually assaulted, evicted, fired, arrested, unbelievably challenging circumstances that they were being stoic, and private, about. It's striking how often withdrawn behavior is assumed to be ego or laziness, instead of considering the obvious choice. Which is, they may be going through something that the ensemble either cannot or should not be a part of. Having the private conversation gives you the opportunity to offer them support, or to clarify concerns (do they need professional help with something?).

## Behavior 5: Self-involved Focus

The very nature of ensemble requires us to turn our energy outward, giving to the group and to the goal. Of course we have an individual role in whatever story we're telling (the story of our education, of this theatre company, etc.), but if our primary focus is on our role, and not the story, then the goal is at risk. Is a previously generous ensemble member:

- seeking excessive reassurance for choices they're making?
- seeking agreement from others in all things?
- becoming a poor listener? (When trouble's afoot, listening is usually the first thing to go)
- assuming the worst of scene partners? For example, a partner's new offer is interpreted as a rejection of something *they've* done?
- becoming excessively self-deprecating?
- using phrases such as:
  - "Is this what you want?"
  - "Is this right?"
  - "I'm doing the same thing she's doing and you didn't say anything to me … ?"
  - "I'm the worst at this." Often followed by tears and/or a swift exit from the room.

### *Possible causes?*

They may:

- have recently suffered a rejection or failure and are inwardly "re-playing" what happened to try to understand what they did "wrong";
- have had their Comparison Button triggered. Either because of a recent failure or someone else receiving praise, the ensemble member gets caught in a self-involved cycle of, "Look how good Gillian is with taking risks; why can't I do that?" or "Samantha has such amazing access to her emotions; I wish I had that."

Now. Before you dismiss this because "Rose and David are talking about students here. They're more insecure. I'm a working professional." Stop and ask yourself: when was the last time you beat yourself up over something that was beyond your control, or held yourself up to an unreasonable comparison to someone else? We'll bet that it's more recent than when you were a college student;

- not have worked for a while, and this could be their first acting job in some time. They might be analyzing everything they're doing to try to:
  - be amazing so you'll re-hire them in the future;
  - figure out why it's been so long since they've worked. What have they been doing wrong?
  - be here to be told how good they are, not to create with others or to be taught by you;
  - be looking for "home" for the wrong reasons. They may be seeking "a parent" (either for approval or to rebel against), or a family that will support their habitual way of doing things instead of challenging them.

### *Potential actions*

1. Speak privately to the individual (see Behavior 1).

2. Do an exercise that focuses on giving and trust.

Conduct an exercise that requires them to focus on another person. If you're in production and you don't feel you have time, please try it. Just once. It will address the problem and the cast will be pleasantly surprised that they've been given "play time" to explore something that they can directly apply to characters/relationships. You can choose an exercise that will break the self-focus and reveal something about the play (bottom of p. 168). Others include:

- Blind Offers (Appendix A). Each actor *must* make an offer to their partner and the structure of the exercise requires a "thank you" after the offer has been received. This reinforces that every offer is needed and every offer will be (and must be) accepted for the story to be told.
- One Word at a Time Storytelling (Appendix L). Literally, the story can't continue without each person's contribution.
- Sound and Movement (Appendix D). This exercise draws everyone's energy forward. Each person is given solo time to explore; they're asked to translate that into an abstract sound and movement, and then they give it to someone who *accepts* it. Each member is asked to accept someone else's sound and movement and allow it to transform. In that process, several things are accomplished:
  - The exercise requires private exploration in a public setting, and *sharing* that through an external, committed physical choice. The entire ensemble then accepts the choice. It mirrors the path you need the individual to take to become a contributing member of the ensemble again.

146

- Provides reinforcement *against* fears of rejection; everyone says "yes, and ... "
- Provides reinforcement that the group needs every individual's contribution.
- Emphasizes each person's unique abilities; everyone's sound and movement is specific to who they are, so comparison to each other is useless. It's more fulfilling to *celebrate* the differences.
- That it's possible to transform and *be* transformed. Sometimes when an ensemble member is caught up in a self-involved cycle, they fear they won't find their way back. Being given vulnerable offers from partners that they *must* say yes to helps them understand the risks that others are taking. When that vulnerable offer is made, and repeated *until* they accept it, they have no choice but to be present for their partner. In accepting that offer, they're much more likely to let go of the isolation of the self-involved cycle.

## Behavior 6: War Games

War is an insidious game that can be played between ensemble members or with you. It can come out of a conflict between members where both decide "I'll show you how professional *I'm* being." It can also arise out of a disagreement between you and whoever the natural leader *within* the ensemble is, usually over struggle for control. Have you observed:

- two members who have not previously been close, suddenly inseparable (think bad high school movies) to the exclusion of everyone else?
- two members who have previously *been* close, suddenly no longer speaking?
- that after giving feedback to a particular ensemble member, you notice an exchange of knowing glances between that person and another?
- that one of those in conflict asks you a question whose answer has the potential to embarrass the other party in the conflict? For example, Sarah crosses away from a prop instead of having it in hand when Mervyn needs it; an honest mistake in rehearsal. Mervyn asks in front of everyone, "If the script says a character is supposed to take a knife out of the other character's hand, then the actor should have the prop, right?"
- that if you're the one they're playing War with, they ask you a question they know you can't possibly have the answer to yet?
- that when you ask that ensemble member a question, they begin their response with "Well, you said before ... " and conclude with " ... or don't you want that anymore?" They want *you* to appear guilty of indecision or error. And guess what? Sometimes you *are* wrong and you need to readily admit it (see "Ego" in Chapter 3). You can apologize or admit that you're wrong and still maintain your leadership status. It's not always easy, but the ensemble will respect you all the more.

War Games can challenge your leadership skills perhaps more than any other behavior listed. Your sniffer is essential to figuring out who's playing. They've had a head start on a plan of attack, and the potential for big emotion and even bigger ego is huge. It's exhausting to even think about the permutations, so why might an ensemble member be engaging in this?

### *Possible causes?*

They may:

- feel they've lost control (in the ensemble, personal relationships, or work) and they want to regain power. And because Ensemble = Home (Home being the place that when you go there, they have to take you in … ) the ensemble becomes a safe place for that behavior to play out;
- realize that they've either joined the wrong ensemble or joined the right one for the wrong reasons. Ego and pride inhibits them from confronting this. Playing War becomes a convenient reason for them being asked to leave and they avoid taking responsibility for the decision;
- feel they've been slighted by you or a member and will play War until they get an apology. It begs the question as to why someone feels it's more satisfying than simply saying,

> "Hey Steve, did you know you're blocking me during my monologue?"
> "Gee, I didn't realize. Sorry, mate."
> "Cheers, no problem."

Done. But because some find War Games soooo satisfying, it could go on for days or weeks if you let it.

### *Potential actions*

1. Address the ensemble (see Behavior 1).

Make a broad statement about mutual support, and that should a conflict arise, the ensemble is strong enough for everyone to be able to freely communicate their concerns. Optimistic? Always. Does this work? Sometimes.

2. Address the individual(s) (see Behavior 1).

This behavior is fairly obvious, so denial is harder. You can be more direct from the get go. Try the following:

- "I've noticed some tension between you and Mike; have you spoken to each other about what the problem may be?" (Then ask Mike the same question.)

If they haven't communicated: "You need to talk to one another and find a solution. I'm happy to be present at that conversation." *Be sure to say,* "I won't be there to tell you who's right or wrong; my presence is to make sure you're communicating clearly with each other." Now, if one of them is *clearly* in the wrong, you need to state that too. "So Adam, let me get this straight; you agreed to meet Ugo to run lines and you blew him off? Don't be a chowderhead; apologize and start earning his trust back."

- "I've felt some tension between us lately; is there something you want to talk about?"

*Don't* begin the conversation by offering an apology; you may not have done anything you need to apologize *for,* and if this person is seeing offense under every rock, a blanket apology reinforces negative behavior. If they further the game by saying, "I'm fine," you have two choices:

- Choice 1: Say, "I noticed you seemed upset when ... " and give them specific behaviors that you observed. They'll likely be pleased that you noticed and will either:
  - admit to the behavior now that they're getting the attention and you'll be able to sort out the misunderstanding, or ...
  - ... they'll be pleased and say, "Nope. *You* misinterpreted. I'm fine." If the latter, give them a day or two to see if your acknowledgment defuses the conflict. If the War continues, follow up with a meeting that will hopefully result in a Peace Treaty. Or in a Victory for the ensemble by your asking them to leave.
- Choice 2: After they say, "I'm fine," respond with, "Okay, my mistake." And get up to leave. If they don't stop you, go. Chances are, they'll quickly jump in with, "Well, since we're here, I was bothered that you haven't been giving me as many notes as Rosanne. ... " Now you have a starting point for discussion, and solutions.

3. Address a subset of the ensemble.

Pros:

- You and the individual have the support of these ensemble members in working together to improve commitment and behavior. There's strength in numbers.

Cons:

- There's strength in numbers. If the person is in denial, and they're persuasive, the subset may "side" against you. Or, if the person is one of the weaker members, the subset may come to their defense – even if the behavior clearly isn't in the ensemble's best interest. Their impulse to protect may override common sense.

4. Divide and conquer.

### Rose

I once inherited an acting class that had been together for several months. They hated each other. I mean, *hated*: they sabotaged, withheld, guarded, you name it. There wasn't an *ounce* of trust in the room. At first, nothing worked: they dug in their heels against each other all the more. I met with every person one on one. I didn't care what had caused the hate, but they sure did. I listened to each of their complaints and my ears were scorched from the accusations they hurled at one another. By the end of each meeting, they had calmed down simply because they'd been listened to. I finished each meeting by saying, "Look, you've obviously been through a lot these past few months. *Please don't tell the others*, but can I ask you to help me? Next class, I'm going to introduce an exercise, and I'd like to call on you first. Your leadership could make all the difference. When I call on you, can I ask you to make choices that are only positive, active, and light? Choose a scenario that's funny, romantic, or make it hilarious if you want. And – this is the hard part – if anyone tries to purposely throw a monkey wrench into what you're doing, can you act as if it's the best Christmas present you ever got? Don't let anyone co-opt it for their own nefarious purposes. Would you do this?" They were thrilled to be empowered, delighted to be in on a private mission, and loved that they were considered a potential leader. Yes, *I* resorted to nefarious behavior. Was everyone I spoke to considered a leader by the group? Good grief, they hated breathing the same *air*. But by the time every single person had led an exercise, each of them discovered leadership skills – and ensemble-building skills – they didn't know they had. By focusing on positive choices, there was no opportunity to use scenarios to take out their aggressions on each other. By focusing on the work, they weren't focusing on each other's *motives*. More work got done, and the behaviors were positively re-directed. They still didn't love each other, but after a few weeks they respected, and felt respected by, one another. That created just enough trust for them to be more willing to learn from each other, enabling them to grow and learn together.

## Behavior 7: It's in the Eyes

You and the ensemble find so much simply in one another's eyes. Can this very intimate window tell a lie? BFA acting student Arthur Kriklivy was asked how he knew when a problem was brewing in an ensemble:

> When you see people watching other people's work, you see the looks that reveal what their disposition is toward that person. When we observe our peers doing good work, we're proud of them. If there are petty problems on a personal level, you see others watching and judging. You feel the vibe changing from a supportive one to a judgmental one.

During the work, have you observed an ensemble member:

- avoiding direct eye contact when you ask them a question?
- challenge you with confrontational eye contact vs. open and receptive eye contact when asking *you* a question?
- avoiding eye contact with others during their work?
- glaring with judgment at another ensemble member while they're working?
- communicating one thing with their body language and giving a contrary message with their eyes and words?

### *Possible causes?*

They may:

- have an interpersonal conflict within the ensemble (see earlier discussions on this issue)
- be feeling slighted by you
- feel that preferential treatment is being given to another ensemble member
- believe that *they're* being judged, and so are either protecting or playing "good for the goose, good for the gander"
- be using drugs, but *not* alcohol. This has absolutely no sociological or scientific basis; our personal observations are that someone on drugs works harder to maintain eye contact to show how straight they are, and an alcohol user avoids close contact because of the noticeable scent.

### *Potential actions*

1. Speak to the individual.

Because eye contact (or lack thereof) is subtler, consider whether it's connected to one of the other listed behaviors: are they withholding in their work? Self-involved? If you can't put your finger on it, ask: "I've observed some changes in your work lately. Is there anything you want to discuss?" If the answer is "no" or the telling "you-know-what," follow up with, "I notice you've been more guarded in your work. What do you feel you're protecting against?"

## Behavior 8: Anything Extreme: Immediate Action Required

Sometimes you have to call out an ensemble member in front of the group (see Lateness: Possible Actions). Yes, this is thoroughly unpleasant, but there are times when you don't have the luxury to reflect on an action between rehearsals, classes, or meetings. Sometimes, someone has broken the "Three Strikes" rule. A remark or action is so egregious that if you don't address it immediately, you'll lose the ensemble's trust and empower the offender. Stop your rehearsal, class or meeting in the following circumstances:

- A violent action. In one memorable run-through, an actor slapped their partner during a verbal fight scene, something that was obviously *not* choreographed. After stopping the run and helping the partner off the floor, the Slapper was asked why in the world they would do such a thing. "I was caught up in the moment and really *felt* it." (FYI: this was a much taller woman slapping a much smaller man. Physical violence isn't limited by gender.)
- A violent word (racist, homophobic, sexist, personal cruelty). We all know what they are.
- A sexually inappropriate action. During one of Rose's improv classes while conducting the exercise The Bear (one group is playing dead while another group tries to get them to react), a male "bear" tried to get a female "hunter" to stop playing dead by unbuttoning her blouse. A verbal caution addressing this terrible breach of trust has been included in her introduction to this exercise ever since.
- If the person is a Repeat Offender of "no, but ... " (vs. "yes and ... "), and individual meetings haven't changed their behavior. A willful and repeated pattern of rejection must be acknowledged in the moment. Otherwise, it may never stop.
- Destructive or unpredictable physical/emotional behavior caused by being drunk or high.

### Rose

I was teaching an improv class and we were doing a round of Hunter/ Hunted (see Appendix G). A student volunteered to be the Hunted (whose goal is to get out of the room). He was huge, built like a linebacker. One of the rules is that the blindfolded Hunter/Hunted move slowly for their safety and for the safety of the spotters. The Hunted began behaving erratically, moving very fast, not listening to my calls to "slow down!" Just as I was about to stop the exercise, he broke into a dead run. While blindfolded. The much smaller spotters wisely jumped out of the way as he plowed through their line. He became momentarily airborne, flying off the stage area and into the desks and chairs below. I raced over; he removed the blindfold and I could see in his eyes that his pupils were nowhere to be found. He was high. And laughing uproariously. Not a scratch. The spotters were upset, having barely missed being knocked over by this hulk. I don't know whom I was madder at: him, for not being hurt at all; or myself, because I didn't figure it out sooner. The student felt invulnerable; but his obliviousness to others made them very vulnerable. If you suspect someone is high or drunk, don't permit them to participate. If you're in a rehearsal, I understand you might give them the benefit of the doubt to keep things moving. But if they're chronic users, things will need to stop, eventually. And on that note ...

## Drugs and alcohol (and attendant behaviors)

We all should educate ourselves regarding possible signs of drug and alcohol abuse. We (David and Rose) don't endorse any specific resource, but have found useful information through the National Council on Alcohol and Drug Dependence (http://www.ncadd.org) and the National Institute on Drug Abuse, a component of the U.S. Department of Health and Human Services (http://drugabuse.gov/NIDAHome.html). Any current or aspiring ensemble leader should gather information about this and other areas of health and safety (fire and emergency procedures, etc.). Educate and prepare yourself, speak to a trained counselor, and/or seek someone you know who is in recovery. Trust us, they *will* help you. If you're in an academic setting or professional organization, find out their official policy on drugs and alcohol, what resources are available to the user/abuser, and whether you're permitted to even broach the subject. Your good intentions could get you fired, inspire a lawsuit, or worse, inhibit the user/abuser from seeking the help they desperately need.

Drugs and alcohol can be why a member shows up shattered just that one time, or why another member exhibits increasingly chronic erratic behavior. They can appear completely sober in one rehearsal and falling apart in the next. Occasional social drinking is one thing; that's usually solved by making a group statement about everyone showing up ready and able to work, or by the hangover itself. Rose had an incredibly responsible acting student come to a morning class after his all-night 21st birthday party. He had one of those excruciating hangovers; he could barely hold his head up from the desk, his brow was knotted like a pretzel, and his skin was the color of wheat paste. His classmates laughed and ratted him out about the party (with great love and affection). There was no need to tell him not to come to class this way again. This hangover was epic and everyone recognized it as a single event that wouldn't recur. The ensemble was profoundly supportive and got to tease this organized and seemingly flawless student about his discovery of, well, being human. He was trusted to self-correct and was back to his usual vibrant self the next day.

Chronic substance abuse is much harder to recognize without educating yourself about it. Speaking *from personal experience only*, we list some potential signs here. Please remember that these may be symptoms of many different things, from a medical condition to personal distractions. Note the behavior, but please don't jump to hasty conclusions, or try to effect any treatment yourself. Possible signs include:

- Serious lack of focus.
- Leaving early or arriving late, complaining of being sick "again."
- Lack of control: their internal censor is out of whack. This can range from their ability to be on time to saying insensitive things out loud.
- Their memory becomes poorer.
- Growing secretive; usually because more and more parts of their day involve using or drinking. They stop talking about their lives for fear of revealing something.
- The opposite may happen; their stories become more outlandish over time. They met a famous person after rehearsal last night and hung out with them, their landlord is suing them and taking them to court (this one *might* be true ... ).
- Their creative judgment is out of whack. They're shocked when given a critical note on a scene, as they thought they had a great breakthrough.
- Unpredictable overall behavior. You might observe moments of brilliance in their work, but it's there and gone. They may be able to maintain stability for a solid week, but then start exhibiting the same behavior that made you consider drugs/alcohol to begin with.

### Rose

I once worked with a student who was smart, talented, and eager to learn. At one point, he became withdrawn from class discussions and occasionally showed up late and disheveled. In our first meeting, he assured me he was simply going through a "tough time," and promised to change. Briefly, he did. The pattern continued, and each time it got a little worse. I invited my friend Mickey Ryan to be a guest artist in our class to administer a specific exercise. Mickey had worked extensively in therapeutic theatre, conducting workshops in prisons, drug rehabilitation centers, etc. When we sat down to discuss the student's work, he said, "You know he's using, right?" I was so naïve about drugs and alcohol, it never occurred to me that the student was on anything other than an emotional rollercoaster.

I made the beginner's mistake of letting it go on too long. Having grown up with alcoholics, I fell into my personal pattern of "they're trying and they just need another chance." "Chances" won't help an addict unless that chance involves professional treatment. I required the student to seek professional counseling and though he was over 21, to make full disclosure to his parents. (He denied everything, until he recognized how much attention he was getting. That should have been a Big Clue.) I literally placed phone numbers for the campus counseling center in his hand. For a brief time, he received treatment, and stayed sober.

Then I was contacted by one of his instructors who said that he'd started showing up late again. I arranged a meeting with the student and purposely set the time early. He raced into my office 20 minutes late, unwashed, and reeking of alcohol. In that moment, I changed. I couldn't keep forgiving the addict for letting himself down; it was dangerous for him and for the ensemble. I told him, "You've been lying to yourself, to your classmates, and to me. You're suspended from the program and you must get the treatment you need. We aren't what you need right now. Get help." He yelled at me for falsely accusing him, then said I was right and begged for another chance, then became angry and challenged me by saying, "Another teacher told me I was brilliant!" He eventually wore himself down and I asked him to go immediately to campus counseling.

When told the news, his class remained sympathetic and respectful toward him. However, they came to me privately to reveal past horror stories about his drug and alcohol use. He was functioning just well enough that they'd be on the cusp of telling me, and then they'd back off when he assured them he was "just going through a tough time." It was an important discussion for us all. It was also when I learned the hard lesson that I couldn't help everyone, nor should everyone be encouraged to stay in an ensemble.

## If an ensemble member questions whether they should stay or go

Most of the time, it simply takes a thoughtful discussion to help get the clarity that you *both* need to make this important decision. If an ensemble member tells you, "I want to quit," begin by asking the following:

- "Why now? Why at *this* moment in time?" Don't accept generalities such as "it's not working for me," or "I don't know" (which usually means "I'm scared"). You do them no favors by letting them leave with vague notions that perpetuate unhealthy habits of avoiding responsibility for themselves and their choices. Follow up: "Tell me what was happening at the exact moment you first had this thought of leaving."

- Were they in conflict with another ensemble member?
- Were they working on a scene that raised personal issues?
- Did they make a risky choice that they felt was rejected by their partner?
- Were they observing a terrific exchange that a favorite "playmate" in the ensemble was having with a "rival?"

Help them identify what was happening in that precise moment and you have a greater chance of guiding them to a "Eureka" moment. In group work, so much is happening so quickly, there's no time to analyze (nor should we, *in the moment*). After a troubling experience, a person can be left only with the sense that they don't feel good about something. And they can be reluctant to examine it too deeply, because they fear losing the magic if they analyze too much.

If you discover that their thought of quitting occurred during a moment of personal jealousy or frustration, help them learn not to throw the baby out with the bathwater. If the "quitting thought" happened during a personally challenging moment, try to track the breakthroughs they were having, or were about to have. If you believe that they're abandoning ship just because the waves are getting higher, *tell* them that. If you hear that they don't trust them*selves* (vs. not trusting the *ensemble*), *tell* them, and help them understand the difference. Here are some questions to ask:

- "What initially drew you to this ensemble?" and "Why do you want to be here?" Get them to re-examine their original reasons and to be specific about what's changed.
- Do they still believe in the goal? If not, what has gotten in the way?
- Do they feel that the goal itself has changed (you may have some soul searching of your own to do)? If so, at what moment did they first have that thought (see previous note)? The bigger question is: has the ensemble changed or have they changed?
- Have they lost their way in pursuing the goal or do they only *feel* as if they have?
- Do they feel the ensemble is growing faster than they believe they are and rather than risk the embarrassment of being the one who "holds everyone back," do they imagine they're throwing themselves on their sword for the good of the group?

If their commitment to the goal is strong and they *want* to stay, but worry that their staying will harm the ensemble, then guide them through the definition of what ensemble *is*. It's often as simple as this:

"Are you aware when a fellow ensemble member is struggling?"
"Oh yes! We've gotten so close, we know right away if someone needs help."

"What do you do when someone is struggling?"

"I help them any way I can, I support them."

"How does that make you feel?"

"I feel really honored that they trusted me with what they were struggling with, and trusted me enough to let me *help* them."

"And ... "

Pause. Change of facial expression.

"Oh."

Note: this line of questioning reveals a weird insecurity we sometimes encounter. We feel as if there are limited I-Need-Help Dollars in the bank, and we need to save them all for a rainy day – even when it's pouring buckets outside. So we don't ask for help. Because we might need these Dollars for a time when we *really* need help. Guess what: if you're thinking about quitting an ensemble that you care about, it's raining ...

Ask, "Have you had any conflicts with other members?" Sometimes a single cruel remark can put a person into a tailspin that they can't get out of. (As playwright Meron Langsner writes in *Lying Makes Me Feel Like a God*, "My words affect people, and people *act* on people.") Help them discover why the words held so much power and determine if the remark was part of a pattern or a single event. If a single event, ask if they're willing to give up the ensemble for a single moment of bad judgment on the other person's part. That might lead to a larger discussion of *why* they're willing to give up something they care about. Is there an unhealthy competition between them and the one they're in conflict with? Were they romantically involved and now it's over?

If they would prefer to remain in the ensemble, but feel they can't stay because of the other person, having the above information will guide you to solutions for the ensemble itself. Tell them, "It stops here and now. The ensemble is not your personal boxing ring." You can use the information to be aware of when the conflict is flaring up and redirect the energy.

### When to encourage them to stay

Often, someone considers quitting just when things are getting good. Someone wants to leave a show, a class, or a company at the very moment they're making real breakthroughs, because they're afraid to let go of the safe and familiar ways of doing things. We all resist a little when asked to give up something that makes us feel more secure, whether it's our old teddy bear or a habitual way of protecting ourselves. To make room for the greater risks that ensemble requires, some things need to go. This is pure physics: something new can't occupy a space that's already filled with something else.

The most common reason for someone wanting to quit is because they're asked to let go of something (whether literally or figuratively). They may resent the ensemble for making them realize that their old habits aren't working anymore. They may resent you because you've been encouraging discoveries that they would rather leave in their psychic basement. Or they may realize what's needed, but doubt their ability to ever be able to break through.

Most of the time, talking it through helps them discover how much they *do* care. By offering guidance on actions they can take, you are in a sense talking them into staying in the ensemble. However, it's important that they understand that they *can* leave, at any time. But don't let them leave without understanding *why*, or without them taking responsibility *for* those reasons. If they agree to try your suggestions before making a final decision, give them a clear time frame. For example, "Try what I'm suggesting until next Monday. If you feel the same way, I'll help you transition out of the group and with whatever you may need." A clear deadline helps them feel safer to try things. Knowing where the Exit is in case of emergency can provide for more confidence building than we may realize.

If after making every effort, the person still feels that this ensemble is not "my tribe," then be a good leader and help them *find* their tribe. However, if their choice is to remain in the current ensemble, you'll need to step up the guidance. Remind them of their responsibility to serve this ensemble's goal, not to try to change it into something it's not. This is probably the greatest challenge of all, because what you're really asking them to do is to *accept who they are.*

### *When to let them go*

We felt everyone's collective gut wrench of recognition and pain even as we wrote that sentence. It's one of the hardest things for you to decide, and to do. We're not helping anyone by talking them into staying if they really shouldn't be in the ensemble, especially the ensemble itself.

Let them go if they've outgrown the ensemble or their interests have changed and they can no longer commit to the goal. People evolve, grow, and continue to make discoveries about themselves and their creative process. They may have been a good fit for the ensemble at the beginning, but have since found something else they're more passionate about.

Listen carefully to their response to, "Do you want to be here?" It will give you everything you need. They may breathe a sigh of relief that you asked so they didn't have to *quit.* They may have felt it was egotistical to say, "I've grown as much as I can here and I need to move on." They may have felt that they're somehow betraying the ensemble members because they've developed new interests. By asking the direct question, you're not firing them, and they're not quitting either. You're working on a mutual decision for them to move on. It may be a sad decision, but ultimately positive for everybody. And if you're feeling bad about it, remember that you're not rejecting them, you're redirecting them.

Now: try not to take a departure personally (we know, good luck with that), but remember, it's not about you. Finding your tribe is a lifelong experience for everyone. As we discussed in Chapter 2, we're born into a tribe and we belong to many different tribes in our lifetime. This search, discovery, bonding, and parting can be fraught with personal issues. Loyalty is declared and personal commitment is invested. When we find our tribe, we say, "I know who I am now. Everything makes sense." However, sometimes we either outgrow the tribe or realize we joined simply because we were welcome and fit in – at the time.

### *If they (or you) realize they joined for the wrong reasons*

An ensemble member might be playing out an old psychodrama that was written long before the rest of you came into their lives. The "play" is reaching its usual conflict and you're about to find yourself in a role you didn't even know you were cast in (father, mother, former teacher, etc.). This psychological minefield is dangerous territory. Remember Chapter 3: it isn't your job to heal them. However, it *is* your job to require everyone to take responsibility for themselves, the goal, and the ensemble, and to help them leave if it's the right decision. If they've been using the ensemble as a surrogate for something else in their lives, help them find what they really need. Again: *it is not your job to heal them.* Please, say that five times or until you quiet the voice that says "But I *have* healed someone in the past" (luck) or "But I can't just let them be in pain" (recommend a doctor). You aren't trained for that and you may do more harm than good if you try.

### Tell them to go if they're an Ensemble Killer (see Chapter 5)

The most common case for ensemble killing is when an ensemble knows there is a prescribed ending, such as a class that will graduate. The Ensemble Killer begins to destroy things so that the goodbyes won't be as painful. They start the separation process early, so that there isn't an ensemble left to mourn. Please look back to Chapter 3 for times when the Ensemble Killer may be you: "I created it, I can destroy it."

### Rose

When I first started teaching, if an Ensemble Killer walked into my office and told me they wanted to leave, I stupidly talked them into staying, thinking all they needed was more confidence. They did even *more* damage thereafter, because they felt empowered ("they can't live without me"). It infuriated the ensemble and I realized too late that I had let *them* down. The ensemble re-formed into one against a common enemy: the Ensemble Killer, and me as a distant second. But, I had to acknowledge that I made the enemy list, and that I deserved to be there!

One Ensemble Killer had students flooding my office: "He never shows up for rehearsals," etc. When I removed him from the program and announced it, astonishingly, a wave of sympathy came over everyone. "Oh gosh, I didn't *really* think he'd get kicked out – what will he do now? He's such a lost soul … " I couldn't believe it. I did a lot of group work that day to help them experience what the ensemble could be without the Ensemble Killer. It allowed them to mourn the loss of what he had initially contributed, and helped them realize that his absence made them feel safe to take risks again. No one was making judgmental comments about their work anymore. They trusted those who *were* in the room and they discovered how much they had been holding back because of the Ensemble Killer.

If you're an early career ensemble leader, time and practice will give you confidence in making these decisions. And Ensemble Killers are Master Blamers, do *not* let them make you or the ensemble responsible for their *ir*responsibility. When I was recently reminiscing with an alum, she asked, "Why did you let that guy *stay*? You gave him more lives than a cat." I said it was because I couldn't bring myself to take away what I *thought* would be his last straw. The alum laughed and said, "Are you kidding? He's performing Off Broadway right now!"

The last time an Ensemble Killer walked into my office and announced, "I'm thinking of leaving the program," I said, "That's great! *I* was just about to call *you*. You haven't addressed the issues we've previously discussed, you're not meeting your academic responsibilities, and I know you're capable of so much more. Clearly you're unhappy here, but I'm sure you'll thrive somewhere else. Would you like to speak to your classmates first or shall I handle it for you?" They were stunned; their ego (which had wanted to be begged to stay) was deflated and they asked me to speak to the class on their behalf. The remaining students celebrated: not because they disliked the Ensemble Killer as a person, but because the Killer had selfishly sucked the energy out of the room: a classic Black Hole.

### If the ensemble itself should end

Theatre companies, improv groups, and long-running private classes can be faced with the frightening question, "Should it end?" Those of you asking yourselves this question about your own ensemble, we heard your stomach flip over. There's *so* much personal and psychological investment tied to this answer. We fear there is failure in endings (not necessarily), we fear that all life forms should live forever (they can't), we worry that we've somehow not done our best if an ensemble reaches a natural conclusion (that's up to you). How can we evaluate if the ensemble has evolved as far as it can? How do we recognize the difference between evolution and extinction? Is it time to evolve further or time to allow it to die so it can be reborn in some other form? The same skills you use to observe individual behavior will help you decide if it's time to allow this particular ensemble to shuffle off this mortal coil. Just as important as nurturing an ensemble, guiding it to its end is an action that you must take with the full participation of the ensemble. There's a reason that couples going through divorce continue to see a counselor; it helps everyone understand *why* it's ending and how to strengthen chances for positive relationships for the future. And in many cases, it salvages the good things that brought those people together in the first place. Ever stay in a relationship too long?

Sometimes the simplest life forms have the longest life (relatively speaking). We all go through times when we want a particular collaboration to last forever. This is a beautiful response to a creative experience that fulfills us artistically, personally, and psychically. If the goals are clear, the structure sets us free and keeps us healthy for a long time. However, as long as that ensemble thrives (or at least remains functioning) we can't begin anything new. We tend to lose sight of the fact that by denying an inevitable or necessary end, we're preventing something new from coming into being. Fighting the inevitable can harm the good that was created by the ensemble (and may contribute to one of those awful endings that you talk about someday over pints of Guinness). We fight the natural order and we fight to keep something alive that others may want to let go. Loyalty is something that is passionately stirred in ensemble; it's to be treasured, and never taken for granted. Along with the mantra "there is no failure in death," we should also remember "there is no disloyalty in moving on." We're asked to truthfully create the life force and human nature in artistic creations. Nature's most powerful force following birth is certainly death. Productions close, students graduate, storytellers say "the end." Why should ensembles be exempt?

### Sudden death of an ensemble

Sometimes circumstances beyond anyone's control can herald the end for an ensemble. Economic woes may force you to close your doors.

### Rose

I was invited to direct for a repertory theatre company about a year before they ended their thirty-five-year existence. Some company members had been with them for decades. Though they fought valiantly to stay afloat, their crushing debt was too much. Everyone in the ensemble knew it was the end, they *knew* they were dying, but management denied it. They made promises that the ensemble knew couldn't be kept and made decisions that fractured what had been a dedicated company. The artistic director resigned, actors were told that they had to re-audition for their long-held jobs, and some board members tried to salvage the good while others tried to press personal agendas. It was incredibly painful to witness. Had the leadership simply brought the ensemble together and said, "We've done our best, but we're ending. There is no failure in death," the company would have had the dignified wake and funeral it so richly deserved. By focusing on everything except the actual goals of the ensemble, the management left a wake of broken hearts and bad feelings. If you find yourself in economic straits and the end is nigh, trust us: everyone knows. The ensemble only wants the truth and for you all to come together one more time so you can end with dignity.

### *Sudden death of a founder, leader, or teacher*

Sometimes an ensemble's identity is so connected to the values or identity of their leader that the sudden loss of that leader means the ensemble should end. It may be a production that a director had a specific personal vision for, or an improv group or class that was led by someone with specific methods. When the leader's identity is so linked to the ensemble's identity, it's better to end that ensemble and create something new. Starting from scratch may seem impractical in the moment, but the ensemble will thrive more in the long run.

## Ensembles with specific needs

Everything in this chapter is applicable to all forms of ensembles: no matter if the ensemble is a seasoned group of Equity actors or a class of teenagers creating devised theatre for at-risk kids in their school district. Some dynamics are universal. A friend who practiced tenant law in New York City once said: "Landlord's attorneys are the same kids who broke your crayons in kindergarten." Lateness, withholding, it can happen in any setting; however, certain behaviors are found in some settings more often than others. Let's look at the actions you can take to ensure the health and wellbeing of ensembles in the classroom, in production, improvisation groups, or a theatre company.

### *Caring for and maintaining classroom ensembles*

Some programs are purposely structured to accept a greater number of students than they can accommodate and at the end of the first year, they "cull" the herd. Your school might believe that students will benefit from these heightened stakes.

While that may be possible, it might also have devastating effects on your ability to care for and maintain your ensembles. An anxiety-ridden, competitive environment can displace a student's focus. "Will a full year of my education (and my parents money) be for naught?" The pressure of knowing that some members of their ensemble will inevitably be cut may serve to focus some individuals, but they will be precisely that: focused *individuals*, or worse, *competitors*. While Rose was still an adjunct at Brooklyn College, a culling process was in place; BFA students could be culled one year, and sometimes *two* years, into their training. Their level of anxiety was maddening. Each year when that "evaluation audition" came round, she saw fear, fights, and even physical illness. When she was hired full time, her first action was to change the BFA structure to institute regular evaluations and a structured probation system if warranted. As long as students were successfully meeting their academic and artistic responsibilities, there would be no culling process. The atmosphere in the classrooms changed immediately; with the anxiety gone, students collaborated more, worked *harder*, and grew together with confidence.

If you don't have a culling process, then we're sure you have strict academic and artistic requirements and that you have a process for probation and expulsion. You may have a student who isn't ready for this high level of work: they could be a double major torn between two loves, or they may be trying to major in partying. If after a series of meetings that involve guidance and goal setting, you find it still isn't working, you may have to suspend them. The class ensemble has to reconstitute itself while moving forward in their training, and several things could happen:

Pros:

The class recognizes the problem student long before you do. They see them in social settings and they experience the "uncensored" version of things. If they're a cohort class, they're also in every class with them instead of the one class that *you* might be experiencing the behavior in. Most of the time, the ensemble wholeheartedly supports the decision to expel the student. The remaining ensemble benefits from:

- seeing that you're willing to protect the work
- knowing that their work and commitment has been respected and acknowledged
- knowing that you're willing to make hard decisions to keep the ensemble strong
- being able to take risks again in an environment that is safer and everyone is committed.

Cons:

The ensemble might feel sympathy for the exiting student. They might ask you to give them one more chance, even if they've complained bitterly about them in the past. Tell them sensitively, but clearly, why the student was asked to leave (without sharing confidential details of course). Keep it simple: "Troy was struggling to meet the challenges of the program and we mutually decided he would benefit from studying elsewhere." "Belinda was struggling with her ability to commit; we decided that she should take time off from school until she felt clearer about her choices." These statements are open but specific enough for the remaining students to understand the reasons why. Without having this information, they might:

- have increased anxiety, wondering if they're next on the chopping block
- start gossiping. Remember; storytellers *love* to create stories, especially juicy ones. And it takes their mind off their own anxiety
- rebel against you because they're feeling vulnerable. They remember that yes, this is an ensemble, but in a pinch, it's not a democracy either
- consciously/subconsciously start self-sabotaging in the belief that their success is somehow disloyal to the friend who was asked to leave.

Training theatre students in ensemble skills teaches them mutual respect and support, and gives them a healthy structure that they can strive to create in every future job. If you begin the process from the very first audition, you'll have a healthier ensemble and they will have a stronger education and job future. The student you remove will have the opportunity to find the ensemble that *is* right for them and you'll have given them important guidance on what they must work on to pursue their goals.

### *Most common reason for fractures in the class ensemble*

Dust-ups in the classroom are inevitable and they tend to start the minute students are permitted to participate in productions on campus. It's their first taste of "not everyone will receive the roles they want" or "not everyone will receive roles, period." This becomes an important early lesson in maintaining the integrity of the ensemble in the classroom. From the beginning, you need to stress that they're in training to obtain the skills necessary for a professional career in acting, they're not here just to perform. Productions exist to give them opportunities to *apply* their current skills, not to reward them for good behavior. The production structure itself conveys that each ensemble member has something unique that makes them appropriate for some roles, but not for others. At first, it's inevitable that a student actor feels disappointment at not being cast. Try to steer them in the direction of: "I'm learning what distinguishes me as an individual." Helping students identify what makes them the unique actor they are, while insisting that they maintain equality within the ensemble, can feel as if you're talking out of both sides of your mouth. How do they return to the ensemble each week where equality is stressed, when they feel they're being excluded from a production that should be the very definition of another ensemble?

We've all felt pangs watching students at the callboard when cast lists go up, wondering how the casting will affect the positive atmosphere in our classroom. It's a slow and sometimes painful process to get acting students to trust us during casting. Casting a young actor in a role they aren't ready for can be more harmful than *not* casting them. Remember, athletes in training are taken care of by their coaches and they're never sent in to play the game if they're not ready. They can be injured and ruin an otherwise successful future.

Having said that, there's a range of definitions for what a student *may* be "ready for." Everyone needs to be given an opportunity to apply their training in a production setting at some point. Otherwise, why were they accepted into your program? A student might lack some traits for what's required of a particular role; but they may have *some* of the ingredients needed. Sometimes you need to take a leap of faith and give them the opportunity, and support them so that they'll grow. You accepted that student for a reason and your responsibility as their teacher is to train them, including in the productions.

These can be challenging conversations to have with your fellow teachers and directors, and mutual support of your mission is key. You're an educational institution that also produces shows. Do you consider yourself a learning institution that uses a model of a professional theatre company? Or are you a program or department that presses for the highest quality always, even if it means occasionally sacrificing educational opportunities for students? Is it educational goals, or ticket sales and reviews that drive your productions? Your ensemble of faculty will need to clarify the relationship of productions to your mission. As we touched on in Chapter 3, ask yourselves some tough questions about your own motives in working with the ensemble. Are you part of a faculty, but what you really wanted was a career in professional theatre? Are you committed to educational goals, or are you trying to create the acting/directing career you actually wanted but in the academic setting?

If your school includes productions, then the casting process is invariably going to create bumps in the class ensemble. To ensure that this process honors the ensemble and the academic goals, use the following actions to preserve that group bond and strengthen their focus on academic goals during the production process.

### *Before the audition*

Clarify audition requirements and review all audition monologues in advance. If you work with every student using the same criteria, you give them equal preparation and ensure the equality promised by the ensemble itself. Working from established criteria creates clarity on casting results and helps eliminate potentially bone-headed speculation on casting decisions. For example, "He stole my monologue!" or "She got more time with the directors 'cause her monologue ran over time!" Few things ignite our "Protect the Ensemble" genes more than hearing the words "my" and "she/he" instead of the person's name being used. You can hear the fissures of division cracking and spreading like the San Andreas Fault. Use the following to establish consistent criteria:

- Is the monologue appropriate for this student at this moment in their development? Is it age appropriate, a role they would reasonably be cast in? Do the character's traits connect to what this actor can uniquely bring forward?

    A word about age appropriate monologues. We understand that many teachers see the value of having students tackle monologues such as Rose from *Fences* or Willy Loman from *Death of a Salesman*. In some classroom exercises, there is value in exploring the language and emotional world of these rich characters. However, in an audition, it sets the student up for failure. They can't possibly know the emotional complexities of a person more than ten years older than themselves; why risk that they'll be focused on convincing the director that they can "be" this 40-year old person vs. allowing their energy to be devoted to action and objective? There are many rich characters written for 18–25 year olds; they're out there and worth the effort to locate. Examine the qualities that first drew the student to the older character, and translate that to a character closer to who they are.

- Don't permit a "recycled" monologue. Actors (especially those in training) grow and evolve, and something that was a good fit six months ago may not be now. More important, when they last worked on this piece their abilities were at another stage of development; they've moved away from those prior bad habits. Why work on a piece that could tempt those bad habits forward?

- Is another student already working on this monologue? Make every effort to avoid duplicates within the class. It can foster unhealthy competition and anxiety.

- Don't permit them to do a monologue from the play they're auditioning for, unless requested by the director.

- Is the action of the monologue clear? For younger actors, err on the side of monologues with strong objectives instead of narrative memory pieces.

- Does the monologue meet the time requirement? New York actor and acting coach Patricia Randell has a 30-second rule: give them 30 seconds less than what they ask for. It's a genius rule and directors will love you for it.

- Does the monologue have a clear listener? If not, help the student choose a specific one. Don't let them settle for, "I'm talking to a friend." Best friend? New friend who you're confessing this to? Specifics, specifics, specifics.

- Have them answer The Passover Question: why is this night different from every other night? Why must this character say these words at this moment in time to this listener?

- Does the monologue give them opportunity to create a clear physical life for the character?

- Do they *like* the monologue? Are they excited by the prospect of tackling it?

These criteria (or additional ideas and structures of your choosing) will get everyone on the same page and will ensure that they are collectively as prepared as possible. They won't avoid disappointment in casting, but they will create conditions that will prevent that disappointment from being turned against the ensemble.

### *After cast lists are posted*

If you've prepared your students using these guidelines, they'll take greater responsibility for their audition and even their education. If they take responsibility and acknowledge the equality of the preparation time, they're on their way to being prepared to accept the results. Preparing together gives everyone the opportunity to be mutually supportive of one another, which will help everyone do their best work at the auditions.

So the results are in: some people are happy, some are despondent. They might agree with the casting and may simply need time to work through their disappointment. They might be disappointed in themselves for not preparing enough. (Another good reason to give everyone equal guidance for their preparation. There's nobody for them to look at but themselves.) After the lists go up:

- If everyone in class has been cast, simply say, "Congratulations to everyone on a job well done." And then get right to work. Don't use class time to discuss specifics of casting. It can dilute the message of the training being the priority over production.
- If you attended the auditions, require every student to meet with you privately for audition notes. Specifically relate those notes to the classroom training and give them goals to work on for next time.
- Whether students were cast or not, speak to the director(s) and get feedback about their callbacks. This keeps you informed as to how they're applying classroom work.
- Don't permit teasing about casting, pro or con, in the classroom. A student cast as the guard in *The Crucible* might have coveted the role of John Proctor. If you overhear him saying to the actor who *is* Proctor, "You might be the star, but I get to bring you to the gallows and watch you die!" stop them. We know there's a lot of good-natured razzing that goes on, but have them do it on their own time. Likewise, don't allow comments in the classroom seemingly filled with praise. "Wow! You're playing Savage? That's the role of a lifetime! You're going to be incredible!" Though meant as praise, this can be just as divisive as negative remarks. The actor cast as Savage may be feeling guilty about getting a coveted role that seemingly sets them apart from the ensemble, or they might be feeling nervous about the undertaking. What if a student is cast in an iconic role, such as Hamlet or Medea, and they're freaking out about the inevitable comparisons? Neither teasing nor praise will help. The class needs to win and lose as a team. Encourage individual achievement in the context of the class work, but step very carefully about permitting individual public praise or teasing where casting is concerned.

- Bring in some group work after cast lists have been posted. Make the exercises fun, challenging, and ones that will reinforce the bonds. Make certain they're specific to the material you're working on vs. obvious "let's get happy" exercises. Trust us, they'll know the difference. Nothing takes a young actor's mind off of disappointment like the thrill of discovering something new with the support of the ensemble. Even if an actor wants to be left alone, require them to engage in the work and with each other. Trust that you're giving them an invaluable lesson about acceptance and not allowing disappointment to interfere with their work.
- Don't console someone who may express their disappointment to you. Consolation implies that there was an individual prize that should have been theirs. Support acknowledges their feelings and gives them guidance toward the primary goals of commitment to themselves, their education, and the ensemble. You're not helping by agreeing with them that they were "ripped off." Even if they were.
- Make sure that your personal opinion of how the casting should have gone doesn't color the ensemble. Period.
- If *you* are the director and you've cast some people from your class and not others, be sensitive to speaking about rehearsals while in the classroom. Exception: if students are cast in different productions that semester and you're discussing overall examples of how they're applying a particular lesson to building their character in production.

### *Caring for and maintaining ensemble in production*

By their very nature, rehearsals and production tend not to last long enough for ensemble problems to occur on a regular basis. If you've cast well, followed the suggestions we made in Chapter 4, problems will be rare. Seriously, when you're out with friends, don't you often find yourselves talking about great ensembles you've worked with in productions? Devoting time for ensemble-building within a rehearsal schedule has never failed to make a stronger cast, or a stronger story. The following suggestions will maintain and enhance those ensemble bonds to make for a better party. That is, production.

- Begin each rehearsal with a unifying warm up, something that allows everyone to work through, or set aside all that their day has been, up to now. It's amazing how often a crappy rehearsal is simply the effect of real life intruding. Either through a regular rehearsal ritual or warm-up, give actors the chance to let go of the stalled subway car or the fight with the landlord. Creativity doesn't have an on/off switch, so have realistic expectations that there is always something you can do to change the energy in the room.
- Bring in a specific exercise that helps the actors get to where they need to be for that specific rehearsal. When Rose was rehearsing *Take Me Out* by Richard Greenberg, on nights when she rehearsed the baseball game scenes,

the ensemble played several rounds of "Capture the Flag" as a warm-up (see Appendix K). The play demands actors be believable not only as seasoned baseball players, but as a successful professional *team*. The exercise was physically demanding and required them to physically challenge one another while continuing to *support* their "guy" who was "up" in each go-round. Doing this exercise immediately got the actors into the spirit and mindset needed, and helped them drop into the bodies of athletes while reaffirming their connection as a team. Design an exercise that will help the actors explore the specific needs of the scenes you're rehearsing as a group. You'll gain more ground than if you'd done a straight text rehearsal.

- Set aside time for specific, structured character work, allowing the characters to interact "off script." This gives actors the opportunity to connect with each other's characters away from the structure of the play and helps them flesh out character relationships and traits that the script may not give ample information about. Psychologically, non-text character work also emphasizes that everyone's role in the story is essential to the telling of *that story*. Focusing on character work in the ensemble framework will help actors keep their character alive and reinforce the need for every single character's piece of that story.

### Rose

When I was directing a production of *The Crucible*, I conducted an exercise called Circle Cross (see Appendix M). The structure frees the characters to express things that are beyond the text, deepens relationships, and demands a trust within the ensemble itself (as fairly risky things can be said between characters). It give characters an opportunity to say something to another that isn't found in the text and allows them to speak to a character they might not be in a scene with.

The most moving moment came when the actor playing Francis Nurse called in Rebecca Nurse. If you haven't read *The Crucible* in a while, we see scenes where Francis is fighting for his wife's life, we see Rebecca accepting her fate while with other characters; but they're never *together* in a scene. The actor playing Francis called the actress playing Rebecca into the circle. They stood for a moment, and it wasn't until then that we all realized, "Oh man, this is the first time they've been together." They looked at each other for several moments and Francis said, "I love you." They started crying, we all started crying, and they exchanged places in the circle. Though the tragedy of Rebecca and Francis Nurse is a sub-sub plot in *The Crucible*, if you ask any of our cast members today about their experience, they'll all remember that as a defining moment in our journey. It reinforced that the story belonged to *every* character, and to the ensemble.

- Set aside a discussion night several weeks into the rehearsal, even if you feel everything is being covered during rehearsals. After you've reached the point of a first stumble-through or run-through, give the actors time to share discoveries about the play, characters, relationships, and larger themes of the story. Even when we've answered the question of "why am I telling this story at this moment in my life?" we find that after several weeks of rehearsals, a light bulb goes off and we shout, "OH!! *That's* why I'm telling this story." We discover things through and with each other.
- If during a rehearsal, a "sidebar" conversation begins, take a moment to consider its value before saying, "OK, back to work." Are they talking about a current event that connects to the material itself? Are they new to each other and simply shooting the breeze for a moment in the way that people just getting acquainted at a party might do? Consider that by allowing seemingly "non-relevant" discussions to happen, you may actually be deepening the bonds of ensemble, or gaining ground in the understanding of the relationships or story itself. Many side conversations are not only useful, but can strengthen the work. Allow that five-minute "sidetrack" and you could cover more ground in the rehearsal itself.

### Caring for and maintaining ensemble in theatre companies (including improv groups)

Theatre companies are created in many different ways and their journey can determine the special considerations you should have for their health. Many are created by students graduating from a school or people who clicked when they met through a workshop or production. Many companies begin with people who already have established friendships. And even if they haven't begun as friends, after working together for a while in a theatre company structure, friendships are quickly formed. This is a good thing; they have a shorthand together, they have knowledge and respect for one another, and they've already collaborated, so they know a thing or two about each other's work habits.

However.

When bumps appear such as artistic differences or financial challenges, what happens when friends disagree about solutions? It's one thing to disagree in daily life ("Hey Roger, you wanna go see the new Matt Damon movie?" "Sounds like punishment to me"). When friends are working together, the stakes are higher and the bumps can get complicated. Established theatre companies take on a family feel more than a class or a single production. There is a depth of investment and commitment that runs deeper over time. So when you need to make practical decisions, how do you care for and maintain both the company and your personal relationships? Remember, your theatre company ensemble is being created from your ensemble of friends and each ensemble has a completely different objective. For the health of your company and your friendships, consider the following:

- In all company matters, the goals of the theatre company ensemble take precedence over the goals of the friendship ensemble.
- You're directing the next production and your best friend Terry covets the lead role. Terry isn't right for the role; someone else in the company *is*. Trust that she'll understand. If she asks you about it, keep the conversation professional, and no matter what, *don't apologize for not casting her.* You can be sorry she's hurting, but not for making the right choice.
- You're the artistic director and your best friend/company member has brought you their new script to consider for production. You read early drafts, you've already told them you love it. The managing director reads it and tells you it's too expensive to produce. You look at every angle to bring down production costs, but it simply isn't affordable. Don't be tempted.
- Resist being over-protective of the company ensemble; new blood is not only good, but also necessary from time to time.
- A new member has joined; at a company meeting, they raise the point that the system used for tracking audience responses is woefully out of date. They suggest dynamic new technology that will be invaluable to your fundraising efforts. You created the old system. Don't get defensive. The new member is trying to make a positive contribution to the future of the company; celebrate that.
- Don't take change personally.
- The membership decides that given the current economic climate, this would be an ideal time to sell your building (which you own free and clear), and use the profit to purchase a smaller space, and invest in a more secure financial future. This is the only home the company has ever known; you were on the committee that secured financing to make the initial purchase. Your gut reaction is that the company wants to throw away its past. It doesn't; it wants to create a better future. Change can feel like a rejection of what you've done before. Remember, it's not about you.
- Stay open to company members taking occasional departures from the group.
- Another company is doing a production that has a terrific role for Ed. He auditions, gets the role, and can't audition for your company's production. You feel a little betrayed. This is your fear talking; you're afraid Ed will like the other company better and won't return. Keep it positive; he'll return with new ideas, he may not have had the chance to do this kind of role in your company, and he'll return satisfied and fulfilled. He's also building goodwill between artistic organizations.

Rose's first introduction to Synergy Ensemble Theatre was actually being taken to *another* company's production. She had wanted to meet some of the membership before holding auditions for a production of *Fool for Love* that she'd been hired to direct. She was taken to see a different company's production that featured several Synergists. After the show, she learned that Synergy fully supported members performing, designing, and stage managing for other theatre companies. They believed that this created an influx of new ideas, kept everyone working more, and created "good neighbors" between arts organizations potentially competing for the same audience pool.

- Be patient with the differences in everyone's personal processes. Long-established companies who enjoy an almost psychic form of communication in the ensemble can sometimes be impatient with individuals who are struggling ("You're slowing us down, man!"). Redirect that energy: ask the ensemble to make a gift of their strengths to the one who's struggling, because their time will come. Never leave a man behind, no matter how good it feels to be sprinting ahead.

## Conclusion

This chapter has been a bit like an all-night party that nobody wants to leave. The more we wrote, the more we realized we had to say. Like when you look up at the clock and see it's 2:00 A.M. and the subway ride is going to be awful anyway, so why not tell one more story before calling it a night? Then you all have some more fun, realize it's 4:00 A.M., and as it gets closer to dawn you say, "What the hell, it's almost light. Why not stay?" So, this chapter has been about cleaning up the bottles, making sure the birthday cake stays hidden until the appropriate time, and perishable food gets wrapped and put back in the fridge after everyone's eaten. It's been a great party; and what's the last thing we do before we leave? We ask the host(s) for their recipes ...

# 7

# ENSEMBLE MAKING: SPECIFIC RECIPES

## How to get cookin' for future parties

So, we've spent most of the night talking about the important ingredients: identifying goals, creating a supportive atmosphere, listening, recognizing and redirecting behaviors, knowing why you're in the room, asking what the ensemble needs, and more. Now, let's look at how to bring these ingredients together and adapt them for different kinds of parties. Here are some of our favorite recipes:

## Recipe 1: joining an ensemble

### *You've been hired as artistic director of an existing company*

You've read a lot in these pages about creating and maintaining new ensembles. What about when you're invited to join and *lead* an existing one? The party has been in session for a while; you know about it, you understand its purpose, but you don't know anything about the dynamics that hold the guests together (or may be driving them apart). Think about creating ensemble in *reverse*: you need to find out what kind of party it is (or what kind they want it to be), who is already at the party, if the guests are having a good time or not and *why*, what's needed to make it a better party, and then, what you can do to make that happen. Here's our recipe:

- Get a copy of the company's mission statement and any grants that define the company's identity and stated artistic focus. Check when it was written, if the authors were company members or independent hires.
- Meet with board members, staff (including volunteers), and performance company; separately for first meetings. Ask how long they've been together and what their understanding of the company's mission is. Those who perform in the shows may have differing perceptions from those who market and budget the shows. Ask about recent production experiences; how do they feel the plays connect to their understanding of the company's mission? What do they feel their roles are within the *company* (not the actual plays, if an actor is responding)? Tell everyone what drew *you* to want to work with *them*, and

what your current understanding is of the company and its mission. Be sure to tell them that, as the new person, you're relying on them for guidance. Though this might seem obvious, stating it out loud is a reassuring commitment from you to this ensemble.

After you've gathered this information and given yourself time to digest it, this would be the time to hold a full company meeting at which you ask:

Does everyone support the stated mission of the company?

Misunderstandings about the company's mission, or *competing versions* of that mission, are two of the most common problems behind troubled companies. Your job is to unite everyone through a common vision so that all members in all departments (administration, production, artistic areas) can mutually support one another and be able to articulate the mission through word and deed. If you discover significant discrepancies in the collective understanding of the mission, ask the following:

- How long ago was the mission statement written? Does it need to be re-defined to suit a cohesive vision that has organically evolved through the years? Has the company evolved to something different?
- Do the differences break down across artistic and administrative lines? Are the acting company, the technical staff, and the production staff clear on the company's mission, but the administrators not? How often has the administrative staff been asked to observe rehearsals (we assume they attend all productions)? Have they become disconnected from the creative process and its relationship to the mission? If so, this can have several detrimental effects:
    - The administrative staff is marketing, promoting, writing grants, and developing audiences based on incomplete or incorrect information as to the company's creative output. This can have a profound impact on audience expectations and on grants (what we say we do vs. what the funder finds you *actually* do).
    - If the administrative staff is unaware of the wonderful artistry that makes this company unique, then whatever makes this company special isn't being presented to prospective funders or audience.
- Did your predecessor make changes to the artistic mission, but fail to formally rewrite the company's documentation?
- Were you hired precisely *because* your predecessor was taking the company in a direction it didn't want to go, and confusion remains?
- Did the company drift from the mission because of personal problems with your predecessor? The message and the messenger may have become entwined. The company may still be committed to the party, but has lost trust in the host and wants someone new who will make sure that the bachelor

party doesn't become a baby shower. Given the chance, most folks are more than happy to talk about problems when the person is no longer in the room. However, don't allow the company meeting to descend into a "bitch session" against your predecessor. There is value in allowing a company to let off steam, to a point. Be ready to redirect the energy from what has happened, to what *can* happen now.

• Conversely, were you hired precisely because the company was evolving, but your predecessor wanted to adhere to the original model?

This is the time to either reaffirm the company's original mission or commit to a new direction for the future. For example, what if, when the company started ten years ago, the original mission was to create artistic opportunities for an underserved community, but now that community is thriving with numerous artistic institutions? Does the company want to identify another underserved community? Do they want to stay in this now thriving area, but focus on developing new plays? If you find that everyone is in agreement with the mission, or once you have created or reaffirmed the mission statement, the next step of this recipe might read, "stir well." That is, start to create ensemble dialogs that will support the goal and the ensemble itself. Ask:

What do you feel your role is in the company? What do you feel you contribute to its success?

We don't mean, "I'm the publicity director"; that's their title. As a member of this ensemble, how do they practice the company's mission for themselves? For instance, Lisa may be the marketing associate for Rattlestick Theater Company; their mission is to develop new playwrights and plays that are deemed too risky for other companies to produce. She might say, "I write grants and create marketing materials to promote the company and its mission. I *personally* take risks in my own work daily, believe my choices support the company's mission, strengthen it by living that purpose in my work, and hopefully inspire my fellow ensemble members." Can a company member be fully committed if they're not "walking the walk?" Everyone will become more deeply invested in the mission, and in the company, by examining and articulating their roles within the ensemble. It also gives *you* the opportunity to identify who on your administrative or artistic staff is your Sparkplug, your Glue, your Rock, or your Rebel.

And though this may seem like an obvious question, do *not* end the meeting before asking:

Do you all know what every company member here *does*?

Invite actors to spend time in the administrative offices; let them watch folks create publicity materials, or spitball ideas about audience development. Do the actors know how many hours of phone calls, discussions, and Internet searches go into creating a single press release? Invite the administrative staff to sit in on rehearsals; let them watch the actors break down a moment, or repeat a confrontation scene three times to discover the stakes. Does the head of box office know how many hours of rehearsal go into ten minutes of a production?

The responses to these questions will help you develop your plan of action. A few additional questions you may want to tuck away for yourself for future care and maintenance include:

- Did they feel abandoned by your predecessor? That is, what might you have inherited that doesn't belong to you?
- Was your predecessor the creator of the company? Did the ensemble come together specifically because of that person?
- Did the ensemble unite to rebel against your predecessor? If so, why?
- Do ensemble members get time off from one another? Do acting company members come and go?
- What's the identity of the acting ensemble itself? Are they like a big Italian family in that they know how to fight big, but how to love even more? Are they a company of misfits, accepting of everyone?
- Is the company what David calls a "Successful Ensemble, Plus One?" That is, a great ensemble and the Asshole? Despite the difficulties Assholes can create, this group accepts them, embraces them, and likely finds them amusing on most days. You'll need to decide whether you try to change their dynamic or if you let sleeping dogs lie.
- This will be unpleasant, but: is there anyone you need to fire and replace? Is there an ugly drunk at this party who's been knocking over drinks and insulting people, but nobody wants to be the one to take away their keys and drive them home? Guess what – you've been hired to be the most sober person in the room. Make the necessary decision and keep the following in mind:
  - The ensemble might become afraid that they're next; then again they could be greatly relieved that the guy is gone. Listen carefully to everyone's responses.
  - When you hire the replacement, get the ensemble excited about the new blood coming in to pre-empt any fears of, "Uh-oh, she's firing us and bringing in her own people ... "

## Recipe 2: cultivating ensemble as an educator

### *Invited to teach a single course (any subject)*

The life of an adjunct lecturer is ridiculously challenging. In the current economic climate, more and more of us are hired to join and support existing ensembles within college or high school departments to which we have no solid ties. We have to learn each department's identity, goals, and how they play together (our friend Valerie calls this "commitment for hire").

You've been hired to host a party that others decided to throw and unless it's an advanced course, it's likely that neither you *nor* the party planners had anything to do with the guest list. People simply registered; total strangers are coming, and nobody has any idea what they might be bringing to the party.

Can you still apply ensemble principles in this strange setting? Of course. "But it's not an acting class," you say, "I'm teaching Intro to Theatre, it's a weekly lecture." Creating ensemble in a room where the desks are bolted to the floor may seem like a weird idea at first, but it works. Everyone's learning is enhanced through emphasizing the ensemble principle of committing to the goal through committing to each other (remember The Excruciating Five Minutes in Chapter 3?). You may still be saying, "Look, this doesn't apply to me. I can't collaborate with 100 people in a lecture hall. This class deals in absolutes. We don't collaborate on an answer – there *is* an answer. Shakespeare will always die in 1616."

True. But you *can* collaborate on how everyone learns the material together. You *can* create a collaborative process that supports deeper ownership of the learning, and supports each student's ownership of their personal learning process. The more open-minded each individual student is to the group, the more likely they are to commit to the goal, feel responsibility toward others, and learn from others. Does that take more time? Sure. Is it worth it? Always.

### Before you enter the classroom

Review the questions and principles posed in Chapters 3 and 4 and apply them here.

- What makes you the unique instructor that you are? What's your personal investment in the goal? Are you willing to show how much you care and are willing to invest?
- What is the goal of this party? What's their mission?
- Who is expected at the party? If it's a class for majors, can the head of the program give you preliminary information about the students enrolled and what their needs are? If it's a class for non-majors, can the department chair find out what types of majors have traditionally enrolled? This helps you with planning: e.g., if creating team projects, do you have some business majors you can pair with communications majors?

Before you enter that classroom, the most important principle to remember from previous chapters is that you *need* something from them. That need is a giant step toward engaging them. Your goal is to get them to invest in their learning. Consider how an actor clarifies their objectives: make your goal *active*. "I want them to understand" or "I want to tell them" are passive objectives. "I want to *ignite* their curiosity" – now *that's* something you can sink your teeth into.

## Now *you enter the classroom*

- As you would at a first read-through (see Chapter 4), create a supportive atmosphere. Infuse the space with the energy you want it to have. Visit the room in advance to make sure it's clean, equipment works, etc. Talk to the students as they enter the room; don't wait until 9:20 on the dot to "begin" the class. Identify and articulate the goal together on that first day. Why did they register for this class? Be a good listener and observer.

- Ask, "What do you want from me?" It helps them understand and articulate what *their* role is in the learning process, what their responsibilities are to themselves and their education.

- Describe what excites you about the subject matter and why you want to work with them. Sharing your personal investment communicates that you're willing to go where you're asking *them* to go. It's a partnership.

- Refer to "Your opening remarks" in Chapter 4. Stress the importance of collaboration and mutual respect, and that you'll do everything in your power to create a safe and supportive environment for them, so they can do their best work and take risks in their learning. Define the rules and structure of the "world" of the class. What do *they* need to contribute to the creation of that safe environment? Turning off cell phones? Being on time? Discuss *everyone's* collective responsibility for the goal and how they will be rewarded for their investment – and we don't just mean grades. Their reward is deeper learning, more fun, and a chance for them to be their true selves rather than playing the role of "student" (which they can hide behind).

- In fact, steer them from an intense focus on grades to an intense focus on *learning*. Grade obsession is often connected to an unhealthy sense of competition. "Who got the highest? Who's the best?" implies that only one student can be successful at any given time. This is usually because they lack trust in themselves, in each other, or the teacher. This is no different from our earlier example of a selfish cast member: if the focus is on individual achievement only, the goal is lost. In this case, if the focus is only on getting a high grade, they're not connected to their actual learning *process*. Whether this is an acting class or not, use the acting process as a model. We encourage actors to avoid going for the result, right? We ask them to be present so that they can listen and be responsive to their partners and to their own instincts. Doesn't that sound like a terrific process for *all* learning? Nurture trust by encouraging collaboration, equal participation in the goal, and by clearly defining expectations.

- Define what failure is and isn't. Nothing shuts someone down faster than feeling that they "got it wrong." Tell them that you expect, and hope for, a certain amount of failure: that it's essential to their growth and learning.

- Remember the sniffer section in Chapter 3: allow for a "wrong" path to be pursued in discussions – even if it would save time to cut them off, don't do it. Helping a student figure it out teaches them that they have permission to try, fail, and most important, that they'll be given the chance to try again. If you quickly supply the answer, you're telling them that you'll be imposing a "right" answer instead of teaching them how to *find* the answers.

- Play your objective and your actions: to inspire, to stimulate, to ignite, whatever you've chosen. But above all, *need* something from them instead of *delivering* something to them. Expect them to engage and they will *want* to engage. Remember the hilariously boring teacher in *Ferris Bueller's Day Off* who quizzed the classroom: "The government, in order to alleviate the effects of … Anyone? Anyone? The Great Depression, passed the … Anyone? Anyone? Tariff bill which … Anyone? Anyone?" Cut to the room of slack-jawed students sliding out of their chairs, drooling, and clutching their heads. It's funny because the teacher had absolutely no expectations of the students; he asked and answered all his own questions. Commit to your objective, need something from the students, and they'll respond and engage with you and each other.

- Once the ensemble has formed, know when to get out of its way. You don't always need to have the high status. What would happen to everyone's investment if you allowed a student to have the higher status? There's a reason students fantasize about taking over a classroom; they crave empowerment. It boosts their confidence, and by golly, it's just plain fun to have power over your teacher. When Johnny Depp was filming one of the *Pirates of the Caribbean* movies in London, he received a letter written by a little girl from a nearby school who asked him if Jack Sparrow would come to help them mutiny against their teachers. When he showed up in her classroom in full pirate regalia, it was covered by media outlets across the world. The teachers supported the "guest mutiny," and it empowered the children and taught them to take risks. Now, we're not advocating chaos; but if the students' rising status seems connected with their grasping of the learning, get out of their way. When you give up your status this way, one of two things is likely to happen:
  - The students will realize how hard it is to do your job and will gain greater appreciation of you and your work, or
  - They will do a marvelous job and *you'll* learn something from *them*. You might find yourself fearing that they won't need you anymore. But remember, you *gave* them the status; they didn't have to *take* it from you. They won't have anything to prove, because they'll see you as benevolent and willing to listen and incorporate their ideas. In actuality, your status will *rise*.

- Acknowledge those who raise their hands, but encourage in equal measure those who don't. Everyone learns more by listening to others. The more you reinforce that all are expected to contribute equally, the more the group will support and encourage each other to respond.

- Assume the best, not the worst of the students, and keep framing the goal in active terms: what you *do* want instead of what you *don't* want.

- Go back to The Excruciating Five Minutes story in Chapter 3. It focuses on students learning about collective responsibility. A teacher isn't someone who gives out work and expects you to do it; a teacher inspires you to do the work for yourself. For every class, ask yourself: what's my goal for today? How can I inspire them anew to achieve their goal?

## Recipe adaptation: a few thoughts on substitute teaching

How does a temporary/substitute leader differ from the regular leader? The primary difference is that you're entering an existing ensemble and have to adapt accordingly. This presents a unique range of challenges:

- How do you balance a respect for the regular leader and the work they're doing with the ensemble, while giving yourself permission to do what you do best? And how do you communicate that to the ensemble members?
- How do you earn their respect and trust in a short time? You don't have the opportunity to do "first day" type activities. You have to lead them from wherever they currently are, to a new point. How do you meet that challenge?

### David

When Rose asked me to sub for her in her graduate improvisation course, I asked myself those questions. I met that challenge by relying on my confidence in my ability to teach improv, and my willingness to listen to the students, discover who they uniquely are, and adjust to meet them at their current point. Another helpful factor was my background with Rose (having taken the course with her for two semesters). So I knew the kind of situation I was walking into, even if I didn't know this particular ensemble. I had to be aware that even as I tuned into their frequency, my participation would inevitably alter that frequency. A new, slightly different frequency would be born.

I knew what kind of party it was (I had been invited to the same party in a previous year), I knew who the regular host was (she had been host when I attended), and I knew what food was served and what games were played. What I didn't know was who the guests were and how much they'd consumed at that point. I asked myself, "What does the party need?" (Someone who won't mess up a good party now that they're host.) And, "What does the ensemble need from me?" (A clear sense of who I am and why they can trust me to keep this party rockin'.)

If you're invited to substitute teach, ask:

- Who is this ensemble? What is its identity?
- What do they expect from me (as a leader *or* new member)?
- What can I contribute? How does my particular set of skills, talents, imagination, etc., fit in?
- How do I tune into their frequency?
- When have I earned my spot? That is, when am I no longer "the new guy?"

### Rose

I once got a call from a college chair on a Monday night asking if I could start teaching an Intro class the next morning. It was well into the semester and I was told the regular instructor had "stopped showing up." I arrived early to ask the department secretaries what had happened (trust me: they always know where the bodies are buried). The instructor had apparently left for a better job, hadn't told anyone, and after *two weeks* a student finally came to the main office asking, "Do you know what's happened to our teacher?" So I knew that this class had been abandoned; they were probably angry, some of them had likely dropped the class, and I imagined that they were so frustrated they'd be looking for a dog to kick. If you ever need an idea for one of those imaginary enter-the-room-with-circumstances exercises, this is a good one.

I got to the classroom early; erased the blackboard, took out the trash, and sat in front so that students would see me immediately when they arrived. Now, these students were *really* mad – some were emotional, some feigned indifference ("He didn't care about us; I'm sure *you* won't either"). I started by offering an apology on behalf of the department and assured them that I was committed to being with them for the semester. I told them I would do everything in my power to create a safe place for them to learn in. Then I gave them the opportunity to tell me what had happened and how they felt. Believe me, the guy who ditched these great students had his ears scorched that day. I listened, asked them what they *had* learned, and apparently all the guy did was show them videotapes. When they finally finished, they seemed drained; that was the time to infuse something new: "I hope nobody minds if we don't see any more videos." Big cheer. "I'd like to suggest that we use the remaining weeks for some live experience projects. How do you feel about that?" Another cheer. "Give me suggestions of what you're most curious about." Every hand shot up in the air and we were off to the races. I ended the discussion to give enough time for a 30-minute lesson on directing. I conducted a participatory exercise: we pushed the desks aside and switched out volunteers until all twenty-five students had had a turn. By the time class was over, something had been exorcised and something new had begun to take its place.

I had asked: what kind of party is this (a disaster), who's at the party (angry, abandoned students), what does the party need from me (a committed host who will take care of the guests), and what does the ensemble need from me (to listen, to nurture, to reassure in order for them to recommit to their goal). You might argue that they were no longer an ensemble, but quite to the contrary. They had become a potent ensemble united against a common enemy who they hated with a passion, and they completely had each other's backs. They *transformed* into an ensemble that was open to being guided by a new host, but only when they realized it was an entirely different party.

## Recipe 3: creating an ensemble

### *Starting your own theatre company*

Everyone reading this book is already an ensemble leader, an ensemble member, or someone who wants to start their own ensemble. Let's say you found a party that you liked, a lot, but it's over now and you want more. You all want to start a theatre company; what does that mean? It means you want a new version of a familiar party.

You've had a taste of what your own party *could* be, as you've likely met your fellow prospective guests at a *previous* party, and though the host told you it was time to go, you didn't want to. Did you meet in college? In a production? Did you bond through a trial-by-fire internship where you built sets all day, ran lights for evening shows, then performed in midnight cabarets? Were you all in a workshop taught by an incomprehensible "artiste," and you hated the artiste but liked each other? There was something in the bonds you formed at that previous party that made you want to get everyone to come together for another round of fun.

At some point in our lives, we've all yearned to be part of a theatre company made up of people we love to work with. We've either heard about or been a part of companies with legendary success, companies with brief but magical periods, or of course, horror stories of when the train jumped the tracks.

So how can we plan a party so that we emerge with friendships and artistic souls intact? If you've never started your own theatre company, talk to some of the great people out there who've done it successfully, read books that will tell you how to manage, budget, plan, etc. For a terrific practical guide, read *Performing Arts Management* by Tobie S. Stein and Jessica Bathurst. Now, we're coming at this from a more personal angle. What are the essential guiding questions to ask yourselves in those precious early days?

### *Why Am I In the Room? and then Why Are We In the Room?*

Identify what it is that's making you consider this. Start with the personal exploration (that's easiest) and then consider the idea that brings you together and unites you (more challenging). What is it that makes you want to work together? How would you describe your bond? And don't stop at, "Well, I *like* everybody in this room. I'm tired of working with sucky people." Recognize that you have two-ensembles-in-one here: the ensemble of friends, and the professional ensemble that wants to create artistic work together. Sure, it could get a little mushy to articulate your relationships out loud, but it will create a stronger and clearer foundation for *both* ensembles. Be clear on the first ensemble before moving on to the second. If the endeavor fails, your friendships will stand a much better chance of enduring if you do this work now.

Next, explore the *idea* of this ensemble. What is the passion that you share, the values that brought you together on this idea? Why must it be with these people at this moment in time? Why do you feel the need to start something instead of joining an existing company? You might realize that you don't necessarily want to start a company, but you *do* want to find a way to continue working together; those are two entirely different things. Your collaborative group dynamic may bring you work with*out* starting your own venture. When interviewing Barefoot Theatre Company's artistic director Francisco Solorzano, he said that half of their large cast for a production of *Raft of the Medusa* by Joe Pintauro was made up of a group of actors who had graduated together from the same program. "I've always tried to create a community, create a family. Especially with the cast of *Raft*, there's trust that's automatically built in, so you see that in the production. It makes the work more compelling to watch ... there's a family dynamic that's built in."

Now, if you *do* confirm that what you want is to start your own company, that leads us to ...

### *What kind of party do we want this to be?*

Doesn't that sound more fun than "we need to write a mission statement?" You know you want to work together and now you have the opportunity to create your own party. Do you want to develop original plays or produce classics? Do you want to effect political change through your work? Is there a specific population you want to serve? (We recently heard of a young director who is working on creating theatre by and for children with autism.) Discussing this will help you create a mission statement. Make sure you're specific; if you find yourself writing, "Our goal is to do quality theatre," that may be true, but it's generic. What distinguishes *your* ensemble? There's a reason you're not all packing up the car to go to someone else's party. Identify your goal, and what's going to make your party unique.

*What are the house rules of the party?*

Creating a structure early on will solve many a problem down the road.

- How often will you meet?
- Will you require your core group to participate in every production, or in a minimum number of shows annually?
- Is everyone guaranteed the opportunity to fulfill their desired position (directing, acting, etc.) at least once a year?
- Will company members be given priority casting in all productions, and outside actors only used in special situations?
- What values do you all hold that will be your guiding principles?
- Most important, how will you collectively handle the leadership needs? Will you have a traditional delineation of administrative and artistic roles? Will there be term limits and you'll all rotate responsibilities?

Of course there are business questions that will come up (profit vs. not-for-profit, grant writing, and fundraising, etc.), and those will be more readily answered after you've defined the house rules for your party. Once you know whether it's a birthday party or baby shower (and make no mistake, you *are* about to give birth ... ), you need to determine:

*What am I bringing to the party?*

### Rose

When my wonderful husband Mike and I threw our wedding reception before flying off to Ireland to get married, we decided we wanted it to be a casual pot luck to which everyone brought their favorite specialty dishes. I coordinated with over 100 people to make sure we wouldn't end up with a hundred pumpkin pies. We had the most delicious assortment of foods, each one made with love and pride because it was that person's specialty. Everyone remembers that day less for the lashing rain, but more for the unique food and fellowship under the tent.

You've got to make sure you don't end up with a hundred pumpkin pies. What are your specialties that you can bring to this party? Ask each other more Chapter 4 questions:

- What do you feel you uniquely bring to this ensemble?

- What primary role do you play in an ensemble? Are you the Rock or the Sparkplug?
- What are your greatest strengths and challenges in an ensemble setting?

Be honest about this last one and don't let each other off the hook. Better you confront Louise now about her funny habit of creating a mess wherever she goes, before it becomes Louise losing your 501(c)(3) documents. Justin's charming ability to always show up on the wrong evening may not be so charming when he's forgotten to invite your board members to opening night. By considering everyone's unique abilities early on, you'll be able to plan ahead and avoid that awful tension that comes when someone is perceived as not pulling their weight. This way, Ramona can say, "Hey, I'm very organized, I'll take care of mailing lists. But I stink at budgets." Ian jumps in with, "Terrific! I'm good at crunching numbers. I'll keep our books, but I'm terrible at networking." Melanie says, "Brilliant! I love asking rich strangers for money. I'll do the main meet and greet, but I can't stand writing follow-up letters to donors." The three A's apply here too; awareness and acknowledgment are fine, but the actions you take to embrace everyone's unique abilities instead of focusing on what they're terrible at will strengthen your company for the long term.

So, you've got the goal, who you are, and what you're bringing to the party. You are the collective hosts at this moment in time. Next:

### *How do you plan the guest list?*

This is exciting, and can be verrry sticky. Have you included everyone from the previous party where you all first met? If not, why not? This is not the time to be shy. We all know that the potential stress of starting a company with people you *do* get along with is tough enough. You don't want to *willfully* invite the Black Hole and the Complainer to the party. You'll end up with the New Year's Eve party that everyone leaves before the clock strikes twelve. What if there are others from the previous party that you don't want to invite? Maybe you just want a subset of the previous group. Or, what if you can't all agree on who should be invited? After identifying your goal, and what you're all bringing, who and what else you need should be clearer. And if someone is still advocating for the Black Hole who will feel left out if they're not invited, ask the practical question: *What would they bring to the party?* If the answer is "the ability to clear the room," there's your answer, and an end to the disagreement.

If you've thrown a successful party that goes on for months or years, what next? Do you want to stay with the core group that created this and invite others in for specific projects only? Do you want to build the company over time, and as you meet others who share your values and commitment, invite them to join? You can revisit this at your regular meetings too.

And what about the extended guest list? It's not only the party of the ensemble itself, but also the audience that you hope will come. What kind of audience members do you want to attend this party? Can audience members be considered a part of the ensemble? Can you create that bond too?

*One model of a theatre company*

## Rose

Some of you may be just starting out in this field, or you work at a college or university in a smaller town, or you're someone who is passionate about theatre and has never been paid a dime in your life for performing or for building a set. The unsung heroes of the arts are the countless community theatres and small colleges who provide artistic experiences for the people of their area who might otherwise never have access to them. These aren't people who want to become stars or paid professionals: they have a desire and commitment to work as an ensemble to create something artistic and meaningful for their community. In that spirit, here is the story of one ensemble's journey.

Synergy Ensemble Theatre of Islip, Long Island, was created in 1985 and chose their name based on the definition "the joint action of separate and different agencies in which the total is greater than the sum of their effects when acting independently." In other words: a commitment to ensemble principles. Their core members met while working on what was supposed to be a "one-off" town-sponsored project. The original company members were teachers, microbiologists, lawyers, social workers, computer consultants, accountants, and even an air traffic controller. I spoke with some of the original Synergists, including Jacquie Kahn, Rosanne Manfredi, Mike Cleary, Mike Cerevella, and Judy and Bill Sellman, and asked how they decided to form their own company. "The town sponsored a children's program every year, and the director put in a proposal for an adult program," said Rosanne. "Judy, me and Cathy (Russo) were all part of that. We did a night of one-acts and called ourselves The Reality Players. That was an incredible experience, but then it was over. We didn't want it to end. A proposal was made to the town to make it permanent. They approved, so we began to assemble people who we liked working with and had a night of auditions."

Jacquie said: "I had just taken my first theatre class – and loved it – in my final semester at C.W. Post (Long Island University) for my business degree." Rosanne added, "I told her if she was interested in more theatre, I could loan her some scripts and such. But if you want a *guaranteed* part, come down to the theatre, we're starting a theatre company." Jacquie said, "I met Mike Cerevella in the parking lot. He was walking around, looking lost, and I was scared. I asked him, 'Are you here for the theatre thing?' The theatre *thing*. And he was. We bonded in the parking lot." Then Judy said (as if finishing a beautiful bedtime story), "and that was the first night of Synergy ... " Judy and Bill were company members for over 20 years (until they moved to Vermont); Jacquie, Rosanne, Mike, and Cathy are *still* members, and to date, Synergy has produced more than 80 productions, plus children's shows, readings, and workshops.

I was invited to direct for them in 1990 and they shattered every cliché of what community theatre is perceived to be in this country. They were committed to creating strong ensemble-based theatre, to learning and growing as a company, and to fiercely supporting each other. Their mission was to provide their community with theatre that was thought provoking, not often produced, and above all, affordable.

Their structure was radically different from any previous company I'd worked with. Rather than a traditional artistic director, managing director, and so on, they annually elected a five-member voting board that made decisions regarding play selection, budget, and schedules. Synergy held company meetings after every production to discuss upcoming events and needs. Anyone who had worked on two or more shows within the season, in any capacity, was considered a voting member. Non-voting members were welcome at meetings, but not allowed to vote in board elections or larger decisions that affected the company. Synergy also seemed to have solved the biggest problem that many fledgling theatre companies seem to face; that is, everybody wants to be *in* the show, but who's going to do the marketing, stage management, set design, and so forth? They required members to participate in *all* activities related to production, and the unwritten rule was that if you came here just to act, we're not the tribe you seek; our members do it all. That doesn't mean that some folks wouldn't come in now and again for a single show; but I observed that someone who *thought* they were breezing in for a single show would then *stay* and join. Even those who didn't return were still welcomed warmly when they attended future shows, and company members would attend *their* productions at other artistic institutions.

In other words, this was a community theatre that defined the best of what that term should mean. They took their role as the resident theatre company in the town of Islip seriously. They participated in town events: parades, you name it. There was also something unique that happened after every show; audience members would stay and wait for the actors to get out of costume and make-up so that they could share their responses with them. Initially, I thought it was friends and family simply waiting to say congratulations. But no, these were audience members who returned over and over because they felt as if they were a part of this company. They wanted to discuss the actors' performances, the story, and moments that made them laugh or cry. It was extraordinary to watch this. They didn't want to leave. They wanted to talk with Bill Sellman who had just played Dennis Shepard in *The Laramie Project* by Tectonic Theatre, and ask him how it felt to play that role after having performed the comedic lead in *Moon Over Buffalo* by Ken Ludwig. They wanted to know how Judy Sellman managed to design and maintain all of the costumes for *Kindertransport* by Diane Samuels while also creating a heartbreaking performance as Helga. They wanted to grab Mike Cerevella, who had played the Mechanic in *Defying Gravity* by Jane Anderson, and ask him: "We have a bet going; didn't you also play the guy in the alligator suit in that weird play *Flukes?*" Through their commitment to ensemble within their company, Synergy had extended that bond and created an ensemble with their audience and community. This is so *rare*, folks; most audiences want to remain anonymous, not wait an extra 15 minutes afterward so that they can continue the experience with the company.

My favorite story about Synergy's special relationship with their audience is regarding Mrs. Beza. She attended the very first Synergy show and became a devoted audience member. She never missed a production and always stayed to speak with actors, directors, and stage managers. After one show, she presented the company with a big fake rubber plant; the kind you see in every office setting. She said, "I was watching that office scene in the last show, saw you didn't have any plants on the set, and I thought, you know? I have this fake plant that would just be perfect for something like that. I'd like to donate it." Company members were so touched by her gesture that every set designer thereafter looked for an appropriate opportunity to include Mrs. Beza's rubber plant in the set. She never failed to notice, and would proudly say to her friends, "Did you see the plant in the waiting room scene? That used to be in my house! It looks so much better on their set!" Sometimes your contribution to the ensemble is being a Rock; sometimes it's a fake philodendron. But no one would ever think that Mrs. Beza was *not* a member of Synergy Ensemble Theatre Company.

Synergy innately understood that to be a true community theatre, your theatre had to be a community itself. For years they held activities for members beyond the theatre itself. Weekly movie nights, outings to other arts events, and wonderful annual retreats in Vermont so that everyone could gather in a relaxed setting to read plays, tell stories, have fun, and oh yes, play "Synergy Jeopardy" for the coveted Jeppie award (which I think was an old bottle of Avon perfume in the shape of a mermaid). Silly? Maybe. But when you produce three to four productions a year, and tensions arise, you work a lot harder to find common ground with each other after you've bonded on a Vermont nature trail.

Though most companies are started by a group of people who are already friends and colleagues, Synergy was a company formed by people who wanted the same thing: to do challenging theatre in a supportive setting with like-minded people. A small number of them were friends when they started, but most showed up because they knew somebody who knew somebody. Everyone *became* friends after they arrived. There have been at least four Synergy marriages (including my own), several babies, and deep friendships that transcend years and miles.

What's the true sign of a great ensemble? You never want the party to stop. Together you do whatever it takes to keep it going, and you all keep coming back for more. Why?

It's just better.

# CONCLUSION

## Last call

As with all great parties, you have to know when to turn out the lights and go to bed. Even if the sun is already up. As hosts, we do most of the work, so now that everyone is getting ready to leave, it's almost time for us to put our feet up. We'll pour ourselves a big drink, survey all that needs to be cleaned up, and say to each other, "We'll do that tomorrow." Then we'll regale each other with tales of what we enjoyed most about the party and our fabulous guests.

One of our hopes for this book is that it serves as a kickoff to a long party season. We hope you are inspired, motivated, informed, and challenged by what you've read. Now it's your turn. Take this and run with it. Throw parties! Try these ideas and try your own ideas born of your passion for this work. Take risks!

And then tell us about your experiences. That's right, we'd *love* to hear from you. Not only do we love to throw parties, but we love to talk about them around the water cooler on Monday. We have established a blog so that we can do just that: http://ensembletheatremaking.com/. So this is a kickoff to a longer and larger conversation that we hope to have with an extended ensemble, including you. Let's share our discoveries, insights, and passion. Let's also use it as a forum to help each other deal with challenges and issues – we know we're not the only two people who have ideas and methods for creating and maintaining ensemble. And the two of us can't possibly have encountered everything that ensemble can throw at us, so please join the conversation.

With that, we'll say "good night." Oops, look at the time. Better make that "good morning." And hey – who's having the party next weekend?

Get home safe,
Rose and David

# APPENDICES

## Appendix A

### *Blind Offers (via Keith Johnstone in Impro)*

Two partners, A and B (group observes).

- Partner A makes a spontaneous, intentionless physical offer/gesture to Partner B and holds it.
- B immediately responds with their own non-verbal response to A's offer and holds it.
- At the moment of the dual hold, Partner A says, "Thank you," then both release to neutral.
- Partner B then makes a spontaneous intentionless physical offer/gesture to A and so forth.
- They take at least three turns each. The offers should be spontaneous and abstract, with no preplanning. The goal is not to tell a literal story, but to make a fully committed offer that is accepted every time. For example, if A points their finger at B, B needn't hold up their hands as if they're being robbed.

The exercise stresses that *every* offer will be accepted, that a partner will *always* be able to "do" something with that offer, and that the offer – and the individual – is not only valued, but is "enough." The "thank you" can sometimes feel awkward to younger students, but it's the most essential portion of the exercise. Blind Offers lessens the fear of rejection and insecurities about "not being enough" and often feels safer because it's non-verbal. Tends not to trigger the "Must Be Clever" switch.

### *Tips*

Be mindful that partners don't rush the "thank you"; encourage them not to preplan the intentionless offer. The time in-between each offer and response will eventually decrease. The exercise encourages holistic listening and creates an understanding of the essential building blocks of trust that comes from true listen/ response between partners. It helps young actors understand that the "yes" is simply accepting a partner's offer; the "and" is what they *add* to it.

### Notes

This exercise particularly helps actors who struggle with harsh self-judgment, about themselves and their choices. Inevitably, someone observes: "I realized that no matter what offer I gave my partner, whether I thought it was weak or stupid, my partner was able to *do* something with it and had a response. And if I was the one responding, no matter how weak I might have thought my response was to their offer, they *always* said 'Thank you.' I need to remember this in all of my work."

## Appendix B

### *Come Join Me*

The group is off to one side of the playing area.

- One person enters the playing area and begins a non-verbal, independent physical activity that establishes a specific environment.
- As other ensemble members recognize the environment, *one at a time*, they enter and make their own contribution to the environment through an activity that would also be found in that environment.
- Once others join, it *can* become verbal. What you *don't* want is the person initiating to announce, "It sure is hot in this *beauty salon.*"

### *Example*

If the initiator is shelving books in a library, the next person might enter and become a student sitting at a desk studying, the next person starts sweeping the floor as a janitor, the next enters and begins scanning books at the check-out desk, and so on. One student might whisper a question to another, an arriving vendor may speak to the receptionist in a normal tone, but no one is *required* to be verbal.

### *Tips*

Adhere to the "one at a time" rule; this way each person observes each choice and it reinforces the question "what is needed?" If someone establishes a school playground, and eight people simultaneously enter as kids playing, you'll never get the teacher, coach, or the drug dealer (trust me, they appear in every environmental improv in New York).

Afterwards, ask each person to identify their *role*, not the characteristics of the person they created. For example, if someone was an irate customer and another person was a drunken customer, both were still *customers*. Ask: whom else, what else, did the environment *need*? Thus, if you had nine customers and only one cashier in a coffee shop, the group begins to understand they could have been a delivery person, manager, health inspector, drug dealer …

### *Notes*

Come Join Me focuses on listening and observation, mutual collaboration, silent agreement, committing fully to choices ("Is he digging a hole or is he raking leaves?"), and most important, that *every role, no matter if it's the primary focus or not, is essential to the scene.* It helps participants understand the essential components of storytelling and that full commitment to every character in the story makes for a better story. The world doesn't fall apart if they commit to a "smaller" role; it is richer *for* it.

## Appendix C

### *What Are You Doing?*

Two people face one another: Person A and Person B. Remaining participants form single file lines behind each of them (same amount in each line if possible).

- A asks B: "What are you doing?"
- B responds by stating a simple physical activity: "I'm brushing my teeth."
- A immediately starts to brush their teeth, while B runs to the back of their line.
- The person who was standing behind B steps up (C) and asks A, "What are you doing?"
- A, *while continuing to do the action they were given* (brushing their teeth), states a new action to C: "I'm bouncing a basketball." Then A runs to the back of their line.
- C immediately starts to bounce a basketball, while the person standing behind A (D) steps up to ask C: "What are you doing?"
- C, while *continuing to bounce the basketball,* gives a new physical action to D, then runs to the back of their own line, and so on.

Do the exercise long enough so that everyone has many turns at this.

### *Tips*

Encourage participants to acknowledge whether they preconceived or not. This helps you support them on the journey toward the time when they *don't* preplan. Discourage them from beating themselves up if they "repeat" an action ("I'm terrible at this; I said 'eating a taco' three times!"). The muscle they're stretching is the impulse muscle and that's more important than not repeating something. Everyone should of course strive for that, but don't be too tough about "repeats" early on.

When participants do preplan, they experience the feeling of having "rejected" their partner's offer and sense their own lack of trust in that they avoided facing their fear of "not having anything." When they don't preplan, they experience "what's the worst that can happen?" (usually two–three seconds of silence at most), as well as the discovery that the well is never dry. They begin to understand that *everything* that comes before their "turn" is part of their inspiration. Their turn is only one component of the larger story, and when they let go of worrying about what will happen when it's their turn, they discover a wealth of inspirational sources that surround them, from actions to sounds to environment.

If someone gives an action that the other person doesn't understand, ask them to commit to what they *imagine* it to be. There was once a student who, in her panic, gave the action in her home language: "I'm veshnoofing ze veshnoofdicator." Her partner paused for a split second, then committed to an action that was inspired by what she imagined veshnoofing the veshnoofdicator to be!

*Notes*

This exercise focuses on the dreaded "preconceiving" monster. It helps participants experience the difference between a preconceived and a spontaneous response. Participants *see* actions that are related/unrelated; e.g., if someone is truly listening and they step up to see someone bouncing a basketball, they may say, "I'm jumping on a pogo stick!" If they've preplanned and step up to basketball-bouncer, they might announce, "I'm drinking a cup of tea" no matter what they see. Now, someone may have a memory of having broken their mother's favorite teacup while bouncing a ball in the house, but you get the idea.

# Appendix D

## *Sound and Movement*

Participants stand in a circle, giving enough room in the middle to allow for physical exploration.

- Person A begins by entering the circle. They explore sounds (not words) and physical motions until they arrive at a sound and movement that connects most closely to what they are feeling at that moment.
- When they connect with a specific sound and movement, and it's repeatable, A brings that sound and movement to someone in the circle – B – to transfer it to them. A moves in front of B and makes eye contact (if possible).

- B tries to capture and take on A's sound and movement.
- When A feels that B has accurately taken on their sound and movement, A initiates an exchange of places (B never initiates the exchange), so that B takes the sound and movement into the middle, and A takes B's place on the circle.
- B then fully explores A's sound and movement and allows it to transform into a sound and movement that connects to what they are feeling in that moment.
- When B feels they have found their own sound and movement, and it's repeatable, they bring that to someone else in the circle, and the process repeats.
- When it's clear that the moment of transference has begun between A and B, the participants standing in the circle then also begin doing A's sound and movement.
- When B moves into the circle to begin their own exploration, the group needs to "fade down and out" so they don't influence B's exploration. You may need to find a gesture to signal the group to "dial it down." The group should not be participating during the individual exploration phase in the circle.

The exercise continues until everyone has gone one or more times. When you determine that the exercise needs to end, instruct whoever is entering the circle to fully explore the sound and movement they've been given, but to eventually bring it to neutral instead of giving it to a partner.

### Tips

When B takes A's sound and movement into the circle, make sure they don't "drop" what they've been given to start a preconceived sound and movement. Everyone must experience the process of exploring a partner's offer, and allow that to *affect* them. Someone may have been feeling blue; what happens if they're given a joyous sound and movement? Can they allow themselves to be transformed? Similarly, when the group is doing each sound and movement, someone may not want to stop because it feels too good or too cathartic.

### Notes

In discussion, participants will observe the primal or tribal nature of the exercise; remind them that the tribe is there to support, always. They may note the intense vulnerability and trust necessary, feeling exposed in the circle. This can also cause an individual to rush the exploration. If they say, "I felt I was taking too much time," that usually means they felt vulnerable and wanted to get the heck out of there. Eventually, participants come to trust their partners and the circle, and experience the moment-to-moment nature of taking an offer and allowing it to affect themselves and their choices.

## Appendix E

### *West Side Story (WSS, via Augusto Boal)*

Two lines of students face each other a la the Sharks and the Jets from *West Side Story.* Try to start with even numbers on each side (it can be done with odd numbers, but that can lead to a meltdown!). Alternating leaders will initiate a structured six-beat sound and movement that their "team" must quickly emulate while moving forward, "pushing" the other team back with the sound and movement, and with its intention.

Begin by teaching the rhythm to the participants and require them to keep their sound and movements within that rhythm (the rhythm itself can slow down or speed up). The rhythm is: "One (beat), Two (beat), one, two, three, four." A sound (not words) and a physical gesture must be created for this rhythm structure by each leader. Imagine someone punching their fist in the air on each beat of this sound: "Yah! Yah! Yah-yah-yah-yah!"

Once that phrase is complete, a leader from the opposite team initiates a repeatable sound and movement that their team emulates while moving forward, "pushing" the other team back. The team that is being pushed back *does not mirror the sound and movement*; they simply receive the energy while walking backwards.

- Select Team A to start: the person at the end of the line is the first leader.
- After the leader of Team A has led their team forward with their six-beat sound and movement (while Team B has been pushed back), then the person on the end of the line of Team B creates their own sound and movement that Team B emulates while moving forward (with Team A being pushed back).
- Without pausing at the end of the final beat of the phrase, the next person in line in Team A becomes the new leader, then the next person in line for Team B is their new leader, and so on.

*Example*

*Table 1*

| Team A | Team B |
| --- | --- |
| Luca | Mena |
| Jan | Steve |
| Maddie | Averie |
| Jackie | Andrew |
| Scott | Joan |

If Team A begins, Luca would lead Team A with his sound and movement first, then Mena would lead Team B with her sound and movement, then Jan leads for

Team A, then Steve for Team B, then Maddie, then Averie and so on. When you get to Joan as the leader for Team B, Luca will then lead again for Team A, then Mena for B, and so on. You can also choose to simply move back up the line: e.g., after Joan has led, then Scott would lead, then Andrew, then Jackie, and so forth. However, the greater challenge for focus and concentration is to go back to the "top of the line."

Now. Whichever team is initiating, that team must step forward *simultaneously and together* with the rhythm, sound and gesture. When Luca is leading, Jackie might say, "How will I see what he's doing from here?" The answer is, she needs to *trust* that the sound and gesture will quickly reach her by virtue of it "traveling down" the line. Jan will immediately see Luca's gesture, Maddie a millisecond later, and so on. However, everyone immediately *hears* the sound, and senses Luca's intention *in* that sound. It's less important to copy the sound and gesture exactly than it is to take on its intention and use it to move the other team back.

## Tips

People initially struggle with the following:

- Getting the sound and movement "right" vs. allowing it to inform and move them forward while the gesture makes its way to them visually.
- Focusing solely on the person directly opposite instead of being aware of the entire opposite team as well as their own team that they're leading forward.
- Hesitating between phrases, doubting whose turn it is to lead. They think the order is changing, but the order of who leads each time never changes. What changes is their focus, which can impact their perception and short-term memory.
- Hesitating when the exchange reaches the end of the line, doubting who's supposed to lead next.
- Stopping themselves before they've finished the six-beat phrase, especially if they're the next one to lead. They're anticipating their turn, preplanning a choice, not trusting that they can be in the moment, and that their impulses will respond.

## Notes

The exercise gives you great bang for your buck. It promotes spontaneous release of impulses, trust (of self and the ensemble), commitment (to choices, to partners, to the "story"), communication, hyper-awareness, physical awareness, listening, issues of preconceiving, and of course physical stamina (a growing problem particularly with young actors). You can see and hear when participants are blocking themselves or a partner's offer, as well as when they are committing fully. You'll also find that WSS:

- addresses the dreaded "enoughs": "What if my choice isn't enough for my partner?" The rhythm structure makes it impossible for anyone to stop to doubt; they must make a choice or everything comes to a halt;
- addresses the classic, "Why do we doubt that we know what we know?" Steve may know that on Team B, he is always the leader after Mena has led for Team B. Why is he stopping himself and suddenly doubting that observation? WSS has the appearance of complexity, but is actually beautifully simple: the six-beat rhythm never changes, someone's turn to lead will always be after the person to their immediate side; so what makes participants stop to doubt?

## Appendix F

### *Kitty Wants a Corner*

Participants stand in a circle with one member in the center as Kitty.

- Kitty approaches someone asking, "Kitty wants a corner?" seeking to exchange places with them.
- The participant responds by saying, "No," and Kitty moves to the next person *in order* in the circle, asking, "Kitty wants a corner?" and so on.
- While this is happening, other members of the circle are trying to find someone to switch places with them. They do this by making eye contact, then establishing *silent agreement* (without gestures or head nods), then they try to exchange places.
- If Kitty gets to one of the vacant spots before the other person does, then the person who lost their spot becomes the new Kitty, and they begin asking for a corner, and so on.

In early rounds, require that the person Kitty is asking for a corner must always say, "No." After you've done it several times, change the structure to allow those in the circle to say, "Yes" to Kitty if they choose. This changes the stakes and strengthens the challenges as their experience with the exercise increases.

### *Tips*

Encourage participants toward true silent agreement, not wildly gesticulating or making big faces to indicate agreement. Remind them that eye contact is only the first step; this compels them to connect more fully to reach the agreement needed to exchange places. Participants don't initially trust the silent agreement and confuse simple eye contact as a signal to "go." Continued focus on the silent agreement strengthens confidence in their ability to do more with less than what they *think* they need.

Those who were Kitty may note (over time) that they sensed when someone was about to change places behind them. This heightened awareness increases confidence. You may observe Kitty defeating themselves: "I'll never find a corner," or giving big exasperated sighs. Discuss this as well; you may find that they were playing the obstacle vs. the objective. For example, an exchanger loses their spot because they were playing "I don't want to get caught by Kitty" instead of "I *want* to get to that spot." Kitty is in the center a long time because they're playing "I don't want to get stuck here" instead of "I want to find an open spot."

In the version where participants can say "yes" to Kitty, you may observe that Kitty is so prepared for rejection, they don't hear the "yes," and they move on to ask the next person for the corner. The most important discovery here is participants finding out that they've been demonizing the "role" of Kitty, and associating that whoever is Kitty somehow has less power than the exchangers. It strengthens awareness of how, where, and when we give away our power, in roles, and in life. This leads to discussions about how participants may be judging roles in other parts of their work, and how they can keep power (instead of giving it away). It emphasizes the equality of every role in a story, and this in turn creates breakthroughs in the understanding of the nature of ensemble itself.

*Notes*

Focuses on awareness, commitment, silent communication, confidence, trust, playing objective vs. obstacle, physical stamina, and risk-taking.

## Appendix G: Blindfold Series

### *The Cobra (via Augusto Boal)*

The group stands in a tight circle.

- Have them put on blindfolds, turn to their right and place their hands on the shoulders and back of the neck of the person now directly in front of them.
- They explore the back of the head, the neck, and shoulders of the person they're touching. Encourage them to be specific in their tactile observations; don't stop the observation at a ponytail (as several people may be wearing ponytails!). Is the ponytail holder plain or decorated? Is it bunched or long?
- After allowing a minute or so for observation, call for the group to break the circle, and move out into the space "bumper car style" (hands folded across the chest, no hands or fingertips protruding straight out into the air where someone can get their eyes poked).
- After a few moments when you see the group has "shuffled" their order, call a freeze, and then ask them to *reform* the circle in its exact order. All without words.

- When they find the person they had explored, they should place their hands on their shoulders to connect that part of the circle, as that person may still need to find *their* person, and so on. It continues until the circle has completely re-linked.
- Once the circle has reformed, call a hold, ask everyone to drop their hands, remove the blindfolds, and see if they have re-formed the circle.

## *Tips*

Remind the group that, when they encounter someone during the seeking phase, they can then break the bumper car pose to carefully examine the partner's neck, shoulders, back of head, etc. If they know who their partner is, discourage them from examining another part of the body that would confirm identify ("I know Lori Ann was next to me and she was wearing that bracelet with the knot work – I'll just identify that!"). Tell them not to dismiss someone who wants to "explore" them, unless there is already a person attached to their shoulders.

You will also have several "segments" that have reformed, with the person at the head of that segment still seeking *their* partner. Be sure that once someone has found their partner and placed hands on their shoulders and back of neck, they *don't drop their hands/arms*. This will guide those who are still seeking their partners to know that this link is complete (many hands will swiftly move over the shoulders and arms/shoulders and arms of a specific link, looking for the end of that part of the chain to see if their person is there). Also, you may need to keep encouraging those at the head of a segment to keep moving to find their partner, but at such a pace that everyone behind them can keep up.

## *Notes*

The exercise explores awareness, listening, trust, observation, and vulnerability. In discussion, note who was self-defeating ("I just knew I would be the last person to find my partner"), who was playing their objective instead of the obstacle, and tactics used. You will rarely have a greater experience than the moment when the circle has reformed and everyone removes their blindfolds. The joy and sense of wonder and accomplishment is a beautiful thing to witness. For young actors, it's a moment of discovering how much they're capable of with the support of the ensemble. For mature actors, they discover that despite years of practical application, the wonder and beauty of what's achievable with the collaboration of an ensemble is still what it's all about.

### *Hunter and Hunted*

Two participants are blindfolded; one is given a rolled up newspaper and is the Hunter, the other is the Hunted. All other participants go to the walls or edges of the room to become spotters.

- The objective of the Hunter is to *tap* Hunted with the rolled up newspaper before they escape.
- Hunted's objective is to escape. If your room has an easily accessible door (or two), Hunted must make it to the door, open it, and begin their exit (obviously, they should stop before walking down the hallway!). If there are dangerous level shifts in the floors of your room, or too much junk for the amount of spotters available to you, you can also clear enough space for an open section of wall at the end of the room, and Hunted's goal is to touch that wall to be "home free."
- Spotters should be given a specific signal (two taps on the shoulder) to identify themselves to Hunter or Hunted; they must be otherwise silent. If spotters are guarding a sharp edge or a protruding architectural element and Hunter/Hunted bumps into them, the spotter taps, then gently turns them away from the danger. Be sure to announce in advance that spotters can't have "a horse in this race." That is, if they're rooting for Hunter, they shouldn't turn Hunted directly toward them. They should turn them away from any danger as neutrally as possible.
- At the beginning, spin and place Hunter and Hunted appropriately in the room, and ask spotters to "cover" by making noise and moving around. Though all specific danger spots should be covered, encourage spotters to exchange places while they're making noise as you spin and place Hunter/Hunted; this way the participants don't mark their place in the room by recognizing someone's voice ("I hear Emme making noise and she was standing about five feet from the door ... ").
- Lastly, tell Hunters that if they find the door first, they cannot use blocking it as a tactic. It's more challenging to explore other options.

*Notes*

The exercise explores the power of simple objectives, simple conflicts, sensory and physical awareness, listening, trust, commitment, and oh yes, trust. The clarity and simplicity of the conflict allows participants to engage in ways that they might struggle with without blindfolds. The blindfolds "erase" the imaginary audience, and intensify focus on actions and needs. In discussion, Hunter/Hunted identify their tactics and what influenced those choices, as well as whether they defaulted to playing the obstacle vs. the objective ("I don't want to get caught" vs. "I want to escape").

This is also one of the best exercises to focus on the role of the spectator. Everyone states that this exercise ranks as some of the most compelling theatre they've seen. The spotters are completely connected to every movement, every choice that Hunter/Hunted are making. The tension is *excruciating* as Hunted nears the door, or as they near the Hunter. I've witnessed spotters nearly *swoon* from giddy tension as they observe Hunted crouch low to the floor, as Hunter sweeps the rolled newspaper six inches above their head, missing them entirely.

Ask the question, "Why were you so completely engaged?" Answers will range from the clarity of the conflict, to the depth of commitment of the Hunter/Hunted, to the primal nature of the exercise and the instinctual responses it triggers. Every human understands "to get" and "to escape;" these conflicts are ancient and universal and trigger something deep within. Hunters/Hunteds describe how they *feel* the energy of the spotters. Inevitably you ask, "How can we strive to create that relationship between the story we are telling and the audience we're telling it to, always?"

## Appendix H

### *Family Portraits*

Divide the group into distinct sections of at least three–five people each. Try to have three or more sections that are now each a "family" (Family A, Family B, Family C, etc.).

- Call on each family to run into the "camera" space, which is where that family will have their portrait taken.
- Each time, call out a word that describes what *kind* of family they are, and then count out loud from one through five. This is the amount of time the group has to pose as the character they've chosen, to find their relationship to their family, then turn out to the camera to have their picture taken.
- After "five," clap or yell, "Click"; Family A runs off and Family B runs on.
- Family B is given a different word that describes their family, then given the five count, and so on.

This goes on until every group has had multiple turns.

### *Example*

Call out "Family A [they start to run into the space], you are the Angelic Family. 1, 2, 3, 4 and 5 … Click! Next family! Family B, you are the Lethargic Family. 1, 2, 3, 4 and 5 … Click! Next family! Family C, you are the Lizard Family …" etc.

### *Tips*

Instruct that it's not simply about them finding a "pose" as an individual, but to embody a character that would appear in that particular family. For example, if they're a part of the Flower family, *who* are they in that family? Are they a flashy bloom? Someone wilted? Once they understand that, be sure they consider who they are *within* the family. Parent? The baby? The Black Sheep? Lastly, did they remember to turn to the camera to *share* their story?

And, if someone doesn't understand what the word means, ask them to commit to what they imagine it *could* be based on the sound of it.

*Notes*

This exercise can be done with five-year-olds or 50-year-olds and is one of the most valuable and fun exercises you'll ever do. It focuses on honoring first impulses, commitment, awareness, physical storytelling, trust, listening, silent communication, and awareness of time itself. *Not* giving people time to think, reject, or reconsider a choice strengthens their awareness of what they're actually doing *with* available time. They're amazed at the fullness of their choices as individuals and families, in only five seconds (in time, reduce that to three seconds!). As the participants discover more and more about their ability to commit to fully realized choices in less time than what they *think* they need, you'll observe increased confidence, both personally and physically. They start to question what they're literally doing with available time in other parts of their work where their time is less limited.

# Appendix I

## *Silly Walk Relay Race (via Marge Linney)*

Exactly what it sounds like: ask participants to create two equal lines, single file. Place an object – or a person who volunteers so that lines can be even – at one end of the room.

- After you shout, "Go!" a member of each team creates a silly walk (not a silly *run*) that takes them to the far end of the room.
- They tap the object or person and continue back.
- When they reach their line, they tap the next person to go, and that person moves with their own distinct silly walk, and so on.
- Each team must cheer on their person; allow the lines to go through two turns each.
- Whichever team finishes first is the "Silly Walk Winner," and their reward should be along the lines of getting to suggest the next group exercise (with Silly Walks comes great responsibility). Make sure any reward is not to the exclusion of the second group.

*Notes*

This exercise focuses on commitment, awareness, physical stamina, impulse, vulnerability, and support. The silliness of it makes it a great candidate to bring in when:

- it's mid-term or finals week and they simply need to cut loose
- the group has been too focused on intellectual analysis to the point where it's inhibited experiential exploration
- there's a high amount of "I'm afraid of looking stupid" which is holding back exploration
- a recent event has caused some sadness or tension in the group (pure physical and comedic release).

## Appendix J

### *Blindfold Freeze Tag*

Participants stand in a line, side by side. Give out bandanas/blindfolds so everyone has them on their person, but doesn't wear them yet. Have the participants warm up with a few rounds of traditional Freeze Tag Improv.

- Two people begin; one initiates a conflict with the other.
- Someone from the group calls "Freeze!"; they do, one of them is tapped out.
- The new person assumes the physical position of the person tapped out, and initiates a new conflict that's inspired by the physical position.
- At some point during "traditional" Freeze Tag, call for the two people up there to hold, remember their physical positions, identify who will initiate a new conflict when they resume.
- Then have them then go to neutral and put their blindfolds on, resume the physical positions, and the new conflict is introduced.
- As before, anyone can call freeze at any time; the new person will tap out one of the blindfolded partners; that person removes their blindfold and returns to the group, the new person puts on their blindfold and assumes the exact physical position and initiates a new conflict with the other blindfolded person.

### *Tips*

Instruct the group that the conflicts in this version should not justify the loss of sight, or acknowledge the blindfolds in any realistic way. The blindfolds are a part of the new structure only and shouldn't be realistically acknowledged (otherwise you'll have twenty scenarios of being lost in a cave).

### *Notes*

Focuses on intense listening, physical commitment, letting go of judging choices, risk-taking, freeing choices. The blindfolds function similar to masks, and help to erase the imaginary audience, and the imaginary judge. Participants become freer in their choices, become more physically expressive, connect with their partners more deeply (you'll notice much more freedom of physical touching), and they let go of any need to control. Because one blindfolded person may be in the playing area for several rounds, they have no way of knowing which person from the group is going to be their new partner. They experience those few moments in darkness waiting, breathing, unable to plan or take the reins in any way.

# Appendix K

## *Capture the Flag*

This version bears little resemblance to the Boy Scout game that apparently it gets its name from! The group divides into two teams.

- One member of each team comes into the center to face off. Each is given a colorful bandana, and the participant tucks one end of it into their back pocket. They should only tuck in enough of the bandana to secure it, not to conceal it; at least two-thirds of it should be hanging from the back pocket.
- At your signal, the goal is for one participant to "capture" the other's bandana by pulling it from the pocket and gaining sole possession of it.
- Each team cheers on their representative, but can't interfere. Whoever captures the bandana remains as that team's representative as the other team sends in a new person.

### *Notes*

Though blatantly competitive and seemingly anti-ensemble, in appropriate circumstances, it encourages physical awareness, physical stamina, agility, focus, commitment, observation, and follow-through on actions and tactics. There are so many close associations between team sports and ensemble-based work that those who've participated in sports will respond to more physical exercises such as this one. Depending on specific needs, this is also a fun way to approach healthy competition, and reinforce the need for team support for every individual. If you have a team member who is physically incapable of agility (vs. "dogging" it), whether because of an old injury or current condition, you can identify that person to be the referee who provides the running commentary. They're also required to stay on their feet the entire time, move about in the space (often quickly) to better observe the action, and they will still get some of the physical benefits the others are striving toward.

As we move forward with what scientists are calling "digital natives" (i.e., those who have been raised with all contemporary technology) physical skills such as agility, stamina, and flexibility, are fast becoming areas in sore need of extra attention in our field. I suspect we'll be incorporating more and more physical work like this exercise into our classrooms and rehearsals over time.

# Appendix L

## *One Word at a Time Storytelling*

Participants sit or stand in a circle.

- Instruct them to create a single story with each person contributing one word at a time, in order.
- Eventually, someone needs to make the decision to bring the story to a conclusion, and all information must be honored.

### *Tips*

You can also do a variation of this exercise in which the group sits like a choir, and you act as the conductor. Point to someone to begin, they speak for a moment or two, stop them, and then point to another random person to pick up the story. In this version, people don't know who will be called upon next, they contribute a segment of an idea instead of a single word, and it challenges the desire to control or push the story in a specific direction instead of where the story itself wants to go.

### *Notes*

Explores listening, commitment, the temptation to control or direct the choices of others, acceptance, and pure collaboration.

# Appendix M

## *Circle Cross (via Dr. Beverly Brumm)*

Actors stand in a circle *in character*.

- One at a time, a character has an impulse to say something to, or to ask a question of, another character. The statement or question is guided by the fact that by virtue of the script, their character *doesn't* have the opportunity to say otherwise (or, not in the way the character wishes they could express themselves). This should be a single sentence, or single question, no more.
- A character walks to the center of the circle, makes eye contact with the character they want to say something to, that character walks into the circle and faces the one who called them in.
- The first character makes their statement or asks their question.
- The other character simply receives, *they don't respond.*
- The two participants exchange places in the circle.

The character who was called in may want to say something that has been informed by that first exchange, but they must wait and call in that character at a later time.

206

## Notes

This is not an interactive improvisation; the character being called in must *silently receive*. This assures the first character that they will be heard, no matter what it is they have to say. The structure frees actors to express things on behalf of their characters, and the exploration deepens character, relationships, and story. It demands a great deal of trust within the ensemble, as sometimes fairly risky things can be said between characters. Maintaining the circle adds the psychic and tangible support needed to support these risks.

Try to bring in this exercise at different times in the rehearsal process. It facilitates discoveries that actors may have been mulling in isolation, and because of the unwritten rule about not imposing your discoveries about a relationship onto another actor, in this forum, the *characters* can "hear each other out." It's especially valuable for characters, or relationships, that have limited stage time and yet demand an immediacy and fullness.

# Appendix N

### *Initiate, Copy, Heighten*

Have the group stand in a line, side by side.

- One person steps forward and begins a simple, repeatable activity. For instance, lifting an imaginary spoon from an imaginary bowl to their mouth, as if eating a bowl of soup (sounds may be included, but no language should be used). They simply repeat the activity over and over without adding anything to it. (Simple choices are best. They need not be funny, clever, or even interesting – actually a seemingly "dull" choice like eating soup works well.) Another possibility is to initiate with an unrecognizable activity such as waving your hand rapidly in front of your face or hopping on one leg while squawking. The important thing is that ANY choice is valid, so long as it is repeatable.
- Once the choice has been established, a second person steps forward and joins in by copying the activity. The goal for this person is to mimic (not mock) the first person as closely as possible. We now have two people doing the exact same thing, in unison.
- A third person steps forward and joins in by performing a heightened version of the existing activity. Simple ways to heighten the activity include doing it bigger, louder, faster, etc. Another way to heighten is by raising the emotional stakes. For instance, if the third soup eater eats her soup while sobbing, an interesting scenario has been established.

*Notes*

This exercise compels members to connect and be dependent on one another. They build a result together from a simple initiation by making a pattern out of it. It empowers them to build upon a simple idea rather than wait for a brilliant one. By repeating this exercise (say, incorporating it into regular warm-ups), the tendency to connect with a partner(s) becomes more frequent. Improvisers may recognize the concept behind this exercise because it is a physical version of the more traditional "yes and" exercises, which tend to be verbal.

# Appendix O

## *The Ad Campaign (via Truth In Comedy)*

Three participants step forward.

- Explain that they are the creative marketing team of the Super Genius Advertising Agency and must work together on a campaign for a new product.
- Once the product is announced they will have to create a name for the product, a celebrity spokesperson and a short slogan that may be turned into a jingle.
- You then announce the team's new product, which should be something fun, but not real (invisible top hats, edible cars, odor-repellent sneakers, etc.).
- Time is of the essence, and you should only give them about a minute to complete this campaign. The time crunch will likely result in wacky ideas; insist that no matter how illogical, or just plain stupid the ideas may seem, everyone must respond with an enthusiastic "Yes!" to any idea offered. No judgment, criticism, or adjustment ("Oh, I like that, but ... ") is permitted.

*Example*

- Imaginary product that was announced by the leader: garlic scented shaving cream.
- Product name shouted out by Member #1: Garlicious Foam.
- All three members shouted, "Yes!" and cheered enthusiastically.
- Celebrity spokesperson named by Member 2: Robert Pattinson.
- More shouts of "Yes," "Brilliant," "I love it," etc., shouted out by all three.
- Slogan concocted by Member #3: Garlicious Foam – it's bloody good.
- More cheering.
- All three then repeated the slogan in a horror movie style jingle. (The musicality of the jingle is irrelevant – no quality is necessary. More important is that everyone enthusiastically commits to the jingle and then sings it together for a big finish.)

*Notes*

This exercise helps break the habit of saying "no" to an idea, shows what is possible through commitment, encourages members to see the value in supporting each other's choices and allows them to practice doing it. The results are surprising and exciting to the members, filling them with a sense of how to unleash their creativity through a process of support, rather than the pressure of supplying an instantly brilliant idea.

# Appendix P

## *The Hot Spot (via Truth In Comedy)*

Participants stand in a circle.

- One person leaps into the center – the hot spot – and starts singing a song – any song.
- Once the song is recognizable, another person leaps in, taps the singer on the shoulder and begins singing a new song. Ideally, only a short snippet of the song will be completed before a new song is started. The new song is generally inspired by the previous song (much like free association).
- This continues with all members taking turns jumping into the center to "relieve" the person on the hot spot.

*Tips*

For those self-conscious about singing, this idea of relief is to be encouraged in the others as a supportive move. This will often be the case with new ensembles. In groups that enjoy singing, the idea of relief disappears and often the whole group will sing along to each song. Encourage the members to change songs frequently. Common themes will emerge, for instance, a whole series of songs about love.

*Notes*

This is a wonderful exercise for bonding ensemble members. It can break down barriers and get members to be more vulnerable with each other (which, in turn, engenders support).

# Appendix Q

## *Untie the Human Knot*

The participants stand in a circle.

- Have them reach out and hold hands. Each person must have the hands of two different people and neither of those people can be the ones standing immediately to their right or left.
- With the hand holding complete, the group has formed a human knot that they must now untie without letting go. To do this, they climb over and duck under each other. They can twist around in each other's hands so long as they don't break contact.
- The exercise is complete when they are back in a circle and the people they are holding hands with are immediately to their left or right. Some may end up facing inward, some outward on the circle. Sometimes two separate circles will be created.

### *Tips*

Every once in a while, a knot is such that it is impossible to untangle. Simply announce that this is one of those occasions and issue a new challenge. Can they accomplish the goal with only one set of hands letting go and rejoining? Two sets?

This exercise works best with groups of at least eight.

### *Notes*

This exercise is an excellent diagnostic tool for the leader. If the ensemble is bonded and well-balanced, the members will work easily together to solve the problem of the knot. On the other hand, bossy people and perfectionists tend to "out" themselves in this exercise. Impatience, lack of commitment, and selfish or controlling behaviors are symptoms to look for. Untying the knot will promote group problem-solving, improve physical familiarity and comfort among members, and produce a group accomplishment (an important step in bonding).

# Appendix R

## *Multiple Pattern Juggling*

Participants stand in a circle.

- One person initiates by looking at another person and saying a word to that person, e.g., "banana."

- The receiver of "banana" free associates on that word and says a new word, perhaps "apple," to a new person.
- This continues until the last remaining participant says their word to the person who initiated the sequence; the cycle is complete.
- Now have them repeat it, exactly, several times. They will say the exact same word to the exact same person each time.
- Once they have this pattern memorized through repetition, have them create a brand new pattern using completely different words. A different person should initiate the second pattern and everyone should avoid sending their new word to the same person they did in the first pattern.
- Again, have them repeat this pattern, exactly, until they have it memorized. Let's say the second pattern begins with "Chevy," followed by "Ford" and so on. So we have a fruit pattern and an auto manufacturer pattern.
- Now challenge them to keep both patterns going at the same time. Start with the fruit pattern and once it has gone all the way around, have them continue repeating it while the auto manufacturer pattern is added.
- To ensure that neither pattern is dropped, every time a member says one of their words, they must watch and listen to make sure that the receiver received it and continued the pattern. For instance, if I say "banana" to Lisa and I don't see or hear her say "apple" to Tom, then I keep repeating "banana" to Lisa until I see and hear her say "apple" to Tom. I don't merely say my word and go back into waiting for my next word. I stay fully vested in making sure the patterns continue beyond me. The key to success is in the members seeing beyond their obvious individual responsibilities (which is to wait for the two words coming at them, and say the words that follow to the next person in each pattern).

*Tips*

After some practice, groups become quite proficient. Here is a list of ways to keep increasing the challenge:

- Add additional patterns.
- Add a pattern that uses sounds instead of words.
- Add a physical pattern such as throwing a ball instead of saying words.
- Once several patterns are being successfully juggled, have the members mix up their order on the circle and see if they can still do it.
- Once several patterns are being successfully juggled, have the members face outward on the circle so they can't see each other and must rely on listening alone.

*Notes*

This exercise provides a healthy mental challenge and forces individuals to look beyond their own agenda. Everyone must share an equal responsibility for the patterns continuing or one or more will be dropped. It increases communication skills because it compels each member not only to send a message, but also to make sure that it was received and passed along. It also helps develop the ability to monitor several shifting points of focus at one time, a boost to listening skills.

## Appendix S

### *Karaoke*

Yes, karaoke. Try it. Rent a karaoke machine or take your ensemble to a local karaoke establishment. They will be excited just looking over the list of available songs and thinking about what choices to make. Everyone will eventually take their turn in the spotlight, the good singers and the bad, the eager and the reluctant. (The eager ones break the ice and the others will all eventually join in.)

#### *Tips*

For someone particularly reluctant, have them sing a duet or backup vocals with one of the eager members. One eager singer may select a song conducive to the whole group (or a subset) singing together.

#### *Notes*

Karaoke is a wonderful opportunity for self-expression and opening up to others. It's also useful for mending ensemble. More than once, I've seen two ensemble members who don't like working together forge an unlikely bond through karaoke. Somehow, they see each other differently after this experience and are able to bring a newfound respect for each other back into the classroom/ rehearsal room.

## Appendix T

### *Falling, Falling, Falling*

Create an open, empty space and have the members move randomly through it.

- When someone feels ready, he stops moving then slowly and clearly says, "Falling, falling, falling." These should be the only words spoken in the exercise.
- After the third "falling," and this needs to be stressed, AFTER the THIRD "falling," that person falls straight backward. Meanwhile, everyone else, upon hearing the FIRST "falling," rushes to get behind the person speaking so they can collectively catch him as he falls, and gently lower him to the

ground, taking particular care to protect his head. The "catchers" need to put their hands on the faller's back, arms, legs, buttocks and head. Everyone crowds together and works to make sure that the faller's safety is assured.
* Once the faller is safely on the floor, the others help him up and the exercise resumes with each member taking a turn.

*Tips*

This exercise is not ideal for initial classes or rehearsals, but better saved until a basic comfort level is reached within the ensemble.

This is a favorite ensemble-building exercise, but it is also potentially dangerous so great caution must be taken. Ultimately, it is your responsibility to decide if your ensemble is ready to do this. If you're working with young children or any other group that this may not be appropriate for, don't do it. Your sense of responsibility, care, and concern must come through in your instructions, your tone – every part of your communication. Never allow joking, side comments, or otherwise distracting behavior from any members during this exercise. Focus on the task at hand is critical.

Some members will feel perfectly at ease with this exercise, and therefore won't anticipate the seriousness of it or the anxiety it may be provoking in others. Be sure to make everyone aware that this exercise can tap into deep-seated fears, and that fear is often covered up by contrasting behavior, so do not assume that ANYONE else is actually comfortable with this. Everyone should be instructed to be overly protective of each other. Literally, they must have each other's back.

You will notice that those who wait to go last are the most fearful. Be gentle and encouraging. The longer they walk around with no one falling, the more pressure the non-fallers will feel – you don't need to provide any additional pressure. Eventually they will probably all take their turn.

### David

Only twice in my years of doing this has a person absolutely refused to fall. It's embarrassing for them and they may lash out at you or the exercise. I then say, "You don't have to fall. What is important is that you're there to catch the others. We will do this exercise again from time to time. Perhaps one day you will feel ready and we will all eagerly be there to catch you." Both of those people eventually fell. One insisted on doing it right after I told him he didn't have to. Be patient.

Be aware that body issues may arise. Larger members may feel self-conscious. Some may not feel comfortable with hands on the back of their legs or buttocks. Again, be patient, or choose a different exercise if this one isn't appropriate for your ensemble. I once had a fellow in an ensemble that I believed to be too large for the others to safely catch and lower, so I never did this exercise with that group.

### *Notes*

With all of the warnings I've issued, you may be wondering why I'm recommending this exercise at all. I've found it to have a great and immediate payoff. It's never worth the risk of anyone's safety, but done responsibly, safely, and with common sense, it's a powerful ensemble-building exercise.

## Appendix U

### *Off My Chest*

Participants stand in a circle.

- In random order, the members "throw" whatever is bothering them "off their chest" and into a pile at the center of the circle. Have them actually use a physical throwing motion.
- This can continue for several minutes with each member throwing multiple "items" on the pile – you'll get a sense of when the pique has peaked (sorry).
- Then instruct the members to mold the pile into a giant ball and roll it out the door together.

### *Tips*

Some examples of frequently heard issues are "my boyfriend," "my parents," "student loans," "ten-page papers," "lack of sleep," etc. Occasionally a deeply personal issue will be revealed ("my parents' divorce"), or an issue that you might find compromising, such as the naming of a colleague ("Professor Bob 'I hate students' Jones"). Where you draw the line is up to you, of course, but these examples are ones you should consider tolerating. It is recommended that you only do this exercise with ensembles that you trust and always announce "what is said in here during this exercise, stays in here" and mean it. The trust among members grows, they become more connected, and the bond strengthens. If any participant uses this exercise to call out another member or raise an issue within the group, that's where you ought to draw a line. There are more appropriate ways of handling those issues.

Try following this exercise with a similar one where they announce what they are grateful for or what they are looking forward to. The throwing motion changes to one of saying thank you or feeling good. Another version has them announcing their wishes and desires – putting them out to the universe. It's all about changing the atmosphere in the room from negative or stressful to positive and hopeful.

## Notes

This exercise gets all of the bad energy, distractions, and stress weighing on the ensemble members out of the room. The effects are remarkable. This exercise is good for established ensembles, but not recommended for new groups. It's useful for relieving stress (right before finals is a popular occasion). Stress has the power to unite or divide and this exercise will help harness the unifying quality of stress and engender support, patience, and understanding among the members.

# Appendix V

### *What I Admire About You*

Participants sit in a circle. Start with one member, let's say Joe.

- One at a time, everyone in the circle says something they admire about Joe, usually as it pertains to Joe's work or contributions to the ensemble, but often it veers into personal traits (which are valuable contributions to the ensemble as well).
- Once everyone has had his or her turn with Joe, move on to the next member of the circle and so on until everyone has been the focus of the exercise.

## Notes

It's remarkable how often members don't realize what they are appreciated for. Confidence is boosted, self-esteem grows, and mutual respect is developed. This can be particularly effective for members who are struggling to overcome bad habits, emerge from a slump, suffering from poor reviews, etc.

# Appendix W

### *The Center of the Earth*

Participants lie on the floor, face up, in a comfortable position, with their eyes closed. They should spread out so they aren't in contact with one another.

- Lead them through a few deeps breaths and strong exhalations or otherwise encourage relaxation through breathing.
- Next, you will lead them on a journey through mental imagery. Tell them to listen to the sound of your voice and imagine what you are describing. There are endless variations on what follows and it is important that you make it your own. Simply reciting the version offered here will ring hollow –

personalize it so that it rings true. What you are about to read is only offered as an example to get you started on creating your version.

- "Start by becoming aware of your core, or center of gravity. It is located directly behind your belly button. Now imagine that you are drilling a well that begins at your core and descends beneath you. It exits your body through your lower back, continues through the floor beneath you, beneath the room below us and successively through each floor of the building. The pipeline continues through the basement, the foundation of the building and into the bedrock beneath the building. It goes still deeper, through the layers of the earth. Through the crust, through the mantle, through the outer core and finally into the inner core of the earth. This is the engine, the furnace, and the source of all energy that lies within the earth. It radiates heat and light. You have tapped into it. Now slowly begin to draw a thin bead of this warm, orange energy up through your pipeline toward YOUR core. Up through the outer core of the earth, through the mantle, the crust, the bedrock, the foundation of the building, the floors beneath you and finally through the floor upon which you lie. Let that energy come into your body, into your core. Let it spread throughout your body. Let it move down through your lower abdomen into your hips and on down your legs, through your ankles into your feet and all the way to the tips of your toes. Let it move up your torso, filling your chest and back, and through your shoulders out into your arms until it reaches all the way to the tips of your fingers. Let it move up through your neck and into your head. Feel the flush in your cheeks, on your lips, and the tip of your nose. Keep going until it has reached your ears and gone to the very top of your head. Now that your body is filled, you can seal off the pipeline. Imagine this bright orange energy that you've captured is pulsing throughout your body. Feel its gentle warmth. You feel good all over: warm, energized, and vibrant. Take a moment and just enjoy how it feels."

- Take a generous pause, a good 30 to 60 seconds, and then continue.
  - "Now I want you to slowly begin to retract the warm energy from all over your body back into your core. Concentrate it into a spot right behind your belly button. Pull it all the way from the tips of your fingers and toes, and from the top of your head. Create a dense, concentrated ball of it. A warm, orange, glowing ball of energy. Just as the earth has a warm, orange, glowing ball of energy at its core, now you have one in your core. It is your engine, your furnace, your source of energy and strength. It is now concentrated and powerful, ready to erupt out into the rest of your body whenever you need it. You are ready to meet whatever comes your way. Take another moment to picture your newly refilled core."

- Take a short pause, maybe 15 seconds, and then continue.
  - "Now over the next minute or so, I want you to slowly come back to an awareness of where you are. Open your eyes, and eventually begin to get up. Bring the very best version of yourself into this space, ready to get started."

*Tips*

As you lead them through the mental imagery, take your time and allow pauses for them to imagine what you are describing. Speak in a soothing tone. Use your words to paint a picture. You are a guide. Put them at ease.

*Notes*

The exercise focuses on changing negativity into positivity and relieving stress, and is especially useful at the beginning of a class or rehearsal if the group has collective fatigue.

## Appendix X

### *Early ensemble-building exercises: forming bonds and trust*

- Come Join Me (Appendix B)
- What Are You Doing? (Appendix C)
- Kitty Wants a Corner (Appendix F)
- Blindfold Series (Appendix G)
- Family Portraits (Appendix H)
- One Word at a Time Storytelling (Appendix L)
- Initiate, Copy, Heighten (Appendix N)
- The Ad Campaign (Appendix O)
- Multiple Pattern Juggling (Appendix R)

## Appendix Y

### *Advanced ensemble building; after the ice has broken and basic comfort level is attained*

- Blind Offers (Appendix A)
- Sound and Movement (Appendix D)
- West Side Story (Appendix E)
- Hunter and Hunted (Blindfold Series) (Appendix G)
- Blindfold Freeze Tag (Appendix J)
- Circle Cross (Rehearsal/production) (Appendix M)
- The Hot Spot (Appendix P)
- Untie the Human Knot (Appendix Q)
- Falling, Falling, Falling (Appendix T)

# Appendix Z

### *Exercises for mending, maintenance, and renewing bonds in times of stress or change*

- Blind Offers (Appendix A)
- Sound and Movement (Appendix D)
- West Side Story (Appendix E)
- Silly Walk Relay Race (Appendix I)
- Karaoke (Appendix S)
- Off My Chest (Appendix U)
- What I Admire About You (Appendix V)
- Center of the Earth (Appendix W)

# BIBLIOGRAPHY

Anderson, J. (2010) *Defying Gravity*, New York: Samuel French.

Atkins, G. (1993) *Improv! A Handbook for the Actor*, Portsmouth: Heinemann Press.

Boal, A. (2002) *Games for Actors and Non Actors*, Oxford: Routledge.

*The Breakfast Club*. Dir. John Hughes, A&M Films, Channel Productions, Universal Pictures, 1985. Film.

Chekhov, A., Friel, B. translator (1981) *Three Sisters*, New York: Dramatists Play Service.

"Happy Birthday Lou!" *The Mary Tyler Moore Show*. MTM Enterprises, WCBS, 22 December 1973. Television.

Cohen, P. (2008) "Two Fathers are Learning Lessons of 'All My Sons.'" *New York Times*, 12 November 2008.

Cohen, R. (2011) *Working Together in Theatre: Collaboration and Leadership*, New York: Palgrave MacMillan.

*Collins English Dictionary* (2009) Complete & Unabridged 10th Edition. William Collins Sons & Co. Ltd.

Cooney, G. (1999) *Irish Prehistory: A Social Perspective*, Dublin: Wordwell Ltd.

*Ferris Bueller's Day Off*. Dir. John Hughes, Paramount Pictures, 1986. Film.

Gellman, M. and M. Scruggs (2007) *Process: An Improviser's Journey*, Evanston: Northwestern University Press.

Goleman, D. "The Must-Have Leadership Skill," *Harvard Business Review*. 14 October 2011. Available at http://blogs.hbr.org/cs/2011/10/the_must-have_leadership_skill.html.

Greenberg, R. (2005) *Take Me Out*, New York: Dramatists Play Service.

Halpern, C., D. Close, and K. Johnson (1994) *Truth in Comedy: The Manual for Improvisation*, Colorado Springs: Meriwether Press.

Johnson, T. (1993) *Johnson Plays I: Insignificance, Unsuitable for Adults, Cries from the Mammal House*, London: Methuen Drama.

Johnstone, K. (1987) *Impro: Improvisation and the Theatre*, Oxford: Routledge.

Jones, C. (2004) *The Burren and the Aran Islands: Exploring the Archaeology*, Cork: The Collins Press.

—— (2007) *Temples of Stone: Exploring the Megalithic Tombs of Ireland*, Cork: The Collins Press.

Kaufman, M. (2001) *The Laramie Project*, New York: Vintage Books.

*King Kong*. Dir. P. Jackson, Universal Pictures, 2005. Film.

Langsner, M. (2010) *Lying Makes Me Feel Like a God*, unpublished play.

Lerman, L. and J. Borstel (2003) *Critical Response Process: A Method for Getting Useful Feedback on Anything You Make from Dance to Dessert*, Tacoma Park: Liz Lerman Dance Exchange.

Ludwig, K. (2010) *Moon Over Buffalo*, New York: Samuel French.

Madson, P. (2005) *Improv Wisdom: Don't Prepare Just Show Up*, New York: Crown Publishing Group.

McTaggart, L. (2011) *The Bond: Connecting Through the Space Between Us*, New York, London: Free Press.

Miller, A. (1952) *The Crucible*, New York: Dramatists Play Service.

Nachmanovitch, S. (1990) *Free Play*, New York: Penguin Putnam.

Pintauro, J. (1992) *Raft of the Medusa*, New York: Dramatists Play Service.

Samuels, D. (2000) *Kindertransport*, London: Nick Hern Books.

Shurtleff, M. (1984) *Audition: Everything an Actor Needs to Know to Get the Part*, New York: Walker Publishing.

Spolin, V. (1963) *Improvisation for the Theater*, Evanston: Northwestern University Press.

—— (1985, updated edn. 2011) *Theater Games for Rehearsal: A Director's Handbook,* Evanston: Northwestern University Press.

Stein, T. and J. Bathurst (2008) *Performing Arts Management: A Handbook of Professional Practices*, New York: Allworth Press.

Sweet, J. (ed.) (1978) *Something Wonderful Right Away: An Oral History of the Second City and The Compass Players*, New York: Avon Books.

Wilson, L. (1998) *The Rimers of Eldritch*, New York: Dramatists Play Service.

# INDEX

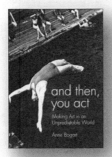

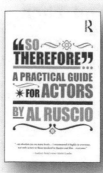